1991

OXFORD MONOGRAPHS ON MUSIC

Haydn
and the Enlightenment

Haydn

and the Enlightenment

the Late Symphonies and their Audience

....•——◆▸—•....

David P. Schroeder

CLARENDON PRESS · OXFORD
1990

Oxford University Press, Walton Street, Oxford OX2 6DP

Oxford New York Toronto
Delhi Bombay Calcutta Madras Karachi
Petaling Jaya Singapore Hong Kong Tokyo
Nairobi Dar es Salaam Cape Town
Melbourne Auckland

and associated companies in
Berlin Ibadan

Oxford is a trade mark of Oxford University Press

Published in the United States
by Oxford University Press, New York

British Library Cataloguing in Publication Data
Schroeder, David P.
Haydn and the Enlightenment : the late symphonies
and their audience. – (Oxford monographs on music).
1. Austrian music. Haydn, Joseph, 1732–1809
I. Title
780.92
ISBN 0–19–816159–X

Library of Congress Cataloging in Publication Data
Schroeder, David P., 1946–
Haydn and the enlightenment : the late symphonies
and their audience / David P. Schroeder.
Includes bibliographical references.
1.Haydn, Joseph, 1732–1809. Symphonies. 2. Symphony.
3. Enlightenment. I. Title. II. Series.
ML410.H4S45   1990   784.2'184'092—dc20   90–6778
ISBN 0–19–816159–X

Typeset by Pentacor PLC, High Wycombe, Bucks
Printed in Great Britain by
Biddles Ltd., Guildford and King's Lynn

To Linda, Emily, and Daniel

Acknowledgements

AT the age of sixteen I had the fortunate experience of singing in the chorus in an amateur production of Haydn's *Creation*. This performance had important consequences for me since my decisions to study voice, focus on music as an undergraduate, and ultimately pursue a career in music all arose directly or indirectly from that youthful awakening. My fascination with Haydn has remained undiminished for over twenty-five years, and in that time I have received assistance, encouragement, and advice from numerous people. A study such as this, like the works of the composer it examines, does not originate in isolation, and I am very pleased to acknowledge those who have taken a personal interest in my project.

At King's College, Cambridge, I found Philip Radcliffe's infectious enthusiasm for Haydn a resource well worth tapping. Symphony numbers meant nothing to him, but when he knew the key and a few notes of a theme, he could play at the piano virtually any part of any Haydn symphony from memory. He was not a music scholar in the usual sense, and possibly for that reason had something very special to offer. I join many in mourning his loss and remembering him warmly.

Along the way I have had the benefit of suggestions from friends who have read preliminary studies or with whom I ·have simply enjoyed discussions. Special mention must go to Julian Rushton, Philip Downs, James Webster, Roy Howat, Walter Kemp, and Dennis Farrell. While I originally had only a vague sense that Shaftesbury belonged in this study, I owe my awareness of broader implications to suggestions made by M. H. Abrams. More recently, while spending a year at the University of California at Berkeley, Daniel Heartz was gracious enough to read the entire typescript. He was able to balance his numerous valuable suggestions for improvement with a spirit of warm encouragement.

I have enjoyed the hospitality of numerous libraries and archives where rare books and manuscripts were put at my disposal. These include the British Library; the University Library, Cambridge; the Gesellschaft der Musikfreunde, Vienna; the Universität Bibliothek, Vienna; the National Széchényi Library, Budapest; the Library of Congress; the Loeb, Isham, Weidener, and Houghton Libraries of Harvard University; the Beinecke Library, Yale University; the Killam Library, Dalhousie University; and the libraries of the University of California at Berkeley. At the Burney Project, McGill University, I enjoyed not only access to typescripts of Burney's unpublished documents, but also lively discussion with Professors Klima and Troide.

Without the support of a Research Grant from the Social Sciences and Humanities Research Council of Canada and two smaller grants from the Research Development Fund at Dalhousie University, my travel to these libraries would not have been possible.

Acknowledgement is given to the written work of other authors throughout in footnotes and other citations. While that type of recognition is normally sufficient, it must be noted that a study such as this is dependent on the availability of a large body of archival and editorial work. In this case, I have H. C. Robbins Landon to thank for the staggering amount which he has made accessible. All quotations in musical examples from Haydn's symphonies are taken from his edition (*Joseph Haydn: Critical Edition of the Complete Symphonies*). For string quartet examples I have used the edition by Georg Feder and Sonja Gerlach in Joseph Haydn, *Werke*.

Some of the ideas which are used in this study have appeared elsewhere in print. I would like to acknowledge the publishers of the following three of my articles for permission to include passages or ideas here: 'Melodic Source Material and Haydn's Creative Process', *Musical Quarterly*, 68 (1982), 496–515; 'Haydn and Gellert: Parallells in Eighteenth-Century Music and Literature', *Current Musicology*, 35 (1983), 7–18; and 'Audience Reception and Haydn's London Symphonies', *International Review of the Aesthetics and Sociology of Music*, 16 (1985), 57–72.

I am indebted to Bruce Phillips of Oxford University Press for his interest in the idea for this book and in seeing it through to completion, and for his valuable advice at all steps along the way. I am also most appreciative of thorough and careful editing by Robert Peden and Veronica Ions.

Nothing leaves my word processor without having been read by my wife Linda, and in the case of a book, without having been read numerous times. Her fascination with this study has never flagged, and many happy hours of discussion have served to nurture the project more than she is aware. For her encouragement, tolerance, and very practical suggestions I am most grateful.

D. P. S.

Contents

Abbreviations of Sources

Certain sources are cited frequently throughout, and citations for these, instead of being placed in footnotes, are identified in the text in parentheses with page numbers, volume numbers (if applicable), and the following abbreviations:

Aris. Twining, Thomas, *Aristotle's Treatise on Poetry, Translated, with Notes, and Two Dissertations on Poetical and Musical Imitation* (London, 1789).

Bibl. Hörwarthner, Maria, 'Joseph Haydns Bibliothek—Versuch einer literarhistorischen Rekonstruktion', in *Joseph Haydn und die Literatur seiner Zeit*, ed. Herbert Zeman (Eisenstadt, 1976), 157–207.

Char. Shaftesbury, Anthony Ashley Cooper, Third Earl of, *Characteristics of Men, Manners, Opinions, Times*, 4th edn. (3 vols.; London, 1727).

Chron. Landon, H. C. Robbins, *Haydn: Chronicle and Works* (5 vols.; London, 1976–80).

Clas. Rosen, Charles, *The Classical Style: Haydn, Mozart, Beethoven* (New York, 1972).

Cor. H. C. Robbins Landon (ed.), *The Collected Correspondence and London Notebooks of Joseph Haydn* (London, 1959).

Mem. Burney, Charles, *Memoirs of the Life and Writings of the Abate Metastasio* (3 vols.; London, 1796).

Nach. Dies, Albert Christoph, *Biographische Nachrichten von Joseph Haydn*, in Vernon Gotwals (trans. and ed.), *Haydn: Two Contemporary Portraits* (Madison, 1968).

Not. Griesinger, Georg August, *Biographische Notizen über Joseph Haydn*, in Vernon Gotwals (trans and ed.), *Haydn: Two Contemporary Portraits* (Madison, 1968).

Sub. Crotch, William, *Substance of Several Courses of Lectures on Music* (London, 1831).

Theat. Holcroft, Thomas, *The Theatrical Recorder* (2 vols.; London, 1805).

Introduction

THE advent of an Austrian Enlightenment occurred much later than in most other nations, and until recently there has been no agreement on the very existence of such a phenomenon in the Habsburg empire. Scholarship of the last two decades has confirmed, however, that the existing social order was challenged by a new outlook on issues such as education, religion, and social justice.[1] Literature played a major role in the process since it was the most effective means of satirizing the old order or providing concrete demonstration of the new sense of morality. Haydn reached his own artistic mastery at the time of this intellectual and social ferment in Austria (c.1770–90), and it seems highly unlikely that the man who ultimately gained an international reputation as the greatest living composer would have been immune to these powerful forces.

Haydn's statements on such matters are infrequent and not direct, and therefore have the possibility of leading us in any one of a number of directions. For some observers, the essence of Haydn is to be found in the following statement made to his biographer Georg August Griesinger: 'I was set apart from the world, there was nobody in my vicinity to confuse and annoy me in my course, and so I had to be original' (*Not.* 17). Original, to be sure, he was, but the image of complete isolation evoked here is another matter. These remarks, of course, are a reflection of only one facet of his experience: during the months of each year that he spent in Vienna, his social commitments were fairly heavy, since he was much in demand at literary and musical salons. At these gatherings he came into contact with people such as Gottfried van Swieten, Franz Sales von Greiner, Johann Baptist von Alxinger, Aloys Blumauer, Michael Denis, Lorenz Leopold Haschka, Tobias Philipp Gebler, and Ignaz von Born, and through them he became acquainted with the dominant aesthetic and social trends of the time.

The purpose of this study is to attempt to show that Haydn was thoroughly committed to the goals of the Enlightenment, and like his literary compatriots, used his works to serve these goals. While this

---

[1] See, for example, Ernst Wangermann, 'Reform Catholicism and Political Radicalism in the Austrian Enlightenment', in Roy Porter and Mikuláš Teich (eds.), *The Enlightenment in National Context* (Cambridge, 1981), 127–40.

could be demonstrated in almost any type of composition at almost any point in his career, the focus here will be on works written between 1780 and 1795, and in particular the English Symphonies (which Haydn preferred to call them, rather than London Symphonies). The relationship of the artist and his audience is of critical importance if enlightened goals are being served, and these symphonies offer an extraordinary insight into the effect of this relationship on the works themselves.

The idea of examining Haydn's works in the context of the Enlightenment is by no means new, but there is, it must be acknowledged, resistance to this approach as well. Recent research involving Haydn's associations with literati, his attendance at literary salons, or his personal library has by no means convinced everyone that these activities or acquisitions had any effect on him worthy of notice. The enduring impression of Haydn, fostered by his own acquaintances, appears not to suggest a man well versed in literary, social, or political matters. Griesinger informs us that he was inarticulate, that 'anyone hearing him speak of his art would not have guessed at the great artist in him' (*Not.* 60). And further, Griesinger believed that Haydn 'did not himself know how he found within himself the ideas for [the products of his genius]'. Haydn's presence at the Greiner salon made no impression on Caroline Pichler, Greiner's daughter, who noted that both Mozart and Haydn had 'an ordinary cast of mind' and 'made flat jokes'. Furthermore, Adalbert Gyrowetz, observing Haydn at a musical salon, could say nothing more than that he laughed 'somewhat archly'.[2] Concerning Haydn's personal library, it could be argued that it served no purpose other than being decorative, or that the books were simply gifts from visitors as payments of respect. As for Haydn's involvement with a person such as Greiner, the lack of supporting evidence is an issue which must be addressed. Haydn refers to Greiner only twice in his correspondence, and in fact only to complain about Greiner's negligence in returning texts. The lack of convincing documentation, then, has confirmed for some scholars that any revision of the prevailing impression would be premature.

What is the bearing of these matters on Haydn's works? Griesinger tells us that 'his theoretical *raisonnements* were very simple: namely, a piece of music ought to have a fluent melody, coherent ideas, no superfluous ornaments, nothing overdone, no confusing accompaniment, and so forth' (*Not.* 60). Once again there is little or no documentary evidence to modify this over-simplified impression. The issue at stake here concerns the relationship of documentation and interpretation. If specific or sufficient documentation cannot be found to support a particular hypothesis, that position, some would argue, is necessarily relegated to the 'suspect' category. Surely the fact that a composer was

---

[2] See Joachim Hurwitz, 'Haydn and the Freemasons', *Haydn Yearbook*, 16 (1985), pp. 33–4.

not a prolific writer of letters, diaries, or other documents which would reveal his opinions does not mean that he did not have opinions. The specific issue of Haydn documentation, in fact, is presented to us by Charles Burney in a way that sheds some light on the matter. Upon receiving a copy of Burney's *A General History of Music* and the poem of welcome shortly after arriving in England, Haydn intended to write Burney a letter of thanks, but meeting Burney at a concert, 'he took the opportunity', Burney writes, 'of making *fine speeches* innumerable, *viva voce*, and by that means saved himself the trouble of writing a letter, as he told me he intended to do'. And, upon being taken home after the concert by Burney, Haydn 'repeated and added more *fine things* on my present, than he could have written in ten sheets of paper'.[3] We do not have the ten sheets of paper, but on the other hand we know that many fine things were said, *viva voce*. The reason for the lack of a written document is clearly not that Haydn had nothing to say.

In Haydn's case the presence or lack of documentation does not allow one to build a particularly strong case one way or the other. The issue here is less biographical than it is one of criticism. The question to be asked is, are literary or other enlightened influences apparent in Haydn's music? The only way to discover this is to examine the music itself, devising critical means which allow such influences to be perceived if indeed they exist. What Haydn does not say in words he is prepared to and capable of saying most eloquently in music. The question of literary influence, then, will not be settled on the basis of archival investigation, which is not to say that such investigation is not of great importance. In view of this, an interdisciplinary approach is called for, relying on means which are necessarily speculative. This study thus attempts to embrace cross-cultural issues, confident that 'speculation' is not a pejorative word and that criticism cannot occur without it.

The 1780s were special years for the Austrian Enlightenment, and this was an eventful decade for Haydn as well. In his various types of composition one can notice refinements or new approaches at this time which are in no small measure related to his increased involvement with enlightened thinkers as well as his more direct relationship with the new international audience. With at least one type of composition, the string quartet, he went so far in 1781 as to say that his newest set of six was written 'in a new and special way'. As for the larger, outside audience, Haydn had been conscious of it all along since his works were disseminated through publication and performance. However, this audience remained indefinite and indefinable for him until the 1780s, when he began to receive commissions from specific concert societies.

The new audience which Haydn encountered in Paris and elsewhere

---

[3] MS Letter to Latrobe, dated 3 Mar. 1791, in the Osborn Collection, Beinecke Library, Yale University.

was becoming an increasingly important force. The same audience had already taken hold of the theatre, and works for the theatre had undergone significant changes in response to the new taste. A type of reciprocal relationship came into being between writers and their public as far as social values were concerned: the works reflected the moral values of this public, and the audience had its values reinforced by the works. It is possible to see Haydn's awareness of and interaction with this audience growing, and between 1784 and 1795 it was largely through the symphony that his relationship with the public was cultivated. With the commission for the Paris Symphonies, he finally was able to gain full control over what should reach the audience, and in England, for the first time, he came face to face with his new public. The Paris Symphonies, commissioned by a Masonic concert society at precisely the time of Haydn's own initiation, offered heightened musical refinement and sophistication which challenged the listener in a new way. The primary task of this study is to define these symphonic procedures and place them in the context of Haydn's relationship with his new audience.

As Haydn's public types of composition (the symphony in particular) were increasingly directed to the new audience, an understanding of the works in question becomes more dependent on an awareness of the audience and the composer's relationship with it. The audience, in fact, could have a significant bearing on the works composed for it. Particularly in a situation such as Haydn experienced in England, where he was in regular contact with individual members of the audience and he could observe audience reaction and read reviews, audience reception could play a key role in his compositional choices from one work to the next. New works could be influenced by the reception of existing works, or existing works could go through revisions in response to their initial reception. For no period was this more true than for the eighteenth century, as writers at this time placed the highest possible emphasis on both pleasing and teaching their audiences or readers. Haydn owned a copy of *Characteristics of Men, Manners, Opinions, Times* by the Third Earl of Shaftesbury, one of the most influential English writers of the century, in which Shaftesbury took the view that 'an author's art and labour are for his reader's sake alone' (*Char.* iii. 228). In the case of Haydn, who wrote of his operas as being 'calculated in accordance with the locality' (*Cor.* 73), it was said of him in England that he informed Salomon he would like to study the English taste before composing any symphonies so he could be assured of the approbation of the public.[4]

---

[4] Charlotte Papendiek, *Court and Private Life in the Time of Queen Charlotte: Being the Journal of Mrs Papendiek*, ed. Mrs Vernon Delves Broughton (London, 1887), ii. p. 290. Also printed in *Chron.* iii. 51.

The symphonies written for Salomon's concerts provide an ideal opportunity to observe the relationship between reception and production. Haydn's relationships with people in England and his ability to observe audience reaction allowed him to calculate a very specific effect for each of the newly composed symphonies. The balance between popular features and intellectual challenge is different in each work, generally shifting towards the latter with each successive season. Having gained the approbation of the audience, he presented it with a musical process which required reflective listening and led to contemplation of matters not strictly musical. The more the listeners followed and engaged in this process, the further they were able to advance in the refinement or intelligibility which this process makes possible. Music had the potential, then, of achieving the same elevated moral goals as were commonly recognized in the eighteenth century as being the purpose of poetry, plays, and novels.

A full study of Haydn and the Enlightenment cannot be confined to the symphonies alone. Different types of composition can be interrelated as the composer discovers procedures in one which are applicable to others. While string quartets and symphonies have fundamental differences, they are also sufficiently similar for the quartets to have an important bearing on the symphonies. Opera and symphony are especially close to each other in the eighteenth century, being the primary secular, public types of composition which engage the interest of a listening audience through dramatic means. In opera one can see an important aspect of a composer's literary inclinations, and in the case of Haydn a shift from comic texts in the 1770s to serious ones in the early 1780s can be noted. In moving towards texts derived from Ariosto and Tasso, Haydn was following a course in opera not unlike that of his literary contemporaries such as Alxinger and Nicolay who wrote chivalrous epics or *Rittergedichte*. But upon reaching this point, Haydn abandoned opera. It seems most probable that he moved away from opera for his own artistic reasons rather than external circumstances or impositions. Both his operas and symphonies were beginning to find a much larger international audience, and Haydn may have decided that he could speak to that audience most effectively through the symphony. However, in 1795 he abandoned the symphony as well, and once again focused his energy on vocal music. It could be argued that Haydn's crowning achievements in relation to the Enlightenment were the masses and oratorios written after he had ceased to write symphonies. A fair assessment of these, however, would require a study much longer than this one is intended to be. The late symphonies are the focus of this study, and the rationale for inclusion of chapters on opera and string quartets arises from chronological relationships and the similarities of compositional procedures.

PART I

Haydn and Enlightened Thought

‥‥‥──◆━──‥‥‥

Haydn and Shaftesbury
Music and Morality

HAYDN had been an active composer for three decades by the 1780s, and had thoroughly established his mastery in all facets of composition. The new level of sophistication and challenge apparent in his works at this time, therefore, appears to have implications beyond matters of craft. To suggest that these implications concern the Enlightenment, however, raises immediate problems and questions. One normally associates the Enlightenment with fields such as philosophy, politics, and literature. If music is to be added to the list—and instrumental music in particular—it becomes necessary to proceed with a critical framework which greatly expands what one normally thinks of as the province of a type of composition such as the symphony. One must also be clear in defining what the Enlightenment may have meant to a late eighteenth-century Austrian composer since this phenomenon was international and in some countries had lost much of its impetus by the time Haydn appears to have developed an interest in it. In order to attempt to answer some of these questions and lay the groundwork for responding to others, it is necessary to define as clearly as possible the nature of enlightened thinking which Haydn is likely to have encountered, and establish the sources of his familiarity with this body of thought.

Haydn and Literati

Traditionally, studies which attempt to place composers in a larger cultural context have been of a general nature, viewing the composer in relation to a *Zeitgeist*. This usually involves the comparison of notable contemporaries, but when considering Austria in the late eighteenth century, the usual approach leads to a pitfall. Austria was very much behind Germany in its philosophical and literary development as a result of the strict censorship which persisted until about 1780. Access to the works of Lessing, Wieland, Voltaire, and others had for the most part been restricted in Austria, and with the lifting of strict censorship, the Viennese literary appetite was for the earlier literature of the Enlightenment rather than the contemporary literature which pointed towards romanticism.[1] Reading and discussion in the Viennese literary salons focused less on the *Sturm und Drang* works of Goethe or Klinger than on mid-century writers or contemporaries whose approaches gravitated towards earlier outlooks. Christian Fürchtegott Gellert (1715–69) emerged as one of the favourites, and others in favour included Lessing, Gleim, Ramler, Jacobi, Hagedorn, and Lavater.[2]

That Haydn shared these preferences is evident in a number of ways. In the case of Gellert, Haydn went so far as to call him his hero. Lavater and Haydn knew each other well enough to exchange correspondence in which Haydn commented favourably on Lavater's works. As for the other writers, it is their works upon which Haydn drew most heavily when choosing texts for his solo songs and part songs, and it appears that in making these choices he relied on the advice of people such as Greiner, at whose literary salon he was an occasional guest. Many of the people with whom Haydn associated at the salons were also members of the Masonic lodge 'Zur wahren Eintracht', and since one of the goals of this lodge was to include leading representatives of all the sciences, arts, and letters, Haydn's membership was considered to be very desirable. Haydn himself had the highest regard for this lodge and its master Ignaz von Born, and enthusiastically presented himself for initiation early in 1785. This assembly was unique among Viennese lodges in that under Born's direction its emphasis was on fostering the goals of the Enlightenment in all areas of endeavour. While Haydn attended no meetings after his initiation, this does not suggest that his support for the principles and values held by these persons had diminished, since the lodge in fact was disbanded before another opportunity for attendance arose.

It will be argued in subsequent chapters which focus on Haydn's literary and Masonic connections that certain writers and Freemasons had a decisive effect on his thinking from the late seventies to the mid-eighties. Gellert and Born have been singled out as having had particularly strong influence on Haydn, and it is possible through these individuals to get to the source of the enlightened thinking which Haydn ultimately attempted to apply in his works. In the case of Born, one discovers that he was the inspiration for a book on Anthony Ashley Cooper, the Third Earl of Shaftesbury (1671–1713), by the German writer Johann Georg Schlosser. Item 917 in the catalogue used for the public auction of Born's library after his death is as follows: Schlosser (J.) *über Schaftsbury von der Tugend an Hrn von Born*, Basel, 1785'.[3] Schlosser, whose first wife was the sister of Goethe, spent the years 1778

---

[1] See Roswitha Strommer, 'Wiener literarische Salons zur Zeit Joseph Haydns', in Herbert Zeman (ed.), *Joseph Haydn und die Literatur seiner Zeit* (Eisenstadt, 1976), 97–121.

[2] Ibid., p. 111.

[3] *Catalogus Bibliothecae Bornianae Publica Auctione Ventetur* (Vienna, 1791).

to 1783 in Vienna where his closest associates were the Freemasons Blumauer, Ratschky, Denis, and Sonnenfels.[4] With Born, however, he developed a particularly strong friendship, and his book *Ueber Schaftsbury* reads like an extended letter to Born, periodically addressing him in person. The book is intended to be instructive concerning Shaftesbury's moral outlook, but at the same time it is a recognition that the ideas of the Enlightenment which Born espoused and practised were fundamentally similar to Shaftesbury's thought. Other titles by Schlosser include *Ueber Toleranz* and 'Fragmente über die Aufklärung'. The idea of tolerance was central to Born's scheme and, it will be argued, is also fundamental to Haydn's approach to symphonies in the eighties and nineties. Since it was from Born and his circle that Haydn became fully acquainted with the tenets of the Enlightenment, one can look to Shaftesbury, whose works were well known and admired in Vienna, as a possible primary source of the ideas which had a profound effect on Haydn.

The possible importance of Shaftesbury to Haydn is apparent in other ways as well. Haydn's preference for the works of Gellert has already been noted, and with this predilection he was in good company as it was also shared by Telemann, C. P. E. Bach, and Beethoven, among others. While Gellert was the most popular literary practitioner of moral philosophy in the middle of the eighteenth century in Germany, his outlook was by no means unique and in fact owed much to the ideas of Shaftesbury. In this, Gellert was not alone among German writers: more than one commentator has noted that Shaftesbury's philosophy was more warmly received in Germany than in England.[5] Other German writers with a particular interest in Shaftesbury include Hagedorn, Lessing, and Weisse, all of whom Haydn used in musical settings of poetry. The pious Gellert had some reservations about Shaftesbury since he was not prepared to accept that everything, including religion, could be subjected to the test of ridicule. However, even Gellert in his play *Betschwester* attacks religious ostentation in a very Shaftesburian way. But in spite of some doubts, Gellert's view of Shaftesbury was largely supportive, as can be seen from the fact that his *Moralische Vorlesungen* was an exegesis of Shaftesbury's moral system.[6]

Shaftesbury's notable work (and clearly one of the most influential works of the entire eighteenth century) was his *Characteristics of Men, Manners, Opinions, Times*, a collection of the following six essays in three volumes:

[4] D. Alfred Nicolovius, *Johann Georg Schlossers Leben und literarisches Wirken* (Bonn, 1844), p. 81.

[5] Lawrence Marsden Price, *The Reception of English Literature in Germany* (Berkeley, 1932), p. 96.

[6] See ibid., and Elda Eggert, 'The Influence of Certain English Moral Philosophers upon the Writings of C. F. Gellert', MA thesis (University of California at Berkeley, 1928), pp. 6–18.

vol. i   1. 'A Letter concerning Enthusiasm',
         2. '*Sensus Communis*; an Essay on the Freedom of Wit and Humour',
         3. '*Soliloquy*, or Advice to an Author';
vol. ii 4. 'An Inquiry concerning Virtue and Merit',
         5. 'The Moralists; a Philosophical Rhapsody';
vol. iii 6. 'Miscellaneous Reflections on the said Treatises and Other Critical Subjects'.

Haydn ultimately acquired his own copy of *Characteristics*, although curiously it was an English version published in 1790 rather than the German translation of 1776–9 (*Bibl.* 180–1). With Haydn's limited command of English, it is questionable how carefully he read a work such as this, or whether he read it at all. Possibly of greater importance here is the actual choice of a particular book. Owning a book may very well have been a type of concrete or tangible endorsement of ideas and theories with which he had been familiarized in conversations with friends or at a literary salon.

Shaftesbury's *Characteristics* was an enormously popular work throughout the eighteenth century, as can be seen from the numerous editions in which it was issued. It was directed not only to persons who wished to achieve greater refinement, but also had specific instructions for those in a position to influence others, and artists in particular. Given the importance of this book and the fact that its ideas were so much in the air, it was inevitable that these ideas should sooner or later find their way into the consciousness of a leading artist such as Haydn. That these principles should emanate from an English writer seems most appropriate. Shaftesbury and most other eighteenth-century aestheticians would not have guessed that instrumental music could be an effective means of conveying enlightened ideas. Haydn's achievement at the end of the century showed that music and the Enlightenment were entirely compatible, and it is most fitting that this should have been demonstrated in such an extraordinary way in England.

From the titles of the works in question by Shaftesbury, Gellert, and Schlosser (also speaking for Born), it is obvious that morality is the central issue, even where art works are concerned. Haydn's own comments also confirm this although not in any systematic way. In general, his remarks which have a bearing on morality or the Enlightenment, and the connection of these with his music, tend in some ways to be more tantalizing than informative. Most of these remarks were made during the last ten years of his life, a time when his memory was becoming progressively less trustworthy. Apart from that, of course, one must also take into account the veracity of the persons who chronicled these remarks. G. A. Griesinger is generally considered to be the most reliable of the Haydn biographers (*Chron.* ii. 117), and to

Griesinger Haydn responded 'that he oftentimes had portrayed moral characters in his symphonies' (*Not*. 62). Sketches of 'moral characters' were commonplace in the eighteenth century, appearing profusely in the moral weeklies which abounded in France, Germany, and England.[7] Haydn's choice of the precise term used by Gellert, Johann Mattheson, and the moral weeklies was not coincidental. While it is possible that Haydn may have intended particular movements (especially slow ones) as musical portrayals of moral characters, it seems more probable that his remark was intended in a general sense, indicating that morality in the eighteenth-century context was central to his symphonies.

Shaftesbury is as much concerned with aesthetics as he is with morality, and in fact, aesthetics and ethics are virtually indistinguishable in his outlook. For the most part the application of morality to art concerns literature, but there are occasional specific references to music, and it is remarkable how similar some of these, along with the more general philosophy, are to Haydn's new approach in the eighties. The six long essays of *Characteristics* form a very extensive philosophical and critical work, and the object here is not to give a complete summary. Rather, it is to take key aspects of Shaftesbury's thought and present them in a way that allows one to see similarities with Haydn's new approaches. The similarities are very striking but this perhaps should not come as a surprise. It would, of course, be incorrect to insist that Haydn's symphonic refinements came about as the direct result of the influence of Shaftesbury, Gellert, Born, or anyone else; undoubtedly some of his approaches were self-initiated and just happened to correspond with views that were common currency. The point is that Haydn, in respect to the predominant aesthetic outlook of his century, was not an isolationist but was very much a part of the mainstream.

Shaftesbury's Moral Thought

Central to all of Shaftesbury's thought is the importance of morality and, indeed, morality is the main pillar of the Enlightenment. Morality, however, is not to be understood in a narrow religious sense but is now placed in a secular context where it can be equated with taste. For Shaftesbury, all aspects of the aesthetic process spring from a true grasp of morality. This includes the basis for a relationship between an author and his audience, the definition of beauty, the function of the rules of art, the dramatic conflict of opposing forces, intelligibility, the use of humour

[7] See Ute Schneider, *Der Moralische Charakter. Ein Mittel aufklärerischer Menschendarstellung in den frühen deutschen Wochenschriften* (Stuttgart, 1976), pp. 53–64; Wolfgang Martens, *Die Botschaft der Tugend. Die Aufklärung im Spiegel der deutschen moralischen Wochenschriften* (Stuttgart, 1968), pp. 168–284; and Eric Blackall, *The Emergence of German as a Literary Language, 1700–1775* (Cambridge, 1959), pp. 59–101.

or ridicule, and the arrival at a principle of tolerance. Morality and beauty in fact are seen as ends in themselves. In its secular sense morality is pursued not for self-interest (the rewards of heaven) but rather for achieving a sense of personal satisfaction and the pleasure in contributing to a decent and humane society. Similarly the contemplation of something beautiful such as an art work should be relatively free of utility or functional orientation. In large measure the act of contemplating something beautiful is a step towards improving morality since refinement of the senses was seen as an important step in the development of virtue. Here Shaftesbury coins the term 'moral sense', which in fact is identical to aesthetic sense. But at the same time, the work of art, like an orator's speech, can be designed in a way which accounts for an ethos and maximizes the effect. It is necessary therefore for an author to know his audience and be able to lead it in the appropriate direction.

Shaftesbury's emphasis on morality in relation to literature and all other types of discourse places a responsibility on authors themselves, who should be of high moral character. With this new focus on authors there may be some reason to assume that Shaftesbury was anticipating the similar inclination of the romantics. However, since his interest was in an author's moral character, in this respect there is a stronger affinity to the seventeenth century than the nineteenth.[8]

Morality is at the heart of all Shaftesbury's philosophical concerns, and it is of primary importance to his study to illustrate how it should be conveyed to an audience. Here one finds an equating of the message with its mode of expression, a sense that morality cannot be transmitted except in a context of beauty. This leads further, to a proposition that morality and beauty are in fact identical, and that manners, art, and nature can all be measured by the same standard. In his own words, 'the most natural beauty in the world is honesty and moral truth. For all beauty is truth' (*Char.* i. 142).[9] And further, he states that his main purpose in writing the essays of *Characteristics* was, 'to assert the reality of a beauty and charm in moral as well as natural subjects, and to demonstrate the reasonableness of a proportionate taste and determinate choice in life and manners' (iii. 303).

The standard by which both beauty and morality can be measured is order or proportion. In both art and manners there is a process of self-improvement of which control is the principal element, control which can be achieved through order and proportion: ''Tis a due sentiment of

---

[8] See Scott Selby, 'Soliloquy, Colloquy, and Dialectic: The Rhetorical Strategies of Shaftesbury's *Characteristics*', Ph.D. thesis (University of California at Berkeley, 1982), p. 70.

[9] Shaftesbury's capitalizations and italicizations are not always included in the various quotations given here. Some minor changes in punctuation and spelling have been made.

morals which alone can make us knowing in order and proportion, and give us the just tone and measure of human passion' (i. 278). Order and proportion can also be called 'inward numbers', giving rise to the following observation:

And thus the sense of inward numbers, the knowledge and practice of the social virtues, and the familiarity and favour of the moral graces, are essential to the character of a deserving artist, and just favourite of the Muses. Thus are the Arts and Virtues mutually friends: and thus the science of virtuosos and that of virtue itself become, in a manner, one and the same.' (i. 338)

Music for Shaftesbury was a favourite image in discussions of the parallels between natural and moral order: 'For harmony is harmony by nature . . . So is symmetry and proportion founded still in nature . . . 'Tis the same case where life and manners are concerned. Virtue has the same fixed standard. The same numbers, harmony, and proportion will have place in morals, and are discoverable in the characters and affections of mankind' (i. 353).

The process of self-improvement is one of developing discriminating judgement and being able to apply this to all facets of art and life:

No sooner the eye opens upon figures, the ear to sounds, than straight the beautiful results, and grace and harmony are known and acknowledged. No sooner are actions viewed . . . than straight an inward eye distinguishes, and sees the fair and the shapely, the amiable and the admirable, apart from the deformed, the foul, the odious, or the despicable. (ii. 414–15)

With this description of the mental power which responds to beauty, he is alluding to the moral sense.[10] Just as morality and beauty are indistinguishable in his scheme of things, similarly moral sense can be said to be the same thing as aesthetic sense. Clearly another term which could be substituted for moral sense is taste, a word which normally applies to artistic judgement but could also refer to manners. While taste involves the ability to make instinctive judgements, the instinct should in fact be a reaction to something more rational which is acquired through an educational process.[11]

The aspect of Shaftesbury's thought which links him in spirit with the romantics is his view that virtue or beauty should be ends in themselves, free of self-interest. The application of the idea of 'disinterestedness' to art results in possibly the most significant distinguishing feature separating modern and ancient art, a phenomenon which M. H. Abrams has identified as 'art-as-such'. Abrams points to Shaftesbury as the source for 'the crossing over of these theological terms, especially "contemplation" and "disinterested," into aesthetic theory', although he

[10] Selby, 'Soliloquy, Colloquy, and Dialectic', p. 61.
[11] Ibid., p. 91.

recognizes that the aesthetic theory resulted from the primary task of developing a 'virtuoso ideal of connoisseurship' for the gentleman.[12] God, nature, or art were not to be loved as means to something (reward or possession), but should be contemplated disinterestedly as ends for their excellence or beauty. Shaftesbury himself uses the word 'disinterested', speaking of virtue which results from reason or free choice rather than something enforced by penalty or reward (*Char.* i. 101–2). Love or virtue are seen in a hierarchical scheme, moving from self-love to love of one's family, society, and finally the cosmos.[13] As one proceeds through this hierarchy there is less opportunity for reward and hence a greater measure of virtue is achieved.

There may seem to be some sense of contradiction in an aesthetic view which on the one hand advocates disinterestedness and on the other suggests that art should instruct in matters of morality. The contradiction is removed by the fact that the moral sense unites morality and aesthetics. The way in which the arts instruct in morality, then, is not necessarily direct. Since beauty and virtue are synonymous, moral improvement comes by way of the application of taste which gives rise to a refinement of the person. The rules of art play a significant role here, although rules are clearly not to be taken in an old, pedantic sense. It is through rules that order and proportion can be achieved, and since these form the standard of beauty, the end result of a knowledge of the rules will be a heightened sense of virtue. The process could work either way: learning the rules could be seen as a moral activity which improves one's sensitivity to art, or sensitivity to art can be seen as something which heightens morality.

In a body of thought in which beauty and virtue are equated and emphasis is placed on the moral character of authors, it naturally follows that the relationship between authors and their audiences will also be of the greatest possible importance. Here Shaftesbury held up the author–audience relationship of the ancients as the ideal in contrast to what he perceived as the unfortunate conditions of his own time. As for the ancients, 'they formed their audience, polished the age, refined the public ear and framed it right, that in return they might be rightly and lastingly applauded. Nor were they disappointed in their hope. The applause soon came and was lasting, for it was sound' (i. 264). In contrast to this, 'our modern authors . . . are turned and modelled (as [they] themselves confess) by the public relish and current humour of the times' (i. 264). He mocks the artist or artisan who ignores or disdains the public, but regard for the public did not mean pandering to it. His

---

[12] 'Art-as-Such: The Sociology of Modern Aesthetics,' *Bulletin of the American Academy of Arts and Sciences*, 38/6 (1985), p. 29.

[13] Selby, 'Soliloquy, Colloquy, and Dialectic', p. 231.

advice to modern authors was that 'they should add the wisdom of the heart to the task and exercise of the brain, in order to bring proportion and beauty into their works. . . . And having gained a mastery here [within themselves], they may easily, with the help of their genius and a right use of art, command their audience and establish a good taste' (i. 277). An artist, then, must not only present that which is appropriate to his audience, but he must also aim for something higher, the contemplation of which will result in the elevation of virtue.

The role of the ancient writers, in which, according to Shaftesbury, they formed, polished, and refined the audience, represented to him the ideal writer–audience relationship. In fact, in the essays of *Characteristics*, Shaftesbury attempted to assume this role with his own reading public. The moral concerns of his works are not the philosophy of ethics in the normal sense of philosophical explanation, but they belong, as Ernest Tuveson points out, 'to rhetoric rather than to philosophical discourse, for their intention is to incite men to action: nothing less than a sweeping reform of themselves and society'.[14] As for poetry, Shaftesbury saw its chief purpose in its ability to make people or societies more virtuous, although this would not be achieved through a conventional approach to morality. Persuasion was a key element in the process, but persuasion now involved a new approach to the arts:

It may be easily perceived from hence that the goddess PERSUASION must have been in a manner the mother of poetry, rhetoric, music, and the other kindred arts. For 'tis apparent that where chief men and leaders had the strongest interest to persuade, they used the highest endeavours to please. . . . Almost all the ancient masters of this sort were said to have been musicians. . . . But where PERSUASION was the chief means of guiding the society, . . . there orators and bards were heard, and the chief geniuses and sages of the nation betook themselves to the study of those arts by which the people were rendered more treatable in a way of reason and understanding, and more subject to be led by men of science and erudition. The more these artists courted the public, the more they instructed it. (i. 237–9)

Didacticism, however, has various sides, and one is that poetic pleasure in itself is instructional, reinforcing the sense that virtue can be heightened from the refinement which occurs in the pleasurable experience of contemplating poetry: 'When the persuasive arts were grown thus into repute . . . many geniuses . . . would content themselves with the contemplation merely of these enchanting arts. These they would the better enjoy the more they refined their taste and cultivated their ear' (i. 239–40).

One could argue, then, that the didactic role of the arts was not in

---

[14] 'Shaftesbury and the Age of Sensibility', in Howard Anderson and John S. Shea (eds.), *Studies in Criticism and Aesthetics, 1600–1800* Minneapolis, 1967), p.75.

direct moral instruction, but was in refining and directing the audience
in its ability to read or listen: 'There must be an art of hearing found ere
the performing arts can have their due effect, or anything exquisite in the
kind be felt or comprehended' (i. 240). His own written works provide
writers with a type of model in this regard even though they were not
necessarily intended to do this. His own mode of presentation is that of
soliloquy or, according to Scott Selby, 'an internalized form of dialogue,
in which the audience is walked through the process of self-discovery'.[15]
Thus a special rhetorical relationship is established with the audience,
which Selby observes is similar to informal conversation: 'In this
conversation, Shaftesbury moves the audience to his position through
his *ethos*, through the common premise shared by both author and
audience. . . . From this common ground, Shaftesbury leads his audience by the hand through the process of discovering his ideas and then
putting these ideas into practice' (p. 206). The model which Shaftesbury
provides for artists is not something formalized but rather is a process.
In this process there is a new potential for intelligibility which, when
taken up by a composer like Haydn in instrumental music, has far-
reaching implications.

    One of the strategies of persuasion was humour, and here, by
establishing a particular tone, the author could fortify his relationship
with his audience. The use of humour had not always been held in high
regard, but Shaftesbury argues for poets to be able to 'recommend
wisdom and virtue (if possibly they can) in a way of pleasantry and
mirth. I know not why poets, or such as write chiefly for the
entertainment of themselves and others, may not be allowed this
privilege' (*Char.* i. 134). In part the pejorative association of comedy lay
in the fact that it was normally connected with the lower classes, but
Shaftesbury justified a more universal application in the light of its long
and distinguished history: 'Comedy . . . [was] of admirable use to
explode the false sublime of early poets' (i. 246). Satire and raillery are
fundamental to his own rhetorical strategy, and they are not to be used
except in support of a higher moral objective. Many current writers, he
believed, were unable to see a higher function: 'our satire therefore is
scurrilous, buffooning, and without morals or instruction, which is the
majesty and life of this kind of writing' (i. 266).

    Another strategy of persuasion which can be closely linked with
humour is the manipulation of audience expectation. A change in
expectation could, for example, involve treating a serious subject in a
light manner. Or, it could be much more complex, making use of
paradox in the belief that paradox or uncertainty is good for the process
of reasoning.[16]

---

[15] 'Soliloquy, Colloquy, and Dialectic', p. 28.
[16] Ibid., pp. 199 and 247.

While Shaftesbury associates beauty and virtue with order and proportion, he is also prepared to recognize their opposites and admit the resulting duality into a larger scheme of things. He distinguishes between beauty and deformity, the amiable and the odious, and the harmonious and dissonant, and observes that what one sees in nature is also true of behaviour and actions (*Char.* ii. 28–9). In the arts he notes that the poet is 'a second Maker, a just Prometheus under Jove', who 'forms a whole, coherent and proportioned in itself, with due subjection and subordinacy of constituent parts', and is able to distinguish between opposites. 'Knavery is mere dissonance and disproportion. And though villains may have strong tones and natural capacities of action, 'tis impossible that true judgement and ingenuity should reside where harmony and honesty have no being' (i. 207–8). The presence of dissonance, disproportion, and evil, however, is given an interpretation which allows these to be seen within a larger context of optimism. Harmony is the state towards which the universe in all respects gravitates, and harmony, of course, can be equated with good. Evil exists as a kind of foil against which a better understanding of good can unfold. In works of art, then, dissonance and disproportion serve in a dramatic way to sharpen one's sense of harmony and to lead one through heightened intelligibility to a higher moral plane. Evil exists as a part of a larger whole, and the representation of evil, like darkness in painting or dissonance in music, yields a greater, less superficial harmony. Virtue will not develop unless tested by conflict.

In 'Advice to an Author' Shaftesbury puts forward a fable of a young courtier and a prince in which the courtier, aided by the prince, comes to the realization that there are two persons in one individual self: 'when the good prevails, 'tis then we act handsomely; when the ill, then basely and villainously' (i. 184). The youth is grateful to the prince for extending compassion and allowing for human frailty. Here and at other points in *Characteristics* Shaftesbury arrives at possibly the most significant manifestation of a moral outlook, and that is the importance of a spirit of tolerance. In advocating religious as well as intellectual tolerance, his thinking clearly runs counter to those who hold to any form of 'enthusiasm' or fanaticism. In so doing, he aligns himself with a certain segment of society, one that would hold a similarly enlightened outlook.[17]

In the two chapters which follow, literary and Masonic influences on Haydn will be considered, and it is noteworthy how much of this thought owed a debt to Shaftesbury. Specific matters such as Haydn's interest in humour or his view of artistic rules will be treated in those chapters. The apparent importance attached by Haydn to morality has already been noted and his comment to Griesinger places morality in the

[17] Ibid., p. 155.

context of what he hoped to achieve with his symphonies. It is possible to get much closer to a grasp of this notion by looking at his symphonies in the light of Shaftesbury's views of the artist leading his audience by the hand through a process of discovery, the importance and function of duality, and the arrival at an understanding of tolerance. Full demonstration of this, needless to say, will not be possible until specific works such as Symphony No. 83 or the English Symphonies are examined in detail in Chapters 7 and 12. At this point it must suffice to approach this matter in a more general way. The heightened sense of intelligibility found in the late symphonies in effect involves the building of a kind of lesson in listening directly into the work, thereby placing the audience in a position of being walked through the process of discovery. The process of unfolding, then, is not simply a musical expansion in the sense of close motivic working but it is treated in such a way that its presentation is fundamentally dramatic.

Like Shaftesbury, Haydn places opposing forces within the context of a larger whole, and frequently at the end of first movements in late symphonies the listener is given a special opportunity to contemplate the relationship of the foregoing conflicting forces in a direct way. In many cases this occurs after a fermata or some other attention-arresting device, such as the return of the drum-roll along with part of the slow introduction in Symphony No. 103. The fermata (or other device) is normally followed by some type of fusion of the opposing forces or the presentation of a context which allows one to accept a coexistence of these forces. In so doing, it will be argued, Haydn is presenting a musical demonstration in instrumental music of the idea of tolerance, and it is in this way, consistent with the thinking of Shaftesbury, that he is able to embrace morality in the sense of the Enlightenment.

2

Pre-English Literary Influences

THE historical view of Haydn is that of a composer with a singularly musical mind, not tempted by distractions such as reading literature. Indeed, the opinion advanced by Giuseppe Carpani in his *Le Haydine* (1812), that Haydn was 'an illustrious idiot', seems to have stuck with unusual tenacity for over a century and a half. Rosemary Hughes among others echoes this in her widely distributed study in which she labels Haydn 'the most unliterary of men', possessing a library consisting 'largely of technical treatises on music'.[1] This view of Haydn was altered drastically in 1976 with the publication of *Joseph Haydn und die Literatur seiner Zeit*, a collection of essays edited by Herbert Zeman, treating subjects such as Haydn's involvement in literary salons, the reception of English literature in Austria, and an itemized list of Haydn's library of literary works.

During the 1770s and 1780s he in fact became very much aware of current literary trends as a result of his personal contacts and reading. Aside from his associations with literati noted in Chapter 1 (van Swieten, Greiner, Alxinger, Blumauer, Lavater, Denis, Haschka, Gebler, and Born), Haydn knew Joseph von Sonnenfels. The regard in which Haydn was held by these people attests to the fact that he was no mere entertainer in their view. On the contrary, he was seen by them as an artist whose achievement of order and proportion placed him within the framework of the Enlightenment. His musical goal was not fundamentally different from their own literary goals, and his arrival at that point was in no small way due to their influence.

Gellert

Many of the books in Haydn's personal library were by writers committed to the Enlightenment, and some of those whose poems he set to music include Gellert, Lessing, Gleim, Hagedorn, Bürger, Lichtwer, Gotter, and Ramler. Haydn's real preference was for mid-century writers, and his declared favourite was Christian Fürchtegott Gellert, the most popular German writer of the mid-eighteenth century. We have

[1] *Haydn* (London, 1962), p. 46.

it on the authority of the Swedish diplomat Frederik Samuel Silver-stolpe, who visited Haydn in 1797, that Haydn considered Gellert to be his hero (*Chron.* iv. 256). As further evidence of his keen interest in Gellert we can look to Haydn's part-song settings of a number of Gellert's *Geistliche Oden und Lieder* or the fact that he owned Gellert's complete works in a 1782 Viennese edition (*Bibl.* 177). That Haydn had much in common with Gellert did not escape the notice of his contemporaries. As early as 1766 the *Wiener Diarium* reported that, 'in short, Hayden is that in the music which Gellert is in poetry' (*Chron.* ii. 130). Much later, in 1786, in a conversation between Dittersdorf and Joseph ii, the two agreed that while Mozart could be compared with Klopstock, Haydn had more in common with Gellert.[2] These sugges-tions by contemporaries that Haydn and Gellert had similar outlooks point to the possibility of an interesting comparison.

That Gellert was influenced by Shaftesbury has already been noted, and this can be substantiated further. In England, two of the earliest moral philosophers to take up Shaftesbury's ideas were Francis Hutcheson and David Fordyce, and in some instances Gellert acknow-ledges a debt to these writers rather than to Shaftesbury himself. In the preface to the volume containing his *Moralische Vorlesungen*, he notes that his goal was not to develop a systematic approach to moral philosophy but rather was to focus on key elements, and to achieve this end he drew from writers such as Mosheims, Baumgartens, Hutcheson, and For-dyce.[3] There are various direct references to Shaftesbury in Gellert's works although not all of these are entirely favourable since Gellert had some reservations about Shaftesbury's application of satire to religion. It seems fairly clear that Gellert, whose knowledge of English was good, had read Shaftesbury in English by 1744. He made frequent references to Shaftesburian terms such as 'moral sense', and he accepted Shaftesbury's equation of beauty with virtue.[4] A key source of Gellert's moral thought was English, and it is noteworthy for the purposes of this study that Gellert had a champion in England near the end of the century, in none other than Haydn's friend Thomas Holcroft.

In Gellert's scheme of things, a special relationship existed between the writer and his reading public or audience. Gellert believed that literature should educate, entertain, and improve society in matters of morals, taste, and intellect, all of which were intimately bound together. But the room for improvement was relatively limited since the audience or society towards which Gellert directed his literature was not the

---

[2] Karl Ditters von Dittersdorf, *Lebensbeschreibung. Seinem Sohne in die Feder diktirt* (Leipzig, 1801), p. 213.

[3] C. F. Gellert, *Sämmtliche Schriften*, vi (Leipzig, 1770), p. 5.

[4] See Elda Eggert, 'The Influence of Certain English Moral Philosophers upon the Writings of C. F. Gellert', MA thesis (University of California at Berkeley, 1928), pp. 8–12.

common masses but rather a middle-class audience which was capable of understanding enlightened principles. The special relationship between writer and audience was that the two sustained each other: the writer appealed to a segment of society whose morals and intellect he believed to be exemplary, and the audience had its morals, intellect, and sense of taste reinforced by the writer's literary characters, situations, and moral writings. While this may seem a rather comfortable approach to morality, there is, of course, much more to it.

The advancement of the middle class in literature around the middle of the eighteenth century was a significant step, and called for the formation of entirely new literary genres such as the sentimental comedy and the novel, both of which Gellert was instrumental in developing. Furthermore, while virtue was always reinforced, it was possible to place virtuous characters in impossible situations where correct solutions did not exist. This happens more than once in Gellert's novel *Leben der Schwedischen Gräfin*, in which characters necessarily commit evil regardless of the options they choose. This type of literary situation both challenges the intellect and addresses the issue of intolerance. By showing that a solution may not exist, the writer is demonstrating a need for tolerance and repudiating dogmatism. The same general literary situation could then be applied to ideas, beliefs, religion, or politics.

Although Gellert directed his works towards a specific audience, he nevertheless was a 'populist', believing his literature should be accessible to all. The new genres were, in effect, the result of developing a new literary language, one which had a 'natural' sense about it and was derived from the middle class.[5] Gellert believed his works should have universal applicability and in this respect their prime function was to express and impart lasting values.[6] A literary work would achieve its lasting value through its didactic approach and consequently would be of use to the world in making it a better place. This view was also put forward by Johann Georg Sulzer (another German aesthetician influenced by Shaftesbury), who saw the writer in his *Allgemeine Theorie der Schönen Künste* as an educator, prophet, and benefactor to the nation.[7]

At the centre of Gellert's concept of betterment was his emphasis on taste. For Gellert and the eighteenth century, taste was not the ephemeral thing it is for our century. It embraced reason, feeling, virtue, and morals, and consequently was the corner-stone of social relevance. In his own words, taste is 'eine richtige, geschwinde Empfindung, vom

---

[5] See Eric Blackall, *The Emergence of German as a Literary Language, 1700–1775* (Cambridge, 1959), p. 204.

[6] See Heidrun Arnason, 'Christian Fürchtegott Gellert's Literary-Critical Ideas', Ph.D. thesis (University of Waterloo, 1976), p. 22.

[7] See Bruno Markwardt, *Geschichte Deutschen Poetik*, ii (Berlin, 1956), p. 151.

Verstande gebildet' (a genuine, immediate feeling, shaped by intellect).[8] A particular type of taste was 'moralischer Geschmack', and to cultivate this he presented portrayals of moral characters. Of course it was possible to portray evil characters as well, but in teaching virtue, their use was severely limited because only their negative characteristics could be shown. In plays, both virtue and vice would be present in different characters in order for drama to exist.

Taste serves to mediate between feeling and reason, and when also applied to works of art, taste must arbitrate between impulsive expression and artistic rules.[9] In an age which spawned Anacreontic poetry, rules were to be taken seriously. Gellert's view, which closely resembled Pope's in the *Essay on Criticism*, was that the creation of great works of art precedes the rules, and hence, the rules are derived from the works themselves. While a knowledge of the rules was essential to the artistic process, an assiduous following of them would probably yield nothing more than a dull, insipid work. Each work demands its own rules and the rules will be determined by the conditions of the work.[10]

The middle class saw itself as the purveyor of morality, but being politically confined, its emphasis was placed on the family circle and small social gatherings. In tailoring his works to fit the sensibilities of his middle-class audience, Gellert needed to avoid certain traditional literary types as well as achieve special balances. The sentimental comedy avoided that which was heroic or tragic or had other aristocratic leanings, using language, characters, and situations appropriate to the humbler classes. Similarly, farce and comedy using ridicule were avoided although it was still common to include silly characters who could be contrasted with virtuous ones. The extent to which laughter in the theatre was permissible sparked considerable debate, and Gellert's view was that while decorum should prevail, humour should not necessarily be excluded.[11]

Gellert was a deeply religious person but his religious goals became intertwined with those of the Enlightenment and found their more convincing expression in secular forms. The final aim of this entire process of education, refinement of taste, and moral instruction was a more dignified and happy life. Along the way certain balances were perceived as being necessary, including those between imagination and reason, and between heart and mind.[12] A work of art should be both

---

[8] 'Wie weit sich der Nutzen der Regeln in der Beredsamkeit und Poesie erstecke', *Sämmtliche Schriften*, v (Leipzig, 1769), p. 174.

[9] See Arnason, 'Gellert's Literary-Critical Ideas', p. 36.

[10] Ibid., pp. 44–5, 48, 55.

[11] See John Van Cleve, *Harlequin Besieged: The Reception of Comedy in Germany during the Early Enlightenment* (Berne, 1980), pp. 118–19, 129–30.

[12] Arnason, 'Gellert's Literary-Critical Ideas', p. 272.

instructional and entertaining: if it failed to entertain, its didactic purpose would probably be ignored. While one should strive for unity, diversity was essential, and in fact various writers, including Lessing and Blumauer, did not believe unity was possible to achieve.[13] A contrived unity, then, was unsatisfactory; a much higher form of unity was an ability to allow conflicting forces to coexist.

While social class may have been a factor in the development of a new literature, similar distinctions would be much more difficult to draw in music. The middle class did indeed become a factor, able to attend concerts as a result of the new concert societies which emerged in various countries. However, in the shift from court music to concert societies, the aristocracy remained of key importance, for both financial support and concert attendance. Instead of an isolation of social classes in the performing arts, there appears to have been an integration. This integration is of course reflected in other facets of life, particularly in Austria where leading political reformers were often from the ranks of the nobility, and the balance of membership in progressive organizations such as Masonic lodges was probably tilted in favour of the aristocracy.

While Haydn came from a working-class background, his education, abilities, and living experiences in effect removed him from any distinctive class. His socially confined existence at Eszterháza was in many ways distasteful, but this was counterbalanced by the attractions of Vienna, which included his friends such as the Genzinger family, van Swieten, and Greiner, as well as the musical and literary salons. As his letters to Maria Anna von Genzinger attest, one of his favourite pastimes was attending the small social gatherings which involved good food, conversation, and music. The audience Haydn was attempting to reach, then, was one he knew well since it was made up of people of various backgrounds such as those with whom he liked to associate in Vienna. Many of these were active reformers in Austria and were clearly receptive to music or literature which attempted to serve enlightened goals.

In devising a musical language to achieve these goals, literary models nevertheless appear to have been of considerable importance. Just as Gellert developed a more natural language, Haydn gradually drew more heavily on source material which could appeal to a broad social spectrum. In symphonic first movements, for example, he progressively made greater use of themes derived from folk sources. Haydn's 'populist' approach and wish for his works to be universally accessible is affirmed in his letter to William Forster concerning *The Seven Last Words*: 'Each Sonata, or rather each setting of the text, is expressed only by

---

[13] See Henry E. Allison, *Lessing and the Enlightenment* (Ann Arbor, 1966), p. 138, and Bärbel Becker-Cantarino, *Aloys Blumauer and the Literature of Austrian Enlightenment* (Berne, 1973), p. 15.

instrumental music, but in such a way that it creates the most profound impression even on the most inexperienced listener' (*Cor.* 60). Central to the thought of writers of the Enlightenment was the belief that the work of art should have a role in the betterment of society and, in Gellert's framework, to do this very directly. Haydn's remark to Griesinger on this subject is very strong: 'I also believe I have done my duty and have been of use to the world through my works' (*Not.* 56).

Gellert's preoccupations with taste, moral characters, and rules are also addressed by Haydn. While Haydn's comments on rules are not systematic like Gellert's, he nevertheless expresses the same point of view. A narrow adherence to rules would, he believed, yield works devoid of taste and feeling (*Not.* 13). But there was a balance: 'Once I had seized upon an idea, my whole endeavor was to develop and sustain it in keeping with the rules of art' (*Not.* 61), implying that the rules related to the context of the work but in no way determined the work. Griesinger further notes that strict theoreticians took exception to Haydn's comic fooling and that Haydn was not particularly put off by this. Comic gestures such as the 'great bassoon joke' of Symphony No. 93 or the 'clucking' theme in Symphony No. 83 could be accommodated in the same way that Gellert believed laughter should not be completely restricted in the theatre. In fact, the fusion of comic and serious elements allowed the new sentimental genre to find its distinctive tone, and one can see Haydn operating on this principle.

Like Gellert, whose religious thoughts were frequently given secular expression, Haydn had no doubt that religious truths could sometimes be expressed best through non-religious means. He argued this point vehemently in his letter to Charles Ochl, refuting the claim by the parish priest of St. Johann that *The Creation* was a desecration of the church:

The story of the creation has always been regarded as most sublime, and as one which inspires the utmost awe in mankind. To accompany this great occurrence with suitable music could certainly produce no other effect than to heighten these sacred emotions in the heart of the listener, and to put him in a frame of mind where he is most susceptible to the kindness and omnipotence of the Creator.—And this exaltation of the most sacred emotions is supposed to constitute desecration of a church? . . . No church has ever been desecrated by my *Creation.* (*Cor.* 187)

Haydn's understanding of morality or virtue was by no means confined to his knowledge of Gellert's works or the influence of Viennese literati. One of the earliest influences on Haydn was *Der vollkommene Capellmeister* by Johann Mattheson (1739). Haydn acquired this text at a formative age, and while he found the exercises dry and dull, he nevertheless worked out all the examples in the book (*Nach.* 96). In the course of studying this text, he undoubtedly encountered Mattheson's ideas concerning affect and rhetoric. Mattheson is not only important to music historians but he also played a crucial role in the development of the moral weeklies. The first of the moral weeklies in Germany, *Der Vernünfftler*, published in Hamburg in 1713 and 1714, aspired to be a German equivalent of the works by Addison and Steele, and in fact many of the articles were direct translations from the *Spectator* or the *Tatler*. The editor of this journal was none other than Johann Mattheson, and the moral thought propagated in *Der Vernünfftler* is still very much evident in *Der vollkommene Capellmeister*. In part 1, chapter 3 of the latter work, Mattheson makes the following statement concerning the purpose of music: 'for it is the true purpose of music to be, above all else, a moral lesson [*Zucht-Lehre*]'.[14]

Concerning the usefulness of his works to the world, Haydn offered some clarification of this in his letter to the Musikverein in Bergen: 'There are so few happy and contented peoples here below; grief and sorrow are always their lot; perhaps your labours [his own works] will once be a source from which the care-worn, or the man burdened with affairs, can derive a few moments' rest and refreshment' (*Cor.* 209). The subject here, like that for Gellert, is happiness, and if it cannot be possessed, at least moments of it should be permitted.

Other writers

Two individuals who appear to have played fairly major roles in Haydn's life, giving advice, providing texts, recommending reading, and introducing him to other literati in Vienna, were Franz Sales von Greiner and Gottfried van Swieten. Both held prominent positions in the Austrian government, Greiner as Court War Secretary and van Swieten as President of the Court Commission on Education, and both were noted social reformers. Greiner has been described as 'the prototype of the enlightened, thinking and active civil servant', and by a contemporary as 'a smooth, right-thinking, understanding, active man, worthy of respect; protector of the sciences and the enlightenment, enemy of hypocrisy and bigotry' (*Chron.* ii. 502). Similarly van Swieten was distinguished by his liberal outlook and his commitment to the ideals of the Enlightenment.[15] It was during the early eighties that he was most active and effective as an educational reformer. His own enlightened views concerning morality and tolerance were very much a part of his plans for education, and he also addressed the importance of rhetoric for the education of the clergy in particular. As a highly sophisticated

[14] Quoted in Hans Lenneberg, 'Johann Mattheson on Affect and Rhetoric in Music', *Journal of Music Theory*, 2 (1958), p. 51.

[15] See Ernst Wangermann, *Aufklärung und staatsbürgerliche Erziehung: Gottfried van Swieten als Reformator der österreichischen Unterrichtswesens 1781–1791* (Munich, 1978).

musician, van Swieten did not overlook the educational value of music as a means for developing taste and hence moral refinement. As a result of his enlightened convictions, literary and musical interests (Gellert and Voltaire were among his early literary favourites), and prominence in the field of education, he was in a unique position to exert an influence on Haydn which embraced much more than purely musical matters.

Concerning Haydn's acquaintance with these men, he wrote on two occasions to his publisher Artaria about Greiner, in fact complaining about Greiner's negligence in returning song texts to him. The fact that Haydn wanted Greiner's 'opinion as to the expression contained therein' (*Cor.* 27) suggests that Greiner was and probably had for some time been an adviser to Haydn on literary matters. Haydn knew van Swieten at least as early as 1775 (*Cor.* 20), and van Swieten provided Haydn with the texts for works such as *The Seven Last Words*, *The Creation*, and *The Seasons*. Both Greiner and van Swieten were highly active in the advancement of the arts and held regular salons to achieve this. In both cases it is likely that Haydn was a more than occasional guest. At Greiner's literary salon Haydn met the most prominent literary people of Vienna and some who were visiting from other countries as well. Van Swieten's salon was musical, focusing on the works of Bach and Handel. While van Swieten was considered by many to be stiff and cold, a warm soul was also recognized behind the formal exterior.[16]

One of the noted foreign writers Haydn met (probably at the Greiner salon) was the controversial Swiss theologian Johann Caspar Lavater. In 1781 Haydn wrote to Lavater, announcing that his new String Quartets, Op. 33 ('written in a new and special way'), were available for subscription, and he stated that he loved and happily read Lavater's works (*Cor.* 32). While his claim of affection for Lavater's works could be put down to good salesmanship, one must proceed on the assumption that Haydn was an honest man. Nowhere do we discover which of Lavater's works Haydn may have known, but aside from his enormously popular study of physiognomy,[17] Lavater was an important exponent of enlightened moral philosophy. In his *Aphorisms on Man* of 1788, he summarized much of his earlier thinking. Concerning the relationship of art and human matters, he stated: 'The enemy of art is the enemy of nature; art is nothing but the highest sagacity and exertion of human nature; and what nature will he honour who honours not the human?'[18] Lavater also saw the importance and necessity of inherent dualities, and

[16] Ibid., pp. 16–17.

[17] *Physiognomische Fragmente: Zur Beförderung der Menschenkenntnis und Menschenliebe* (Leipzig and Winterthur, 1775–8). Lavater had a silhouette of Haydn in his collection, and he wrote the following under it: 'Something more than ordinary I perceive in the eyes and the nose; The forehead too is good; in the mouth something philistine', *Not.* 52.

[18] *Aphorisms on Man*, trans. William Blake (London, 1788), pp. 189–90.

expressed this in various ways in the *Aphorisms*: 'Copiousness and simplicity, variety and unity, constitute real greatness of character' (p. 4); 'The study of man is the doctrine of unisons and discords between ourselves and others' (p. 9); and 'Avoid connecting yourself with characters whose good and bad sides are unmixed, and have not fermented together' (p. 215).

Both van Swieten and Greiner had a particular enthusiasm for the works of Gotthold Ephraim Lessing. Van Swieten had known Lessing personally and had been instrumental in the attempt to secure a position for him in Vienna.[19] As for Greiner, it was not uncommon for plays such as Lessing's *Minna von Barnhelm* to be performed at his country residence during the summer.[20] While Haydn's familiarity with *Minna* cannot be documented, his awarness of Lessing is evidenced by the fact that in later years he set Lessing texts to music both as solo songs and part songs.

While Lessing was one of the strongest advocates of the didactic function of literature, describing the theatre as his 'pulpit', his didacticism by no means presented a view which was entirely Utopian. There is an element of pessimism present in his works, something which is also apparent in the works of Blumauer and even Gellert, and this pessimism about society indirectly argues the need for tolerance. He held the view that while one should strive towards unity among mankind, the full achievement of this was not possible, and conflict remained an inevitability. This he saw as being true for both societies and individuals. For societies, there is the matter of class, and Lessing saw no possibility of a classless society; differences which are intellectually or economically determined were seen as inevitabilities. Concerning individuals, Lessing accepted something which he called a 'perspectival conception', or the limited truth possessed by any given individual.[21] This would put necessary limitations on the ability of any two individuals to be in agreement. The best of all possible worlds, then, is one which must be seen as containing primary dualities. Social evil is inevitable, and disunity and conflict will in fact be a part of the best of all possible societies.[22] As Henry E. Allison points out, 'this evil is seen not as something arbitrary, which can be removed by a better constitution or plan of creation, but as an ultimate and irreducible aspect of reality'.[23] If an actual unity is not possible, the solution must lie in an ability to accept a larger whole in which opposing forces are able to coexist.

---

[19] Wangermann, *Aufklärung und Erziehung*, pp. 10–11.
[20] Caroline Pichler, *Denkwürdigkeiten aus meinen Leben*, i (Vienna, 1844), p. 127.
[21] See Allison, *Lessing and the Enlightenment*, p. 138.
[22] Ibid.
[23] Ibid.

One of the most articulate spokesmen of the Viennese literary circle was Aloys Blumauer, as is evident from his extended essay *Beobachtungen über Oesterreichs Aufklärung und Litteratur* (Vienna, 1782). Here Blumauer spoke of literature as a vehicle for the education or 'enlightenment' of the people, and of the primary importance of dispelling superstition and intolerance (p. 30). As editor of and a contributor to the *Journal für Freymaurer*, the official mouthpiece of the lodge into which Haydn was initiated, Blumauer will be considered at some length in the following chapter.

Another important literary figure of the Vienna circle was Johann Baptist von Alxinger. At one point van Swieten commissioned Alxinger to write a cantata text entitled *Die Vergötterung des Herkules* for Haydn. While Haydn knew Alxinger personally, he did not use the text, the circumstances of which were explained by Alxinger when he had the work published separately in *Die österreichische Monatsschrift* in 1793. The work was probably written in about 1790, since Alxinger first offered it for publication in 1791 to *Der neue deutsche Merkur* after Haydn declined it.[24] The type of heroic text used in this work was not unrelated to the type of opera which Haydn had more or less abandoned in 1783, suggesting perhaps it was a path Haydn no longer wished to follow. It is noteworthy that Haydn's operas of 1782 and 1783 were based on texts of Tasso and Ariosto, and bore some resemblance to the literary *Rittergedichte* genre of which Alxinger was the leading Viennese exponent. Again, van Swieten, for whom Ariosto and Tasso were particular favourites, was not far removed from the scene.

Greiner, like Charles Burney, had a daughter with exceptional literary ability, and it is from her, Caroline Pichler, that one is able to learn much about the tastes and inclinations of the literary group of Vienna. Her fairly extensive correspondence with Lavater and Lorenz Leopold Haschka as well as her autobiography *Denkwürdigkeiten aus meinen Leben* are indispensable sources of information for the people in this circle as well as their ideas. She refers on a number of occasions to the importance of Gellert to her literary friends as well as the effect of Gellert's works on herself, pointing out that in her early years she would in the evening reflect on the day in the context of Gellert's 'Selbstprüfung', or that she compiled her own prayerbook consisting largely of Gellert's Lieder.[25] The person primarily responsible for introducing her to the works of Gellert was the poet Haschka, who also provided Haydn with the text 'Gott erhalte Franz den Kaiser' for the famous anthem. Haschka was fairly typical of the members of the Viennese literary group in that he

---

[24] See D. E. Olleson, 'Gottfried, Baron van Swieten, and his Influence on Haydn and Mozart', D.Phil. thesis (University of Oxford, 1967), pp. 162–3.
[25] Pichler, *Denkwürdigkeiten*, pp. 83–4.

was educated in a Jesuit order and came to Vienna upon the disbanding of the order, whereupon he was accepted by Greiner into his salon.[26] Also in common with his Viennese colleagues was his ambivalence on various matters including the French Revolution, the church, and Freemasonry. He was not one of the more congenial members of the group as he was less than sympathetic to some of the works of his colleagues.

Possibly the most influential of the literary reformers in Vienna was Joseph von Sonnenfels. Haydn was not the only musician who knew Sonnenfels. Beethoven's respect for him was made evident by the dedication of the Piano Sonata in D, Op. 28, to Sonnenfels in 1802. Sonnenfels was particularly influential in the service of Maria Theresa, and with the decline of that influence after her death, he focused new energy on Freemasonry, providing along with Born the intellectual inspiration for 'Zur wahren Eintracht'. Unlike the stream of ex-Jesuits which had flowed to Vienna, Sonnenfels was Jewish by birth and secured an unusual amount of confidence from the Empress, given her narrow attitude.

Of his various tenaciously fought literary skirmishes, the one which occupied him longest and had the greatest effect was his attempt to rid the Austrian stage of 'Hanswurst', the Austrian slapstick version of the principal *commedia dell'arte* figure. Unlike others who had waged this battle purely at the level of literary taste, Sonnenfels turned it into a social issue, arguing that the fundamental problem was with the low level of the public taste. Rather than placing the blame on the comedians, he argued for reform through education of the public. With improvements in the taste and standards of the audience, the quality of the drama and activities of the actors would naturally rise.[27] In general, Sonnenfels did not like comedy, even of the Goldonian type, much preferring serious or sentimental drama. It is of considerable interest to note Haydn's changing approach to dramatic texts for opera, from *Der krumme Teufel* in the early fifties (commissioned by the most famous of the Viennese Hanswursts, Kurz-Bernadon), through his Goldonian operas of the late sixties and seventies, to his shift to more serious operas in the late seventies and early eighties. The possible influence of Sonnenfels on Haydn's embracing of serious opera will be considered in Chapter 4.

One other writer of the various literary people connected with Haydn who should not go unmentioned is Pietro Metastasio. For a few years in the 1750s Haydn was quartered in a house in which Metastasio also lived. Metastasio showed various kindnesses to the young musician,

---

[26] See Eugene F. Timpe, 'Lorenz Leopold Haschka: One Further Contrast', *Germanic Notes*, 10 (1979), p. 56.

[27] See Robert A. Kann, *A Study in Austrian Intellectual History* (New York, 1960), p. 211.

including free board in exchange for lessons for one of his own pupils and introductions to individuals such as Porpora, from whom, Haydn wrote in 1776, he had 'had the good fortune to learn the true fundamentals of composition' (*Cor.* 19). Metastasio was arguably the leading moral poet of the century, and Haydn set one of his librettos, *L'isola disabitata*, in 1779. During Haydn's years in England, his close friend Charles Burney was writing a large three-volume study of Metastasio, a project which Haydn endorsed and aided in a limited way. Burney's work in the 1790s no doubt rekindled the admiration Haydn had developed for Metastasio about forty years earlier. Metastasio will be discussed in Chapter 9, at which point Burney's biography of him is considered.

Various common threads run through the literary approaches of Haydn's friends and those whose works he read. Tying these together is the relationship between a writer and his audience, a relationship which is built on a shared view of a better social order. Not unlike Shaftesbury, these writers considered morality the key to this and it could be fostered by means of persuasion, the most effective of which was the process of refining taste.

3

The Lodge 'Zur wahren Eintracht'

AMONG the eight Masonic lodges in Vienna before the end of 1785, one in particular stood out as a centre of enlightened activities. As such, this lodge, 'Zur wahren Eintracht', proved to be a natural gathering place for people who were in a position to influence the intellectual, moral, and social direction of the nation. Indeed, it included among its members the leading writers, scientists, and social reformers in Austria, and ultimately Haydn as well. Speculation on the extent of Haydn's interest in Freemasonry has been a matter of curiosity among Haydn scholars for at least a century, but it was not until 1985 that a publication appeared which addressed the issue seriously. Unlike Mozart, who was very active as a Freemason for at least a decade, Haydn's tangible interest in Freemasonry appears on the surface to have been fairly slight. The primary documentation currently available is of very little help. In fact, it seems to cancel itself out as Haydn is seen on the one hand to be professing an interest, and on the other neglecting to attend any meetings after his initiation.

Prior to the appearance of the major article 'Haydn and the Freemasons' by Joachim Hurwitz in 1985,[1] few writers on Haydn were prepared to give more than a sentence or a short paragraph to this subject.[2] It is perhaps notable that writers who have dismissed the subject quickly have generally done so as a result of the belief that Freemasonry was of little or no interest to Haydn. Landon's approach to this subject in 1959 was to sweep it aside with the cursory observation that Haydn's lack of attendance was the result of disappointment with what he found at his initiation (*Cor.* 49). More recently, Landon has been much more prepared to give this subject its due. An earlier dismissal of the issue came from Karl Geiringer, who advances the

---

[1] *Haydn Yearbook*, 16 (1985), 5–98.

[2] The few prepared to go further include Carl Ferdinand Pohl, *Joseph Haydn*, ii (Leipzig, 1882), p. 209; H. Kling, 'Haydn und Mozart und die Freimaurerei', *Neue musikalische Rundschau* [Munich], 1/5 (1908), 6–9; O. E. Deutsch, 'Haydn bleibt Lehrling', *Musica*, 13 (1959), 289–90; Carl Maria Brand, *Die Messen von Joseph Haydn* (Würzburg, 1941), pp. 197–214; Heinrich Eduard Jacob, *Joseph Haydn: His Art, Times, and Glory*, trans. Richard and Clara Winston (London, 1950), pp. 153–7, 274–80; Jacques Chailley, 'Joseph Haydn and the Freemasons', in H. C. Robbins Landon and Roger E. Chapman (eds.), *Studies in Eighteenth-Century Music* (London, 1970), 117–24; H. C. Robbins Landon, *Haydn Chronicle and Works*, ii (London, 1978), pp. 503–8; and Alexander Giese, 'Einige Bemerkungen über Joseph Haydn als Freimaurer und die Freimaurerei seiner Zeit', in Gerda Mraz, Gottfried Mraz, and Gerald Schlag (eds.), *Joseph Haydn in seiner Zeit* (Eisenstadt, 1982), 168–71.

disappointment theory and also suggests that Haydn 'may have been too deeply rooted in the Catholic faith and liturgy to concern himself seriously with the Masonic religious ideas'.[3] This general view is supported by Jens Peter Larsen who concludes that 'for Haydn, unlike Mozart, Freemasonry was apparently only a passing phase'.[4] Rosemary Hughes dismisses the matter with reasons similar to those of Geiringer,[5] and Leopold Nowak asserts that the simplicity of Haydn's nature prevented genuine involvement with a society that depended on secretiveness.[6] The most thorough but also the most aberrant discussion of this subject before 1985 came from Carl Maria Brand, whose personal prejudices and acquiescence to Nazi ideology prevented him from treating it with any degree of objectivity.[7]

The source of the controversy appears to have been the following statement made by Carl Ferdinand Pohl in 1882: 'We are not in the least able to discover whether Haydn found what he had wished and expected in this circle, or whether his joining the Order had any influence on his way of thinking.'[8] That it has taken over a century for Pohl's comment to be addressed or challenged should probably come as no great surprise. A composer who has consistently been described as simple and scarcely more than an *idiot savant* is hardly likely to be thought of as being inclined towards one of the great intellectual and social forces of his century. Thanks to the article by Hurwitz, the issue can now be seen in an entirely new way. Perhaps the greatest value of this article is the thorough presentation of documentation and background along with the cautious and sound interpretation of the available information. For example, Hurwitz settles once and for all the matter of Haydn's lack of attendance after his initiation in response to those who claim this as a sign of lack of interest. The simple fact is that as a result of Haydn's workload at Eszterháza and the *Freimauererpatent* issued by Joseph ii on 11 December 1785, Haydn did not have the opportunity to attend another meeting of 'Zur wahren Eintracht' before the lodge ceased to exist. Even if Haydn had wished to attend the new lodge which emerged from the restructuring (whose register bears his name), he was prevented by his own hectic schedule and the early dissolution of this lodge.[9]

As excellent as Hurwitz's article is, it still presents only part of the picture. Hurwitz is concerned more with 'the role played by Free-

---

[3] *Haydn: A Creative Life in Music* (Berkeley and Los Angeles, 1968), p. 93.

[4] 'Haydn, (Franz) Joseph', *The New Grove Dictionary of Music and Musicians* (London, 1980), viii. p. 341.

[5] *Haydn* (London, 1962), p. 58.

[6] *Joseph Haydn. Leben, Bedeutung und Werk* (Vienna, 1959), p. 298.

[7] See Landon's editorial footnote in Hurwitz, 'Haydn and the Freemasons', p. 39.

[8] *Joseph Haydn*, ii. p. 209.

[9] Hurwitz, 'Haydn and the Freemasons', pp. 42–50.

masonry in the life of Joseph Haydn' (p. 25) than its possible effect on his thinking as an artist, and so must rest his case entirely on archival documentation. His interest in Haydn's music is limited to whether or not Masonic symbolism can be identified, an exceedingly difficult matter since Haydn did not write any music which can be described as being overtly Masonic. Given the severe limitations of the documentation and the potential for analytical sophistry in identifying Masonic symbolism in music, Hurwitz necessarily arrives at a rambling and wistful conclusion.

The approach to be taken here, which will not necessarily yield a more satisfactory response to Pohl's observation, will be considerably more oblique, placing the ultimate burden of 'proof' on Haydn's music written at the time of his greatest Masonic activity. The object here, however, is not to identify specific Masonic features in the music (in particular the symphonies), but to suggest a possible role for Freemasonry in strengthening Haydn in his endeavour to achieve enlightened goals in his music. Contrary to Hurwitz, who believes it is too much to 'expect Haydn to have been much interested in the battle against all kinds of "ignorance, prejudice and superstition" which was the guiding motive among the enlightened activists and supporters in the lodge' (p. 36), this study posits that Haydn was deeply concerned with such matters and that it was his Paris and subsequent symphonies which argue most elequently for tolerance, intelligence, and morality.

The lodge

On 11 February 1785 Haydn's initiation into the lodge 'Zur wahren Eintracht' took place. His letters leading up to the event to the *Hofsecretaire* von Weber and his sponsor Count Apponyi leave little question concerning his attitude, as he writes that 'the highly favourable impression which Freemasonry has made on me has long awakened in my breast the sincerest wish to become a member of the Order, with its humanitarian and wise principles', as well as of 'the inexpressible Joy of being among a circle of such worthy men' (*Cor.* 48–9).

There were eight lodges in Vienna, and one must consider why he joined this lodge rather than one of the others. Narrowing the influence to a particular person appears not to be possible. Mozart was not a member of this lodge although he was a visitor. Greiner and van Swieten clearly had associations with people in this lodge but neither one can be documented as being a member of this or any other lodge. As a guest of the various salons in Vienna, however, Haydn came into contact with some of the most prominent members of this lodge, including Ignaz von Born, and undoubtedly was invited to join in keeping with the policy of the lodge of having the most prominent representatives of different fields among its members. These people were at the forefront of instigating and implementing the ideas of the Enlightenment in politics and literature, both before and after the death of Maria Theresa. Haydn, then, was drawn into the circle of Austria's intellectual élite who had the means to enact social reform and determine the direction of literature after the partial lifting of censorship (indeed, some of them were censors). Social reform and renewed literary activity went hand in hand, and in fact many of the notable officials of government were themselves prominent literati. For Haydn, who enjoyed his associations with these acquaintances in the literary and musical salons, it was a relatively small step to wish to continue this fellowship in the context of a Masonic lodge.

The lodge which appears to have been hit hardest by the *Freimaurerpatent* was 'Zur wahren Eintracht' as a result of its unique focus on literature, science, and moral instruction. Membership declined rapidly as it was absorbed by the new lodge 'Zur Wahrheit' for a variety of reasons, including professional embarrassment and intrigue. Ignaz von Born, *Meister vom Stuhl* of 'Zur wahren Eintracht', was elected master of 'Zur Wahrheit', but by August 1786 he had resigned and abandoned all Masonic ties.[10] Born's withdrawal appears to have triggered an exodus as Sonnenfels and others left shortly thereafter.[11] With the departure of prominent members such as these, it should come as no surprise that an apprentice like Haydn would cease his association in the light of his preference for one particular lodge and the persons who had been members of it. The *Freimaurerpatent* not only limited the major cities of the empire to three lodges each but it eliminated all provincial lodges in keeping with Joseph's plan of centralization.[12] As a result, even if Haydn had wished to attend another lodge at or near Eszterháza (which seems unlikely in any event), the opportunity very simply did not exist.[13]

Haydn's interest in Freemasonry, as expressed in his letter of 29 December 1784, was in its goals and principles. These goals were those of the Enlightenment, and it was at one lodge, 'Zur wahren Eintracht', that he could enjoy hearing these values expressed among men who were for the most part not only prepared to regard him as an equal but also venerated him for his achievements. Since this lodge had a very special attraction for Haydn, it is important to have a clear sense of its goals and scope. Understanding the nature of this lodge is perhaps the most

[10] Ibid., pp. 45–7; and see H. C. Robbins Landon, *Mozart and the Masons: New Light on the Lodge 'Crowned Hope'* (London, 1982), p. 26.

[11] Hurwitz, 'Haydn and the Freemasons', pp. 45–7.

[12] Discussions on the *Freimaurerpatent* can be found in Ludwig Abafi, *Geschichte der Freimaurerei in Oesterreich-Ungarn*, v (Budapest, 1893), pp. 143–80; Edith Rosenstrauch-Königsberg, *Freimaurerei im Josephinischen Wien: Aloys Blumauers Weg vom Jesuiten zum Jacobiner* (Vienna, 1975), pp. 59–64; and Franz Kratter's pamphlet *Drei Briefe über die neueste Maurerrevolution in Wien* (Prague, 1785).

[13] Hurwitz, 'Haydn and the Freemasons', pp. 50–1.

important factor in coming to terms with Haydn's interest in Free-masonry.

Under the guidance of Born, 'Zur wahren Eintracht' became a type of academy or society of science and literature. The special qualities of this lodge are exceedingly well documented. It should hardly be surprising that a lodge filled with prominent literati and educators should be active in the dissemination of Masonic thought. Hurwitz describes these activities in the following way:

Born's lodge convened more than once a week to receive its new candidates and discuss masonic affairs. It introduced the 'Uebungslogen' in which the Instructions about masonic symbolism and morality were followed by lectures for Master Masons about masonic and non-masonic themes. They came to be adopted elsewhere, also by lodges abroad. Above all, 'True Concord' championed learning, and the quality of its scientific and artistic achievements turned it into the intellectual élite lodge which had been the goal of its foundation. The lectures were printed in the *Journal für Freymaurer* . . . and since it [the *Journal*] was meant only for masons it was not subject to official censorship (pp. 16–17).

The Journal

The *Journal* was conceived by Born and Sonnenfels and edited by Aloys Blumauer. Its purpose was to educate fellow Masons about the true purpose of Freemasonry, but it might be more accurate to describe it as an illuminator of 'Zur wahren Eintracht'. It was published on a quarterly basis from the beginning of 1784 to the end of 1786, therefore outliving the lodge itself.

Born and Sonnenfels succeeded in making this the one lodge in Vienna which could be singled out for its link with the literary Enlightenment and enlightened social and political aspirations. Some of the more prominent literary members included Blumauer, Alxinger, Haschka, Leon, Gebler, and Kratter. It has, in fact, been argued that Born turned the lodge into a type of fashionable club for advocates of the Enlightenment.[14] As well as being a mineralogist, Born was a writer of satire and also a contributor to the unending flow of pamphlets in Vienna at this time. He was dedicated to spreading the ideas of the Enlightenment and he achieved this through his own writing and by raising financial support for the needier writers in his circle. Possibly the most gifted of these was Aloys Blumauer, who prefaced the first number of the *Journal für Freymaurer* in the following way:

The purpose of our Masonic journal is to prevent the lamentable

---

[14] See Paul P. Bernard, *Jesuits and Jacobins: Enlightenment and Enlightened Despotism in Austria* (Urbana, 1971), p. 75, and Abafi, *Geschichte der Freimaurerei*, v. pp. 281–3.

consequences of indifference on the part of their often most esteemed members; to present our Order to the Masonry public in its special, most beautiful, and dignified form; to guide the searching spirit of their members only to fruitful paths which run parallel to the welfare of humanity; in short, to provide Masonry with genuine workers devoted to its purpose and through them to give mankind just as many benefactors.[15]

Blumauer's own contributions to the *Journal* emphasize the purpose of the lodge as an instrument of the Enlightenment. In his first substantial article in the *Journal*, 'Rede über den Karakter des Maurers', he discusses the central place of Freemasonry in educating and forming the soul. The first and most essential step before an initiation could take place was moral training, since higher knowledge could not be achieved until this was completed.[16] Morality was, of course, fundamental to the work of every writer of the Enlightenment, and this received the strongest possible reinforcement from Freemasonry.

In various articles Blumauer considered one of the most important features of the order, this being the sense of equality offered by Freemasonry.[17] Unlike the rest of Austrian society which was rigidly stratified by class, Freemasons claimed that wisdom and virtue were to be held as the grounds for equality.[18] In this respect the benefits to a composer such as Haydn were enormous. Not only did he come from a humble social background, but his position as Kapellmeister kept him low in the social order of Eszterháza and left him at the mercy of overzealous, petty officials. The role of educator or moralist towards which the writers of the Enlightenment aspired was for the most part denied to the artist in livery since his social position did not afford sufficient dignity.[19] It is not without significance that Haydn's symphonies, which represent a new point of arrival in his application of enlightened thinking to instrumental music, were commissioned by a Masonic concert society. As their spiritual and social equal, Haydn could address the members of his new audience with the dignity required to be a moral teacher.

The question of the relationship between Freemasonry and the church was a particularly important one for Austrian Freemasons, and Karl Geiringer's assertion that Haydn was too devout a Catholic to take

---

[15] 'Vorerinnerung über die Veranlassung, den Zweck, und die eigentliche Bestimmung dieses Journals', *Journal für Freymaurer*, 1/1 (1784), pp. 9–10.

[16] See Bärbel Becker-Cantarino, *Aloys Blumauer and the Literature of Austrian Enlightenment* (Berne, 1973), p. 39.

[17] This is also discussed by Schittlersberg in 'Ueber die Beobachtung der maurerischen Gleichheit', *Journal für Freimaurer*, 2/1 (1785), pp. 77–82.

[18] See Blumauer, 'Rede über den Karakter des Maurers', *Journal für Freymaurer*, 1/1 (1784), p. 191.

[19] See John Van Cleve, *Harlequin Besieged: The Reception of Comedy in Germany during the Early Enlightenment* (Berne, 1980), p. 115.

Freemasonry seriously must be considered. This issue was addressed by Blumauer in the *Journal*. The new attitude towards religion was clearly non-traditional, and emphasis was placed on the ethical side of religion. God remained very important to Austrian Freemasons, and Blumauer pointed out that man can serve God by doing good in the world.[20] Altruism can have many manifestations, and one is that the literary writer can do good deeds by providing works which have moral or spiritual content. This was an idea which Haydn could support, as can be seen from the statement made to Griesinger which has already been cited: 'I know that God has favoured me, and recognize it thankfully. I also believe I have done my duty and have been of use to the world through my works' (*Not.* 56). Haydn no doubt remained a strong Roman Catholic and saw no particular conflict here with enlightened and Masonic values. The fact that the church did not approve of Freemasonry was no greater a problem for Haydn than it was for hundreds of his compatriots. As well, Hurwitz reminds us that we should not take comments about Haydn's devoutness too literally, since his library did not contain a single devotional book while in fact it did contain various banned books, including at least one Masonic work (p. 75).

The role of literature in spreading and fostering enlightened and Masonic principles was of crucial importance for Born, Blumauer, and the other literati of 'Zur wahren Eintracht'. For Blumauer's view on this, we can return to his *Beobachtungen über Oesterreichs Aufklärung und Litteratur* (1782). While much of this study is an attempt to place the pamphleteering which followed the *Pressfreiheit* into some sort of perspective, he also put forward a direct equation concerning literature and the Enlightenment, stating that the former should serve the latter. It was the duty of the writer to educate the people and attempt to dispel superstition and prejudice (p. 30).

The same sentiments were reflected by Joseph Mayer, whose article 'Ueber die Verbindung der Künste und Wissenschaften mit der Maurerey' appeared in the second number of the *Journal*. According to Mayer, both art and science are primary means of fighting superstition and evil. The deciphering of secrets was seen as one of the most important human achievements, and Masonry, with its progressive steps leading to the level of master, was of course fully committed to this. Science involves the explanation of secrets through the understanding of nature which in turn leads to natural laws and frees humanity from superstition. Through literature, characters can be portrayed in such a way that evil can be given a negative representation or virtue can be reinforced, and in the process secrets about the human condition can be

---

[20] Becker-Cantarino, *Aloys Blumauer*, p. 43.

uncovered. Both science and art are crucial in the discovery of truth, and their function is closely tied to Freemasonry.[21] Mayer gives us possibly the clearest view of the sense of Freemasonry which Born was attempting to cultivate in this lodge.

Born's own lectures and contributions to the *Journal* reflect the preoccupation of Freemasons with secrets, and his first article, 'Ueber die Mysterien der Aegyptier', which directly follows Blumauer's preface to the first volume, is concerned with hieroglyphics. Haydn himself was attracted to these subjects, as can be seen from the fact that he owned a copy of David Hoeschel's *Horapollinis Hieroglyphica* of 1595 (*Bibl.* 182). In fact, there is further evidence of Masonic interest in Haydn's personal library. Most notable is a copy of Gabriel Pérau's *Ordre des francs-maçons trahi* (1744), and indirectly related are Knigge's *Über den Umgang mit Menschen* (1793) and Witgeest's *Natürliches Zauber-Buch* (1762), a delightful book which among other things describes how to make a mechanical car or how to make three asses sing, reading from a score (pp. 136, 45–6)! Mysteries, of course, could easily lead to the area of charlatanism and absurdity.

While themes of the Enlightenment are touched upon throughout the lectures and the *Journal*, the matter is approached directly in Haidinger's 'Ueber die Fortschritte der Aufklärung', which is in the fourth number of volume 2. In his view strides had been made and supporters of the Enlightenment were on the increase, but reformers were reminded to be vigilant against prejudice and other evil or mindless forces which might undermine their work. Again prejudice and intolerance are singled out as forces which must be eradicated, and mankind was to be persuaded to seek illumination in reason.[22]

If the primary function of literature was to further the goals of the Enlightenment, it would not escape the notice of someone associated with the leaders of the Austrian literary movement such as Haydn that music could serve the same function. Mayer's article in fact made no distinction between literature and the other arts but simply used the generic term 'Kunst'. Aside from private exhortations which Haydn may have received in this regard from Born or other friends, he was given a public challenge in the form of an address to himself at his initiation by Joseph von Holzmeister, and the speech appeared in the *Journal* under the title 'Ueber die Harmonie. Bey der Aufnahme des Br. H * * n [Haydn]'.[23] Holzmeister's understanding of music was no doubt somewhat limited but he did nevertheless recognize some important connections between music and Freemasonry. His greatest emphasis

[21] J. Mayer, 'Ueber die Verbindung der Künste und Wissenschaften mit der Maurerey', *Journal für Freymaurer*, 1/2 (1784), 65–104.

[22] Haidinger, 'Ueber die Fortschritte der Aufklärung', *Journal für Freymaurer*, 2/4 (1785), 54–60.

[23] *Journal für Freymaurer*, 2/2 (1785), 175–81. For an English translation, see *Chron.* ii. 506–8.

was on the role which both have in generating unity from diverse and possibly antagonistic forces. He also addressed a number of the basic issues of Freemasonry such as equality, freedom from prejudice, hatred or intrigue, and the pleasure gained from the accomplishment of good deeds and the exercising of the intellect. Near the end of his address, speaking directly to Haydn, he stated that he hoped 'the desire to remain steadfastly true to [his] goddess friend also in this circle' had been awakened (*Chron.* ii. 507). The implication was that Haydn should use music as a means of fulfilling the principles held by the members of the lodge.

Music and Freemasonry

Unlike Mozart, Haydn did not write music for use at Masonic occasions. Similarly, he did not write works such as *Die Zauberflöte* in which Masonic associations are unmistakable. He did, however, bring a new level of achievement to string quartets and symphonies during the 1780s. The new string quartets of 1781 were, according to Haydn, 'written in a new and special way'. His arrival at a new height of realization in the symphonies happened at precisely the time of his initiation into 'Zur wahren Eintracht' (late 1784 and early 1785), and the substance of this arrival, as has already been suggested, was a new level of dramatic intelligibility. This new achievement, which is particularly evident in the first movement of Symphony No. 83, accounted for the audience in a new way in that it demanded a higher degree of reflective listening.

One can see this process emerging in Haydn's symphonies of the seventies and early eighties, but it was not until the Paris Symphonies that its full implications were realized. This set of six symphonies was commissioned by Claude-François-Marie Rigoley, Comte d'Ogny, for the Parisian concert society Le Concert de la Loge Olympique. This was a Masonic concert society which in 1781 took over the activities of the Concert des Amateurs after the financial collapse of that organization. The earlier society had been established in 1769 at the Hôtel de Soubise and was directed by Gossec.[24] While the performers were all Free-masons, attendance at the concerts themselves was not in any way restricted. Landon has speculated (since the correspondence is lost) that the negotiations between Haydn and the Loge Olympique began in 1784 or early 1785 (*Chron.* ii. 592). The arrival of an important commission from a Masonic society at exactly the time of his own initiation may very well have struck Haydn as the ideal opportunity to extend his symphonic language beyond what had already been achieved, allowing these works to play a role in fulfilling those principles held by 'Zur wahren Eintracht'.

[24] See Roger Cotte, *La Musique Maçonnique et ses Musiciens* (Braine-le-Comte, 1975), p. 57.

The type of procedures used in Symphony No. 83 are very much evident in later symphonies as well, written for either Paris or London. While Freemasonry may have been less on Haydn's mind by the time he went to England, it should be noted that Johann Peter Salomon, the source of the commission for the English Symphonies, was a Freemason and member of the London lodge for German-speaking people 'Pilger-loge' No. 238. A further London connection with Freemasonry lay in the fact that the concerts of the Academy of Ancient Music were given at Freemasons' Hall. Not only did Haydn occasionally attend these concerts but his own symphonies were sometimes presented at this hall, and on at least one occasion Haydn himself was asked to conduct (*Chron.* iii. 249, 299). The connection here, as with Paris, lay in the fact the Freemasons were at the forefront of the new social order and their facilities were ideal for reaching the new audience.

The symphonies of Haydn have no hidden Masonic symbolism and there does not appear to be any documented causal connection between his Masonic initiation and his new treatment of symphonic language. In the case of *The Creation*, however, it has been argued that this is a work with special Masonic significance (*Chron.* iv. 349–50), in spite of the fact that it was written only a few years after the *Kriminalpatent* by Francis ii which made all Masonic activity illegal and subject to severe penalty. While such significance is open to question, an unassailable fact about *The Creation* is that it presents humanity in a special way, a manner fully consistent with the thinking of the Enlightenment. Similarly, one could argue that Haydn's new dramatic intelligibility in the symphonies, which makes provision for a heightened process of understanding, allows a comparable type of association.

Haydn's demonstrated interest in Freemasonry lay in one lodge which had a highly distinctive nature. For the members of 'Zur wahren Eintracht', the lodge appeared to be little more than a convenient forum for like-minded persons to share their enthusiasm for the goals of the Enlightenment. When their lodge was absorbed into a larger lodge, many members had no further incentive to remain associated with Freemasonry. Haydn's interest in Freemasonry had similar limitation placed on it; he was attracted to Freemasonry only so long as it could be defined in the context of 'Zur wahren Eintracht'. For the members of this lodge, spreading social reform and enlightened thought was the highest priority, and that is clearly reflected in the literature and lectures which emerged from this circle. Haydn's remark to Griesinger, that he had done his duty and been of use to the world through his works, confirms that he was able to share the aspirations of his fellow members. It would appear, then, that for Haydn Freemasonry and Enlightenment meant essentially the same thing, and attending a Masonic meeting involved seeing one's friends from the literary salons under only slightly different circumstances. When that forum vanished in 1785 (or 1786), the aspirations clearly did not, since Haydn's compositions over the next decade and a half show increased understanding and a steady strengthening of these principles.

4

───◆───

Opera, Rhetoric, and *Rittergedichte*

THE symphony does not stand in isolation among Haydn's productions as the only type of composition with enlightened characteristics. Some of his finest achievements prior to 1785 were in other types of composition, including opera and the string quartet, and it is possible to see his new directions and refinements taking shape in these works. Until fairly recently, opera has been a blind spot in Haydn scholarship, dismissed because it was believed he showed little critical judgement in the choice and shape of librettos, he failed to make his operas dramatic, and he had little aptitude for opera in general. Inevitably a comparison is made with Mozart in which Haydn fares very poorly, and his own remarks to Franz Roth in Prague concerning Mozart's operatic superiority are invoked to substantiate the unfavourable comparison.

In recent years, fairer assessments of Haydn's operatic achievements have been forthcoming, and the key factor here has been the attempt to place his operas within an eighteenth-century context rather than to judge them in the light of the inclinations of major opera-houses in the twentieth century. Operas known in score or recordings only are unlikely to fare well against works which have a permanent place in the repertoire and current musico-dramatic consciousness. Haydn's operas, particularly those of the late seventies and early eighties, are important achievements and have a definite effect on his subsequent application of enlightened thinking to instrumental works.

Opera at Eszterháza

During the early 1960s a number of key studies of Haydn's operatic activities appeared which place the significance of opera in Haydn's musical life in a new context.[1] From 1776 to 1790 he wrote at least six operas and directed the performances of approximately one hundred different operas by the most popular composers of the time, including Dittersdorf, Anfossi, Cimarosa, Guglielmi, Paisiello, Piccinni, Sacchini,

[1] Dénes Bartha and Lázsló Somfai, *Haydn als Opernkapellmeister* (Budapest, 1960); János Harich, 'Das Repertoire des Opernkapellmeisters Joseph Haydn in Eszterháza (1780–1790)', *Haydn Yearbook*, 1 (1962), 9–110; Mátyás Horányi, *The Magnificence of Eszterháza*, trans. András Deák (London, 1962); and H. C. Robbins Landon, 'Haydn's Marionette Operas and the Repertoire of the Marionette Theatre at the Esterház Castle', *Haydn Yearbook*, 1 (1962), 111–97.

Salieri, and Sarti, to mention only a few. Between 1780 and 1790 he directed over one thousand performances at Eszterháza, leaving one to wonder how he found time to do anything else. As director, Haydn was responsible for not only directing all performances but also presiding over rehearsals (including the coaching of singers), supervision of score-copying, and also altering scores to meet the local musical circumstances (and, no doubt, to satisfy himself). In his own mind there was no question that a connection existed between instrumental music and Italian opera. One facet of that can be seen in his taking 'exception to the fact that so many musicians now composed who had never learned to sing. "Singing must almost be counted among the lost arts [to quote Haydn], and instead of song they let instruments dominate"' (*Not.* 61). Given that Haydn put enormous energy into both opera and instrumental music during these years, there can be little question that the two had a substantial bearing on each other.

Considering the amount of operatic activity at Eszterháza, one is inclined to wonder how great the role of the director of music was in both selecting his own librettos and choosing the works of other composers for performance. In the absence of evidence to the contrary, it has generally been assumed that the final responsibility lay with Prince Nicholas. In both Haydn's librettos and the general Eszterháza repertoire, however, there are interesting trends which may suggest that Haydn was not without a voice in the selection process. The trends, in fact, were in keeping with Haydn's new interest in literature, and can be seen to correspond with the literary directions and inclinations of certain prominent literati with whom Haydn came into contact. In his own operas from 1766 to 1777 Haydn used librettos in his Italian operas which are either by Carlo Goldoni (*Lo speziale*, *Le pescatrici*, and *Il mondo della luna*) or are similar to the Goldonian comic model. While there is room in this model for some serious elements (exemplified in *Le pescatrici*), comedy is clearly the dominant force in these works. In his operas after 1777, his librettos are no longer purely comic but either combine serious and comic features or are entirely serious. Three of these, *La vera constanza* (1779 or 1778), *Le fedeltà premiata* (1780), and *Orlando paladino* (1782), are stylistically related as *opera semiseria*,[2] while the other three, *L'isola disabitata* (1779) with its libretto by Metastasio, *Armida* (1783), and *L'anima del filosofo* (1791) are all serious works. Similarly, in the operas produced by Haydn, there was also a notable increase in serious works from 1783 to 1788.[3]

During most of the eighteenth century vocal music was judged to be

---

[2] See Mary Hunter, 'Haydn's Aria Forms: A Study of the Arias in the Italian Operas written at Eszterháza, 1766–1783', Ph.D. thesis (Cornell University, 1982), p. 6.

[3] See Bartha and Somfai, *Haydn als Opernkapellmeister*, p. 27.

superior to instrumental music, and a composer's reputation therefore
rested on his vocal achievements. In spite of his apparent instrumental
leanings, Haydn was well aware of this fact, and in his autobiographical
sketch of 1776 he listed only vocal works among those which had been
received with greatest approbation, beginning the list with three operas
(*Cor.* 19–20). As late as 1784 he was still able to tell his publisher Artaria
that his newly composed opera *Armida* was judged to be his finest work
(*Cor.* 44). In spite of the fact that Haydn almost always wrote his operas
for particular festive occasions at Eszterháza, he no doubt became
increasingly aware of the effect these works could and should have have
on an audience, especially with the post–1776 operas which became very
popular outside Eszterháza. From *L'incontro improvviso* (1775) to *Armida*,
all his operas were translated into German and performed elsewhere.[4]
With the shift towards serious elements in his operas one also sees a
change in the social status of characters, a change which was related to
the wider outside audience. In earlier works, social class tended to be
clearly drawn, with lower-class characters hoping to improve either their
social status or financial position. In operas after 1777 social status is
much more difficult to decipher.[5]

The shift to *semiseria* or serious librettos and the resulting differences in
social status of the characters suggests a deliberate pattern, one which
the composer himself may have had a role in determining. Furthermore,
one can observe other factors involving Haydn's literary friends which
may have had a bearing on his role in the emergence of this pattern. It
has already been noted that Gottfried van Swieten provided or adapted
texts for Haydn's *Seven Last Words*, *The Creation*, and *The Seasons*. Given
his important role concerning these texts, it is possible that van Swieten
had at least an indirect influence on Haydn's choice of texts before 1787.
He returned to Vienna in 1777 from Berlin to take up his duties as
Prefect of the Imperial Library, and in 1781 was given the additional
position of President of the Court Commission on Education and
Censorship. Since he already knew Haydn before 1777, one can assume
that their acquaintance was renewed upon his return and grew from
there. Van Swieten's own literary preferences were for classical authors
such as Homer, Pindar, Sophocles, Euripides, and Plato as well as later
writers who emulated them, including Milton, Cervantes, Ariosto, and
Tasso.[6] Haydn's librettos of 1782 and 1783, *Orlando paladino* based on
Ariosto's *Orlando furioso* and *Armida* based on Tasso's *Gerusalemme liberata*,
correspond with van Swieten's own preference. While this could be no
more than coincidence, it is possible that there is more to it.

[4] See Hunter, 'Haydn's Aria Forms', p. 16.

[5] See ibid., pp. 4–7.

[6] See D. E. Olleson, 'Gottfried, Baron van Swieten, and his Influence on Haydn and Mozart',
D.Phil. thesis (University of Oxford, 1967), p. 15.

Serious opera was very much alive and well in the 1780s, but in some centres, including Vienna and Eszterháza, it was less often performed.[7] For Haydn to write or introduce serious opera into the repertoire was therefore not simply a matter of course. Another person who may have influenced Haydn's interest in serious librettos was Joseph von Sonnenfels. Haydn knew him through the literary salons and 'Zur wahren Eintracht', and because of Sonnenfels's prominence as the leading literary reformer in Vienna during the last two decades of Maria Theresa's rule, it would have been difficult for Haydn not to be aware of his views by the mid–1770s. Sonnenfels's obsessive distaste for Hanswurst and the *commedia dell'arte* has already been noted in Chapter 2, and his argument was more social than literary, in that social development was seen as being dependent on the elevation of audience taste. However, his distaste for comedy did not stop with *commedia dell'arte*, but also included Goldoni. He held all types of comic opera up to comparison with Gluck, and against that standard, in his opinion, they all fared badly.[8] Haydn's shift to the serious is very much in line with Sonnenfels's thought, leaving behind *commedia dell'arte* (except for the marionette operas) at a very early stage, and ultimately abandoning Goldonian librettos as well. One of the works to herald Haydn's new operatic direction was *L'incontro improvviso* (1775), a reworking of the libretto of Gluck's *Rencontre imprévue*. Haydn's final opera, *L'anima del filosofo*, relates to the subject of the best known of all Gluck's operas, *Orfeo*.

As a literary reformer Sonnenfels sometimes went to absurd lengths, but in spite of this he was not without success in achieving in Austria what Lessing had accomplished in Germany.[9] His insistence on propriety in drama went much further than that of most writers, including Haydn's favourite, Gellert. In Sonnenfels's view, any force opposing morality in a dramatic work must be soundly defeated: there should be no unresolved issues at the end. Evil in its various manifestations could be present as a foil against which virtue is highlighted, but this clear weighting in favour of good all but eliminates the possibility of real conflict and hence drama from occurring. The theatre, then, had a mission, which was 'to defend the good, to fight evil, to uphold authority, to obviate subversion'.[10]

---

[7] See John A. Rice, 'Sarti's Giulio Sabino, Haydn's Armida, and the arrival of opera seria at Eszterháza', *Haydn Yearbook*, 15 (1984), p. 181.

[8] See Robert A. Kann, *A Study in Austrian Intellectual History* (New York, 1960), p. 214. Sonnenfels was, of course, partial to Gluck's serious operas.

[9] See ibid., p. 222.

[10] Ibid., p. 213.

Armida

With *Armida*, Haydn used a libretto which came very close to
Sonnenfels's standard. Rinaldo's dalliance with Armida must ultimately
be seen as nothing more than a temporary lapse. When Ubaldo and
Armida pull at Rinaldo, representing the forces of duty and sensuous
pleasure, there is no serious question as to which he will follow (unlike,
for example, Fiordiligi's response to her moral dilemma in Mozart's
Così fan tutte), and hence there is no real drama involving human frailty
or failure.

This apparent lack of drama has of course been largely responsible for
the dismissal of Haydn's operas in this century. Some writers, however,
have defended Haydn's operas against an insistence on a dramatic
measurement in which one finds genuine conflict, human error, and
continuity of action, as one finds in the operas of Mozart. Helmut Wirth,
for one, has argued that Haydn's operas have more in common with
those of Gluck than Mozart in that characters or events are not to be
seen in a continuous flow of human drama, but instead should be taken
as representations of moral positions. He points out that Haydn exhalts
good and castigates evil, presenting a moral lesson to the audience.[11]
While Wirth places Haydn (by inference) firmly within the Sonnenfels
camp, one suspects that Haydn may have had some reservations about
being there. *Armida* was his next to last operatic endeavour, and there is
a hiatus of eight years between this and his final opera.

The opportunity of writing another opera, however, was something
which Haydn would have welcomed. In response to Franz Roth's
request for an *opera buffa* for Prague, he observed that he was not
prepared to give him an existing one since these were too closely tied to
Eszterháza. But, he wrote somewhat wistfully, 'it would be quite another
matter if I were to have the great good fortune to compose a brand new
libretto for your theatre' (*Cor.* 73). His most recent librettos had been
anything but brand-new. Armida (or Rinaldo) was one of the most
familiar subjects in all of opera, and had gone through a number of
reworkings leading up to Haydn's setting in 1783.[12] Haydn's specific
reference to a new libretto suggests that he indeed may have been much
more discriminating than has generally been thought. One would, of
course, like to know what his desired new libretto might have been.
Perhaps he had hopes that one of his literary colleagues would write or
commission a suitable libretto, a libretto which might allow greater
range in dealing with human and dramatic situations.

---

[11] *Joseph Haydn als Dramatiker* (Wolfenbüttel and Berlin, 1940), p. 188. Readers should be aware
that Wirth, in conformity with Nazi editorial practice, identifies all Jewish sources.

[12] See Marita McClymonds, 'Haydn and his Contemporaries: "Armida Abbandonata"', in
Joseph Haydn: Proceedings of the International Joseph Haydn Congress, Wien, Hofburg, 5.–12. September 1982,
ed. Eva Badura-Skoda (Munich, 1986), 325–32.

Orlando

Interest in Tasso and Ariosto was by no means unusual in Vienna during the seventies and eighties, and van Swieten was in good company in this respect. One of the genres of the literary Enlightenment which appears to have been of particular interest to the Viennese was that of the chivalrous epic or *Rittergedichte*. Works of this type exploited the fantastic as a vehicle for the propagation of morality, or 'ein lehrreiches Wunderbares', as J. J. Breitinger called it.[13] The principal eighteenth-century writers associated with this genre were Wieland, L. H. Nicolay, and Alxinger, and their verse epics were based on the older poetic forms of Cervantes and Ariosto. These Renaissance writers had designed their verse epics with Classical models in mind but added a biting satire or irony. Of the various epics which attracted the eighteenth-century writers, the one with probably the greatest appeal was Ariosto's *Orlando furioso* (1515–32) which was based on the French epic of the Middle Ages, *Le Chanson de Roland*. Nicolay used this legend as the basis for his own epics more than once, first in *Galwine* (1773) in which he introduced Ariosto to German literature, and again in his last epic, *Reinhold und Angelika* (1781–4).[14]

Nicolay was no stranger to Vienna, residing there for two years in the early 1760s and returning in 1781. While away from Vienna he maintained contact with various individuals and was able to number Metastasio, Gluck, Denis, and Alxinger among his friends.[15] Aside from the Classics such as Tibullus, Ovid, and Horace, one of the strongest formative influences on Nicolay was the fables of Gellert. At a very early age he entered into correspondence with Gellert and received practical advice from the older poet.[16] In *Galwine*, Nicolay succeeded in capturing the spirit of Ariosto, and inserted his own enlightened values by attempting to expose prejudice and injustice.[17] In *Reinhold und Angelika*, he no longer attempted to illustrate a particular moral but instead used the fantastic as an apparent end in itself. While love (which, of course, is part of a larger moral scheme) is at the centre of this epic, it is treated ironically here, allowing the work to function at a different level.[18] Not unlike Shaftesbury's raillery, love in this case is put to the test. The ultimate effect of the work is not the direct imparting of a moral. Instead, the moral function here lies in the refinement which should result from contemplation.

[13] *Critische Dichtkunst*, i (Zurich, 1740), p. 166.
[14] See Richard M. Ilgner, *The Romantic Chivalrous Epic as a Phenomenon of the German Rococo* (Berne, 1979), pp. 59–63.
[15] See Edmund Heier, *L. H. Nicolay (1737–1820) and his Contemporaries* (The Hague, 1965), pp. 25, 43.
[16] See ibid., pp. 11–12.
[17] See Ilgner, *The Romantic Chivalrous Epic*, p. 61.
[18] See ibid., pp. 68–70.

Nicolay's literary approach endeared him to the Viennese more than most visiting writers, and even Joseph ii gave him a warm welcome in 1781. Haydn was very much aware of this man and his works and in fact acquired a collection of his poems published in 1785 (*Bibl.* 185–6). Haydn's familiarity with Nicolay's works could have been reinforced in various ways, including his own admiration for Metastasio and Gluck as well as his acquaintance with Alxinger. Alxinger was the leading exponent of the chivalrous epic in Vienna, and he expressed his esteem for Nicolay in a poem of welcome in 1781,[19] not unlike the tribute Haydn received from Burney in England ten years later (although decidedly superior in poetic merit). Alxinger's own verse epics were written later in the 1780s and were influenced by his strong Masonic leanings. His exploration of mysterious subjects was entirely in keeping with the practices of Freemasons such as the Illuminati.[20]

The fact that van Swieten commissioned Alxinger to write a cantata text for Haydn appears not to have been a miscalculation, in spite of the fact that Haydn rejected it. This cantata, *Die Vergötterung des Herkules*, is clearly related to the epic tradition, and according to Alxinger it was van Swieten's wish that it should allow Haydn to present an enlightened work in the spirit of Handel.[21] Further indications of Haydn's awareness of the eighteenth-century epic include the fact that he owned a copy of Klopstock's *Messias* published in 1780 (*Bibl.* 169–70), the work which influenced writers like Wieland to launch into the epic, and the admiration which Haydn and Wieland had for each other. Haydn did not appear to own any of Ariosto's works, although he did have a German translation of Tasso, *Das befreyte Jerusalem* (1781), in his library.

While the German literary revival of Ariosto's *Orlando furioso* dates from 1773, this subject was repeatedly treated in music from shortly after the appearance of Ariosto's verses.[22] As an opera it had been set by Lully, Handel, Piccinni, and Guglielmi among others before Haydn took it up in 1782, and it is Guglielmi's setting which Haydn's most resembles. The libretto used by Haydn appears to have been an adaptation of the Guglielmi/Badini text by Nunziato Porta, the new opera stage director appointed at Eszterháza in 1781.[23] Haydn needed to write a new opera for the occasion of the proposed visit to Eszterháza of the Russian Grand Duke Paul and the Grand Duchess. Geiringer has speculated that given the urgency, Porta may have suggested that

[19] See Heier, *L. H. Nicolay*, p. 43.

[20] See Ilgner, *The Romantic Chivalrous Epic*, p. 81.

[21] Johann Baptist von Alxinger, *Gedichte*, ii (Vienna, 1812), p. 141.

[22] See for example Alfred Einstein, '*Orlando furioso* and *La Gerusalemme liberata* as Set to Music during the 16th and 17th Centuries', *Notes*, 8 (1950–1), 623–30.

[23] See Anthony van Hoboken, 'Nunziato Porta und der Text von Joseph Haydns Oper "Orlando Paladino"', in Friedrich Wilhelm Riedel and Hubert Unverricht (eds.), *Symbolae Historiae Musicae* (Mainz, 1971), 170–9, and *Chron.* ii. 544.

Haydn use his own libretto which would need only slight alteration for use at Eszterháza.[24] It would not, however, seem unfair to suggest that Haydn took this project seriously even if time was short, and could see long-range potential for this work beyond the occasion for which its première was intended.

In fact, the visit of the Russsian Grand Duke never did materialize, so the première took place on Nicholas's name day. As Haydn may well have anticipated, the work was very successful both at Eszterháza and beyond, with performances in German translation at numerous Central European locations (*Chron.* ii. 545). Because Haydn could now safely assume that his operas would play to a larger international audience, it is entirely possible that he was as responsible as anyone else for the choice of librettos, and that he chose ones which would be in line with the enlightened literary direction of which he had now been aware for a number of years. The choice of a text based on Ariosto was a very natural one given the interest in Ariosto in Vienna at that time.

The themes of Haydn's *Orlando paladino*, which are love, refinement, and the exorcizing of self-interest, are enlightened ones similar to those of the literary chivalrous epics. Orlando himself is at the centre of the development of these themes. He rants and raves throughout most of the opera, a clear sign that refinement is lacking, and it requires the efforts of the sorceress Alcina, along with Caronte who bathes him in the River Lethe, to calm his ravings. The principal lovers in the work, Angelica and Medoro, are set upon by a variety of hostile forces, not the least of which is Orlando, who would like Angelica for himself. When his rage has abated, Orlando is able to join in protecting the lovers from other wild and unruly forces, and in fact is finally able to offer Angelica his knightly services without the expectation of reward. When this ultimate act of refinement and understanding of a higher form of love occurs, Alcina allows the same resolution in the landscape, as she transforms the forest of wild battle into a cultived garden of love with a touch of her wand. With the resolution of the themes, a didactic function is served. The arrival of a resolution required the intervention of sorcery or magic, and in a sense Alcina's sorcery is a symbol for the musical medium which has the final responsibility for persuading the audience and leading the listener to a higher level of refinement and hence virtue.

Haydn's means of achieving his musical ends in this and other operas written at this time may seem very curious indeed to twentieth-century opera audiences. Act I of *Orlando*, for example, begins with a short introductory ensemble and ends with a large finale, but between these ensembles are nine arias in a row. The balance of the act, then, is most heavily weighted in favour of arias, and many observers have taken this

[24] Joseph Haydn, *Werke*, 25/11/i (Munich and Duisburg, 1972), p. viii.

to be an obvious dramatic flaw, chastising Haydn for not exerting the type of influence on his librettist which Mozart is known to have had. However, as Mary Hunter points out in her recent study of the operas, there is no compelling reason why Haydn's operas should be measured against a standard which Mozart set a few years later.[25] While Haydn wrote extremely fine ensembles, his focus was on arias, and Hunter rightly concentrates on the musical features of his arias. Also, she is prepared to draw conclusions about the musical and social significance of arias. She agrees with Wirth that it is Haydn through the music rather than the librettist who is ultimately responsible for 'conveying the higher moral and social messages of the operas' (p. 31). In discussing the musical procedures used by Haydn in achieving these goals, she makes the following observation:

Such processes are persuasive on stage partly because they are embodied in dynamic yet symmetrical, or aesthetically satisfying, musical forms. Such forms, as Rosen argues, are a direct result of sonata style. One of Haydn's most signal achievements in the later operas, particularly the three *semiseria* works, was to integrate typically sonata elements—long range tonal tension and resolution, thematic development and return, etc.—into arias. (p. 379)

Hunter is well aware of the fact that there are implications here for the understanding of Haydn's instrumental music.

In linking the term's 'persuasive' and 'symmetrical', Hunter under-scores a maxim which is at the centre of eighteenth-century thought. For Haydn in his operas, dramatic continuity is not the concern that it is for Mozart in *Le nozze di Figaro*. Haydn's drama operates at a different level, the conflict being between opposing forces or ideals. The continuity, then, is in the process of leading the listener to a point of heightened refinement. To achieve this, arias work just as well or better than ensembles because of their persuasive power. In another recent study, arias have been called 'operatic speeches' which, 'like their counterparts in spoken drama, tend to be eloquent, colorful in diction and metaphor, articulated into distinct parts, beautifully formed and balanced, growing in force as they proceed, and calculated for their effect on hearers both onstage and in the audience'.[26] This sense of effect corresponds entirely with the notion of rhetoric held by the writers of the Enlightenment in that the aria 'assaults us at length with calculated, forceful language and delivery'.[27]

In the light of Haydn's friendships, the books he read, and the literary activities happening around him, it seems entirely plausible that his

[25] 'Haydn's Aria Forms', p. 26.
[26] James Parakilas, 'Mozart's *Tito* and the Music of Rhetorical Strategy', Ph.D. thesis (Cornell University, 1979), p. 6.
[27] Ibid., p. 9.

embracing of semiserious and serious opera when he did was not necessarily the result of decisions made by his patron, librettist, or stage director. Of the various possible oblique or even direct influences on this direction, van Swieten should not be ruled out. It should be noted that van Swieten, like many of his fellow Jesuit-educated colleagues, was keenly interested in rhetoric,[28] and his passion for and propagation of the music of Bach and Handel is entirely in keeping with his continued interest in rhetoric. It was through van Swieten's salons that both Haydn and Mozart very much increased their exposure to the counterpoint of Bach and Handel, and in this counterpoint one is able to find one of the most significant eighteenth-century applications of rhetoric to music.[29] The sense in which Haydn applied rhetoric to music, however, was not in the strict classical sense of oratorical design. Rather, it was the more modern Shaftesburian approach in which language, tone, or style could have a persuasive effect through elevation, refinement, and intelligibility.

Opera, then, appears to have played an important part in Haydn's realization of the goals of the Enlightenment in music. The fact that he wrote only one new opera after 1783 could suggest that he was not entirely comfortable with the direction in which he was moving. In spite of the hiatus after 1783, his experience as an opera composer and director had an enormous effect on his instrumental works, and the spirit of opera clearly lived on in his works for the rest of his career.

[28] See Ernst Wangermann, *Aufklärung und staatsbürgerliche Erziehung* (Munich, 1978), pp. 37–8.

[29] See Warren Kirkendale, 'Ciceronians versus Aristotelians on the Ricercar as Exordium, from Bembo to Bach', *Journal of the American Musicological Society*, 32 (1979), 1–44, and Eric Chafe, 'J. S. Bach's *St Matthew Passion*: Aspects of Planning, Structure, and Chronology', *Journal of the American Musicological Society*, 35 (1982), pp. 53–4.

5

String Quartets, Op. 33
'A New and Special Way'

In issuing the notice of his String Quartets, Op. 33, Haydn announced to potential subscribers that this set was written in 'a new and special way'. Connoisseurs who knew the Op. 20 set may have found this to be a somewhat inflated claim, possibly suspecting that it was made for commercial rather than musical reasons. Numerous scholars since Adolf Sandberger at the end of the nineteenth century have been prepared to take sides on this issue, some claiming that these quartets represent the beginning of mature classicism in music and others dismissing the remark as mere sales promotion.[1]

Haydn had not issued a set of quartets for nine years, and it is possible that he may have actually forgotten how advanced the quartets of Op. 20 were.[2] What is more plausible, however, is that he knew precisely how the two sets related to each other and that he still believed there was something new and special about Op. 33. The distinction, however, is fairly subtle since what we find in Op. 33 is not a radical departure but rather a refinement of techniques. The process of refinement brought these works to a new level of sophistication which was entirely in keeping with the spirit of the Enlightenment. The procedures in these quartets allow new possibilities for the relationship of the four performers, and Haydn's claim may have had as much or even more to do with the effect on the players or audience than the compositional techniques. Like the symphonies of the eighties, these quartets represent an arrival of refinement and comprehensibility which is not unrelated to literary and social activities.

Before the 1780s, the string quartet was a more private than public type of composition, and as such had something in common with certain types of literary works. With the proliferation of devotional poetry, the new medium of the novel, as well as moral weeklies, reading material was placed in the hands of individuals who could enjoy it in the privacy

---

[1] This is summarized in *Chron.* ii. 578–9.

[2] Haydn's memory of his own works was something less than flawless. See for example his letter dated 13 October 1791 to Maria Anna von Genzinger from London, at which time he could not remember the opening of the Symphony in E flat (No. 91) written less than three years prior to this, in *Cor.* 119.

of their own homes by themselves, with family members, or in small social gatherings. Writers such as Gellert were particularly responsive to this new function of literature, and generated not only intimate types of literature but also focused on intimate situations in that literature. In the initial stages, the social unit most strongly appealed to was the family, since it was here, particularly in the instruction of the young, that moral literature could be most useful. From the family there was an expansion to somewhat larger social units, including learned societies, salons, and clubs, although the literature continued to appeal most strongly to family values. The importance of the family circle was of considerable interest to Haydn, and like Gellert he was well aware of the efficacy of appealing to small social units with intimate works. His success in this gave him special satisfaction, as his letter to Jean Philipp Krüger of the *Musikverein* in Bergen attests: 'you happily persuade me . . . that I am often the enviable means by which you, and so many families sensible to heartfelt emotion, derive, in their homely circle, their pleasure—their enjoyment' (*Cor.* 209). Also, Haydn was drawn into Viennese society when he was in the city, including small musical parties, and literary and musical salons. As is apparent from his letters to Maria Anna von Genzinger, one of his favourite pastimes was attendance at small social gatherings, and it was more than good Parmesan cheese and Viennese strudel that attracted him.[3]

Conversation, wit, and humour

The type of musical composition ideally suited for small social gatherings was the string quartet, an idea confirmed by Heinrich Koch among others,[4] and Haydn may very well have recognized this in a new way with Op. 33. Clearly the nature of conversation was of paramount importance within small gatherings, and an interesting comparison between conversation and the string quartet has been drawn by Charles Rosen: 'The isolated character of the classical phrase and the imitation of speech rhythms in all of Haydn's chamber music only enhance the air of conversation. . . . The eighteenth century was cultivatedly self-conscious about the art of conversation: among its greatest triumphs are the quartets of Haydn' (*Clas.* 142). Rosen gives substance to these remarks with analysis of various techniques beginning with those found in Op. 33. What Rosen finds most striking, in Op. 33 No. 1, for example, is not that any voice can carry the melody (which is a well-established technique in earlier quartets) but that an accompanimental figure can

---

[3] See for example the letter dated 9 Feb. 1790 in *Cor.* 96–8.
[4] See *Versuch einer Anleitung zur Composition*, iii (Leipzig, 1793), p. 325.

change 'imperceptibly and without break into the principal melodic voice' (p. 117).

The cultivation of conversation was indeed a preoccupation of the eighteenth century, and one of the more fascinating treatises on the subject was *Über den Umgang mit Menschen*, by Adolf Freiherr von Knigge, a work which Haydn had in his personal library. This work, published in 1788 (Haydn's copy was dated 1793), gives a systematic accounting of conversation in almost every imaginable situation, and it brought together ideas which were in vogue at least since the middle of the century. While it may appear at first to be a book on etiquette, in fact it was much more than that. It was directed to the middle class, which Knigge recognized as the standard-bearers of the Enlightenment, and spoke directly to moral and social issues.[5] A significant emphasis was placed on conversation with family and friends, as well as with people of one's own social class and those of higher or lower status. Knigge recognized the importance of avoiding stolid moralizing and endeavoured to permeate his observations with wit.[6] The combination of wit and morality in fact occurs in the first chapter, where section 26, entitled 'All people want to be amused. On joking', is followed by a section called 'Quit the society of no person without having told him something obliging and instructive'. The fusion of joking and moralizing is approached in the following way: 'Above all things let us never forget that people want to be amused and entertained; that even the most instructive conversation at last becomes irksome to many if it is not seasoned by occasional sallies of wit and good humour.'[7]

Haydn's use of wit and humour in his music has recently been subjected to careful scrutiny.[8] Various contemporary critics found the use of comic elements in Haydn's works to be intrusive, as Griesinger reports: 'Strict theoreticians meanwhile found much to take exception to in Haydn's compositions, and they cried out especially over the debasement of music to comic fooling' (*Not.* 13). Charles Burney discovered the same thing in his earliest investigations of Haydn: 'The critics in the northern part of the empire were up in arms. And a friend at Hamburgh wrote us word in 1772, that, "the genius, fine ideas, and fancy of Haydn, Ditters, and Filtz, were praised, but the mixture of serious and comic was disliked, particularly as there is more of the latter

---

[5] See W. E. Yuill, 'A Genteel Jacobin: Adolf Freiherr von Knigge', in Hinrich Siefkin and Alan Robinson (eds.), *'Erfahrung und Überlieferung': Festschrift for C. P. Magill* (Cardiff, 1974), pp. 43–4.

[6] Ibid., p. 43.

[7] *Über den Umgang mit Menschen*, trans. P. Will as *Practical Philosophy of Social Life*, i (London, 1799), p. 24.

[8] Gretchen Ann Wheelock, 'Wit, Humor, and the Instrumental Music of Joseph Haydn', Ph.D. thesis (Yale University, 1979), and Steven Paul, 'Wit, Comedy and Humour in the Instrumental Music of Franz Joseph Haydn', Ph.D. thesis (University of Cambridge, 1981).

than the former in their works".[9] The place of wit and humour in works of literature or music as well as social intercourse was much discussed in the eighteenth century, and opinion was divided. Haydn's English friend Thomas Holcroft believed that comedy was more effective than tragedy in serving a moral purpose (*Theat.* i. 142). Gellert, as we have seen, took the view that while decorum should prevail, there clearly was a place for laughter in the theatre.[10] Shaftesbury, of course, had led the way in this debate, drawing a distinction between a type of destructive wit on the one hand, and raillery which is in good taste on the other. It was the latter which provided amusement as well as something beneficial.

Haydn's comic indulgences were readily accepted by critics sympathetic to the ideas of the Enlightenment. Griesinger took pleasure in noting that Haydn could find the humorous side of anything, and as this affected his compositions, 'this caprice is most striking, and his allegros and rondeaux are especially often planned to tease the audience by wanton shifts from the seemingly serious to the highest level of comedy' (*Not.* 57). A. C. Dies expands on Haydn's comic side, quoting at length an article by Herr Triest from the *Leipzig Musikalische Zeitung*, in which Haydn is compared to Laurence Sterne concerning the use of wit and humour (*Nach.* 199). While humour is by no means absent from Op. 20, it is taken much further in Op. 33, giving this set a new spirit. This ranges from actual jokes, such as the conclusion of Op. 33 No. 2, to more general aspects of musical language.

New versus old

Haydn's use of comic features in Op. 33 seems considerably more than harmless roguery. It represents a conscious shift in language, and Haydn was no doubt well aware of the inclinations of the particular subscribers and audience to whom his works appealed in contrast to those who preferred earlier styles. He did not discuss these matters in any great detail in letters or with biographers, and that would have been unnecessary considering how ably the music speaks for itself. In this case, the finale to Op. 33 No. 1, that extraordinary first work of the set, offers a fascinating insight into the transformation. The theme which begins the movement gives the sense of belonging to an earlier generation. This effect is very much enhanced beginning at bar 13 and lasting until bar 30 where the figuration in the first violin appears to be a parody of Vivaldi or one of his contemporaries (Ex. 1*a*). After a

[9] 'Haydn', in Abraham Rees (ed.), *The Cyclopaedia: or Universal Dictionary of Arts, Science, and Literature* (London, 1819).

[10] See John Van Cleve, *Harlequin Besieged: The Reception of Comedy in Germany during the Early Enlightenment* (Berne, 1980), p. 119.

Ex. 1

a.

b.

transitional passage (bars 31–42), Haydn introduces material which has a highly comic spirit (Ex. 1*b*), and appears to snub the preceding material in the earlier eighteenth-century style. At this point, the composer seems to be drawing a line between the old and the new, and by dismissing the old he clearly aligns himself with that which is modern. Disrespect for earlier composers is surely not intended; however, there may be a message here for those players and listeners who valued only that which is from the past and is serious. Haydn's own approaches were being shaped by a new social outlook, and with Op. 33 he clearly recognized his public as being that segment of society which could share his own inclinations and values.

The finale to Op. 33 No. 1 demonstrates the distinction between old and new in another important way, and this is in the exchange of ideas among the parts in a witty conversational style. The source of the figure at bar 43, which established the authority of that which is new, is comic opera, and the same is true for the new conversational style of the quartets. Given the fullness of Haydn's involvement with comic and semiserious opera as both composer and director, it is hardly surprising that these activities should have some bearing on his instrumental works. It was also entirely appropriate that his instrumental compositions should acquire characteristics of the type of works which enlightened critics believed had the greatest moral effect on audiences.

Exchanges between characters in operatic ensembles going back to the Neapolitan intermezzo tended to use irregular phrasings, following the dramatic nature of the text, and also frequently involved series of short, punctuated exchanges in rapid succession, again relating to speech patterns.[11] This type of rapid exchange occurs directly after the material beginning at bar 43, reinforcing the new spirit established at that point. In the development a highly regular and formalized exchange occurs in one-bar units, using the old-style material first heard at bar 13,

---

[11] See Gordana Lazarevich, 'The Neapolitan Intermezzo and its Influence on the Symphonic Idiom', *Musical Quarterly*, 57 (1971), pp. 301–5.

and an intentional monotony results from the sequential extension of this for fifteen bars. In contrast to this, Haydn breaks the pattern of the principal theme with a rest near the beginning of the recapitulation, and against the sequential expansion of that theme introduces a rapid exchange with material derived from the exposition. The result is a complex exchange of three prominent, previously heard themes or motives (Ex. 2), demonstrating the idea of musical conversation at its most sophisticated level.

In the article quoted by Dies, Triest follows his remarks on Haydn and humour with the following assertion: 'If one wished further to suggest the character of Haydn's composition with two words, it would be, I think, artistic popularity or popular (intelligible, penetrating) artistry' (*Nach.* 199). In the lightness and humour of Op. 33 there is clearly a new level of popularity, but this popularity had a new dimension to it. 'Popular', as Triest is using the term, does not imply that which simply ingratiates the composer to a larger public. In appealing to this audience, it was important that an appropriately universal type of language should be used, just as Gellert and other writers had used language suitable to a wider social spectrum and had placed it in a context which allowed for a process of refinement. As for music, the language which could include the humbler classes was folk-music (both song and dance), and in Op. 33 the amount of thematic material derived from folk sources far exceeded anything in quartets or almost any other type of composition by Haydn prior to 1781. Even the designation 'Minuet' with its courtly associations is dropped in this set in favour of the 'Scherzo' which suggests a different class association. The Scherzo of No. 2, for example, has the rustic flavour of the ländler, and the same folk orientation is common in Haydn's later symphonic third movements.

Ex. 2

Musical procedures

The heightened intelligibility found in Op. 33, a phenomenon aptly described by Triest as 'popular artistry', allows for understanding by means of a process of unfolding. In sonata-form movements, the recapitulation involves much more than a stabilizing of the key or a somewhat altered presentation of earlier thematic material, as it must account for problematic areas of the exposition and development. If a dramatic problem has been put forward, it remains for the recapitulation to follow through on this and arrive at some type of conclusion. In the quartets, the dramatic problem often involves the ambiguity generated by the working of motivic and tonal material, and the way in which the recapitulation differs from the exposition reflects a specific dramatic response to earlier events. The initial theme of the opening movement will generally return in the tonic (although not always: Op. 33 No. 3 returns with a seventh in the chord, and No. 6 does not bring back the theme), it will be repeated to a greater or lesser degree, and then Haydn will launch into the new treatment. A good example of this is Op. 33 No. 1, in which the beginning of the recapitulation follows the exposition for six bars only. There is a problem of tonal ambiguity in this passage, and instead of leading to B minor as the exposition had at bars 9–10, the recapitulation extends the tonal ambiguity, using a motivic accompanimental figure. The arrival of B minor is delayed for eight bars.

In addressing the tonal problem in Op. 33 No. 1 as he did, Haydn was adding a new level of dramatic interest which allowed a direct response on the part of the player or listener. This type of dramatic approach is achieved with even better results in Op. 33 No. 5. Once again there is new material early in the recapitulation of the first movement, beginning at bar 208, which is an expansion of the motive derived from the first theme. Further ambiguity is found in the second theme with its extended syncopation (bars 251–8). But the most interesting occurrence is that which follows the fermata at bar 271. The abrupt change to E flat here reflects back on bar 78 of the exposition and bar 152 of the development (Ex. 3), tying together important dramatic points in the movement. This type of sudden shift to the flattened submediant in a recapitulation in response to earlier events is also fairly common in his symphonies. The beginning of the stable conclusion (bar 290) refers back to the rhythmic figure at bars 208–16, and therefore stabilizes material which was previously unstable (Ex. 4), a process not unlike the metric alignment which occurs in certain later symphonies (Nos. 84 and 86).

While Op. 33 anticipates the procedures of later symphonies, there are notable differences as well which have a bearing on the respective treatments of the unfolding process. The most obvious difference is that

Ex. 3

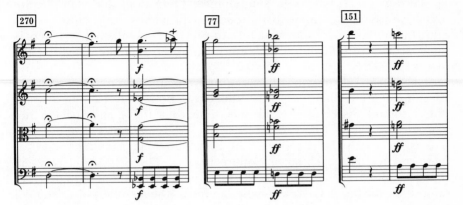

Ex. 4

a.

b.

the quartets do not use slow introductions (Op. 71 No. 2 is the only exception in all the quartets), while the slow introduction ultimately became a fundamental part of the language of later symphonies. Another dissimilarity is the length of first movements, as those of the symphonies are much longer than those of the quartets. Even Op. 33 No. 5, which has 305 bars, is in 2/4 time, and is therefore considerably shorter than any of the first movements in later symphonies. The length of quartet movements prevents certain procedures from being pursued to the same degree as in the symphonies. Transitions, for example, are much shorter, sometimes to the point of providing little more than a direct modulation. Similarly, in an exposition of only thirty bars, there is little opportunity for tonal ambiguity before or after the arrival of the new key.

The musical distinctions between quartets and symphonies relate in large measure to their respective functions. Both were gaining a wider international dissemination at this time, but the quartets were not considered 'public' works in the sense that the symphonies were until the late 1780s, with the sending of the first Tost Quartets to London for performance at the Hanover Square Rooms. The distinction between public and private music concerns those who were best able to perceive and enjoy the musical works—whether it was the members of a listening audience or the performers themselves.

The primary appeal of the quartet was to the players, and this had a strong bearing on the musical procedures used, such as the nature of the counterpoint. In contrast to the type of contrapuntal interrelating of themes which can occur early in the development, as happens in Symphony No. 83, the contrapuntal process of the quartets tends to be one of expanding a single motive, reflecting the potential equality of the parts (or performers). Also, the nature of the motivic elaboration in the quartets suggests a somewhat different emphasis to that found in symphonies. Motivic expansion is taken further in quartets, and, one could argue, constitutes their essence. Further, the expansion is passed from one part to another, allowing all four players to participate equally in the process. In a work such as Op. 33 No. 6, the sense of motivic elaboration is so pervasive that it is sometimes difficult to distinguish thematic material from transitions. By the end of the development section of the first movement, the process has gained such momentum that even the beginning of the recapitulation lacks thematic definition (although the main theme was stated earlier in the development).

In the string quartets, and in a heightened way with Op. 33, the music places four intelligent people in a 'harmonious' setting, sharing both intellectual and heartfelt experience. The ability to share and exchange the important material offers a strong sense of unified purpose, one in which the player is both aware of his individual importance and the role he plays in creating the whole. In a very real way, then, the quartet became a realization of one of the highest goals of the Enlightenment. With accompaniments that can be transformed to melodies and vice versa, there is an apparent recognition of a higher social truth which is that differences do not preclude equality.

6

Theory versus Practice
Aesthetics and Instrumental Music

An intriguing separation inevitably appears to exist between theory and practice, between the thinking of eighteenth-century music theorists or aestheticians and the compositional approaches of a practising musician such as Haydn. Aesthetics, as a branch of philosophical inquiry, has its own principles and procedures, and need not be disturbed by the approaches to art emerging at the same time. Modern aesthetic historians, such as René Wellek, make no apologies for the independence of their discipline and its detachment from the practice of writing.[1] Concerning music aesthetics, Carl Dahlhaus simply states that it is shaped by philosophical or literary considerations.[2] From the historian's point of view, then, the importance of the activity is in no way diminished by a lack of correspondence with practice. It is on this premise that John Neubauer proceeds in his recent study entitled *The Emancipation of Music from Language*.[3] Similarly for the theorists of the eighteenth century, there was not always a necessary link between theory and practice, as their agendas were often determined by prior theoretical discourse or other aesthetic principles.

On the other side, practical musicians have tended to take a dim view of theorists or aestheticians whom they see as being a step or two behind practice, or in any event incapable of understanding the practical or intuitive matters with which composers concern themselves. In the case of Haydn, those who have chosen to see him as untouched by external influences or lacking interest in theoretical, aesthetic, or literary matters have been able to take some comfort in his reply when informed that Albrechtsberger wished to remove all fourths from the purest style. '"What does that mean?" replied Haydn. "Art is free, and will be limited by no pedestrian rules. The ear, assuming that it is trained, must decide, and I consider myself as competent as any to legislate here. Such affectations are worthless. I would rather someone tried to compose a really *new* minuet"' (*Not.* 61).

---

[1] *History of Modern Criticism, 1750–1950*, i. *The Later Eighteenth Century* (New Haven, 1955), pp. 6–7.

[2] 'Romantische Musikästhetik und Wiener Klassik', *Archiv für Musikwissenschaft*, 29 (1972), p. 171.

[3] *The Emancipation of Music from Language: Departure from Mimesis in Eighteenth-Century Aesthetics* (New Haven, 1986), pp. 2–4.

Comments taken in isolation can, however, give a distorted impression. A look at the larger context gives a somewhat different view, and suggests that Haydn was very much aware of current thinking on aesthetics. Haydn's own works were frequently judged by critics in the light of conventional aesthetic standards, and not only did he know this but he also spoke of his music in direct response to this. It appears, in fact, that some of his most important compositional choices may have been made in response to thinking on aesthetic issues. Haydn had in his personal library a substantial collection of theoretical treatises (*Chron.* v. 402–3), and in both Vienna and London knew people who were themselves aestheticians or had knowledge of the views on music of various writers including Lessing, d'Alembert, Diderot, Gottsched, Sulzer, Krause, Daniel Webb, Sir William Jones, or John Brown.

Aesthetic opinion

Until near the end of the eighteenth century, the overwhelming majority of critics held the opinion that instrumental music was vastly inferior to vocal music, and for many the reason lay in the apparent inability of instrumental music to convey moral instruction or, indeed, to attain any level of intelligibility. Haydn, having read *Der vollkommene Capellmeister*, was familiar with Johann Mattheson's description of instrumental music as 'mere noise' and 'useless junk' which displayed a complete lack of moral qualities.[4] The same view was held by Sulzer and Marpurg,[5] and it was argued as well that instrumental music, because it lacked a sense of cause and effect, was ineffectual in communicating moral wisdom.[6]

In England a similar type of conservatism persisted well into the nineteenth century. Thomas Busby relegated Haydn to second-rate status since his symphonies, 'splendid and original as were his conceptions', lacked the fulfilment which alone could come through 'the treasury of the poetic muse'. As a composer of vocal music Busby considered Haydn to be decidedly inferior: 'no critic will compare his sacred masses and oratorios with even the least excellent of the sacred music of his great predecessor and countryman [J. S. Bach]'.[7] Haydn did not fare much better with William Crotch, who considered sacred music to be above all other types and isolated vocal features of melody as the standard for beauty (*Sub.* 32, 35). Only through the combination of poetry and music could both arts reach their highest potential (p. 64). Crotch was prepared to recognize Haydn as being first among

---

[4] See Bellamy Hosler, *Changing Aesthetic Views of Instrumental Music in 18th-Century Germany* (Ann Arbor, 1981), pp. 10–11.
[5] Ibid.
[6] Ibid., p. 5.
[7] *A General History of Music*, ii (London, 1819), p. 395.

instrumental composers, but in the end he deemed Mozart the greatest among modern composers, not because of the operas (of which he preferred the serious to the comic), but because of the superiority of the *Requiem* (pp. 144–5). Crotch considered the current direction in instrumental music as a passing trend perpetuated by a large and unrefined audience; his advice to composers was to look to J. S. Bach and not be discouraged by the censures of a public which had an enormous appetite for trash (pp. 20–1).

Opinion in Germany was very much in line with that in other parts of Europe. Certain writers, such as Gottsched and Lessing, whose influence on Viennese literati in the eighties was very strong, had made their positions in this matter perfectly clear. Johann Christoph Gottsched, the most influential arbiter of taste and morality in Germany during the first half of the eighteenth century, in judging the newer Italian instrumental works, found them to 'mean absolutely nothing: they represent a mere jangle, which makes one neither cold nor warm'.[8] In vocal music as well, Gottsched objected to composers who could not recognize the limitation of music and would not keep it in its proper place. He saw no particular reason for suspending disbelief when experiencing opera, and even if Italians sing in real life, Germans clearly do not. Excessive musical richness in opera simply gives rise to a sensuality which in turn renders opera 'a promotor of lust, and a corrupter of morals'.[9]

The dramatic thought of Lessing has very little in common with that of Gottsched, but where instrumental music is concerned, the two are strikingly in agreement. Lessing endeavoured to be sympathetic to instrumental music, but in the end it simply could not measure up to his standard of dramatic intelligibility. The problem lay in the need for contrast in instrumental music, and he did not believe that a listener could follow the expressive differences without the fortification of words. The result of contrast in music without words was confusion and disorder: 'A symphony which expresses in its various movements different, contradictory passions is a musical monstrosity; a single passion must dominate in a single symphony.'[10]

When Haydn went to England in 1791 primarily as a symphonist, he found that among the people with whom he associated there were only a few notable exceptions to the majority position concerning the role of words in the achievement of musical intelligibility. Among his friends in England (a few of these will be discussed in Part II), some had strong views on the capacity of vocal music to carry a moral purpose. Thomas

[8] Hosler, *Changing Aesthetic Views*, p. 3.
[9] Ibid., p. 53.
[10] Neubauer, *The Emancipation of Music*, p. 158.

Holcroft, who appears to have played an advisory role to Haydn on poetic matters similar to that of Greiner in Vienna, looked at opera as a very useful instrument for moral instruction (*Theat.* i. 215). Thomas Twining subscribed to the conventional view of the superiority of vocal music and found this position bolstered by Aristotle and the ancients: 'the *expressions* of Music considered in itself, and *without words*, are, (within certain limits), vague, general, and equivocal. . . . The effect of *words*, is, to strengthen the expression of Music, by confining it—by giving it precise direction, supplying it with ideas, circumstances, and an *object*' (*Aris.* 48). Twining, however, was prepared to concede that his view derived from Aristotle did not necessarily apply to the present, since instrumental music, he assumed (not actually knowing any music of the Greeks), differed greatly between that of the ancients and that of the present. Christian Latrobe as well, who was convinced that music has spiritual and intellectual capabilites, was in fact referring to vocal music. His interest in instrumental music was in its ability to enhance a text.[11]

Haydn's views

To what extent was Haydn familiar with the prevailing opinion concerning vocal and instrumental music, and would he have cared, assuming that he was aware? Looking at his overall output, one sees an enormous body of symphonies, chamber works, and sonatas composed consistently throughout his career, while his vocal works such as operas, masses, oratorios, songs, and arias were written much more sporadically, concentrated at certain points in his career. Curiously, however, his own comments about his works do not necessarily reflect what would appear to be his priorities in terms of actual composition. Most revealing in this regard is his Autobiographical Sketch of 1776, by which time he had already written over sixty symphonies. As was noted in Chapter 4, when itemizing his works which had received the most approbation, his list begins with three operas (*Le pescatrici, L'incontro improviso,* and *L'infedeltà delusa*). Two more vocal works follow the operas, the oratorio *Il ritorno di Tobia* and the *Stabat Mater.* Finally he comes to instrumental works, but in contrast to vocal works which are given by name, he now lists neither specific works nor instrumental types, as he simply gives the broad category '*camer Styl*'.[12] Eight years later, in spite of the achievements of the String Quartets, Op. 33, and the Symphonies Nos. 61–78, his letter to Artaria of 1 March 1784 does not dispute the contention that *Armida* was his 'best work up to now' (*Cor.* 44). Even in

[11] *Letters to my Children,* ed. J. A. Latrobe (London, 1851), p. 28.
[12] H. C. Robbins Landon and Dénes Bartha (eds.), *Joseph Haydn: Gesammelte Briefe und Aufzeichnungen* (Kassel, 1965), p. 77.

the last years of his life, he led Griesinger to believe that he deplored the practice of composers who wrote for instruments without first learning to sing. About himself, he told Griesinger 'that instead of the many quartets, sonatas, and symphonies, he should have written more vocal music', believing he might have become one of the foremost opera composers (*Not.* 63).

The view of Haydn held during the first half of the twentieth century, that his only serious achievements were his instrumental works, is no doubt still in need of further realignment. However, it is difficult to imagine, in the light of his output, advocating the opposite extreme, as Haydn himself appears to be doing. How could he seriously argue that all his finest achievements are in the area of vocal music, and that he should not have expended so much time and energy on instrumental works? With Haydn himself, there appears to be something of a gap between theory and practice.

As a composer he brought the symphony and string quartet to a point unimaginable to any of his contemporaries aside from Mozart, and he put an enormous amount of energy into these types of composition. However, when speaking about his own music, he assumed the position of virtually everyone in the eighteenth century who spoke about music, and this was that vocal music is superior to instrumental music. Furthermore, if instrumental music is to be taken seriously at all, it must be based on melodic material with a vocal quality, which Haydn appears to have believed he was doing in contrast to many of his contemporaries. To be sure, his earliest training was in singing, but whether or not this led to instrumental works with a vocal quality is quite another matter. It clearly did not lead to the type of musical simplicity which his English critics such as William Jackson and William Crotch had in mind. Haydn, of course, uses themes with a vocal quality in his symphonies, even in first movements, but more often than not such themes are polarized against complexity and ambiguity, placing them in a dramatic context in which they act as one of the forces in a dramatic duality.

In this apparent gap between theory and practice, a view of a somewhat more complex Haydn necessarily emerges. There can be no question that he was intimately familiar with current aesthetic thought and that he actually attempted to emulate it when speaking of his own music. The extent to which this emulation is a distortion is revealing, both concerning the view he wished to be held of his works and his approach to composition itself.

Haydn's musical quotations

Haydn's wish to achieve intelligibility in his symphonies was nothing new in the 1780s, and some of his approaches in earlier works suggest a significant narrowing of the apparent gap between theory and practice. Since it was universally acknowledged that intelligibility was not possible without a text, it seems to have occurred to Haydn at the earliest stages of his career that a possible solution in instrumental works was to quote musical material which was associated with a particular text. The sources of such material could be wide and varied, including opera, folksongs, liturgical sources, or street music. Having used this type of quotation in some of his early symphonies (perhaps more often than has as yet been identified), he subsequently explored more sophisticated possibilities, where textual associations could be present by implication, for example in phrasing or rhythmic patterns which could be associated less directly with a particular text. In this way he established the groundwork for the very sophisticated approach to intelligibility in later symphonies where the associations can become musical *topoi* which need not be specifically identified for the process to function. Haydn may very well have been doing more than attempting to find the sanctioned aesthetic terminology, in commenting on vocal approches to instrumental music. In a number of cases, his quotations with textual associations have definite moral implications, placing his works within the realm of contemporary aesthetics even though his means went far beyond what most aestheticians, critics, or theorists could imagine.

In some of his earliest instrumental works, one sees Haydn quoting well-known melodies. In the Baryton Trio No. 5, the opening movement uses 'Che farò senza Euridice' from Gluck's *Orfeo*. Another fascinating quotation of Gluck has been identified by Daniel Heartz, this being the use of the 'Tabaksgesang' from the Opéra-Comique *Le Diable à quatre* for the first movement of Symphony No. 8 ('Le Soir') of 1761.[13] Heartz points out that this melody was a familiar street song in Vienna, and he also discusses the possible implications of the quotation for the programmatic interpretation of the symphony.

Within a few years Haydn uses quotations again in a symphony, now with strong dramatic and moral implications. In the first movement of No. 26 in D minor ('Lamentatione'), written in c.1768, Haydn quotes at length a liturgical source which provides him with a musical represent-ation of the Passion drama. The quotation, from the *Cantus Ecclesiasticus*

---

[13] 'Haydn und Gluck im Burgtheater um 1760: Der neue krumme Teufel, Le Diable à quatre und die Sinfonie "Le Soir"', in Christoph-Hellmut Mahling and Sigrid Wiesmann (eds.), *Bericht über den Internationalen Musikwissenschaftlichen Kongreß Bayreuth 1981* (Kassel, 1984), 120–35.

Sacrae Historiae Passionis Domini Nostri Jesu Christi, Secundum Quatuor Evangelistas, is very long (twenty-two bars), and is almost without deviation from the source (see Ex. 23, p. 156).[14] The source, as Landon points out, was something with which Roman Catholic listeners in Austria would have been familiar. Haydn, having established the reference in the first movement and surrounding it with music which elicits a suitable response (syncopated material in D minor), referentially determined the content of the second movement as well, now quoting one of the 'alphabet Lamentations' found in the same source (*Chron.* ii. 293). The second movement, then, evokes the appropriate affective and liturgical response to the events of the first movement. The type of reference made in this work (similar ones appear in Nos. 30 and 45) is very forthright, as the quotation itself is the centre of focus. In this case the symphony serves the extramusical function of the quotation rather than the quotation becoming a part of a symphonic texture. The source material here, with texts for the Evangelist, Christ, and the Vox populi, as well as a lamentation of the Prophet Jeremiah, in a sense makes this symphony a type of vocal work without words. Even the instrumentation supports this, as the source material is always in the oboe and second violin parts.

Another type of quotation which was used by Haydn throughout his career is that of folksong. Again through textual associations it was possible for folk-music to have extramusical significance. A case for this is made by Geoffrey Chew who observes Haydn's use of the '*Nachtwächter*' melody in a number of works from the 1760s and seventies.[15] Others have also traced the melody to a number of sources, and one of these, from 1686, has the following text: 'Nichts Irdisch ewig gewehrt / Wie ein Wetterhahn sich verkehrt' (Nothing earthly remains forever / As a weathercock turns).[16] The theme of passing time and decay is one that turns up in Haydn's works and writings on different occasions. The autograph manuscript of Symphony No. 64, for example, bears the inscription 'tempora mutantur etc.' It has been noted by Jonathan Foster that this is probably the most famous epigram by the Welshman John Owen (c. 1565–1622), which is entitled 'O Tempora': 'Tempora mutantur, nos et mutamur in illis: quomodo? fit semper tempore peior homo.' This was translated in 1677 by Thomas Harvey as: 'The times are Chang'd, and in them Chang'd are we: How? Man, as Times grow worse, grows worse, we see.'[17]

---

[14] Landon cites the 1763 Monastery of St Florian edition in *Chron.* ii. 291–4, and also mentions the Viennese (ex officiana Krausiana) edition of 1761.

[15] 'The Night-Watchman's Song Quoted by Haydn and its Implications', *Haydn-Studien*, 3 (1974), 106–24.

[16] See *Chron.* ii. 281, and Paul Nettl, *Das Wiener Lied im Zeitalter des Barock* (Vienna and Leipzig, 1934), p. 42.

[17] Foster, 'The Tempora Mutantur Symphony of Joseph Haydn', *Haydn Yearbook*, 9 (1975), p. 328.

Foster suggests that Haydn may have known this epigram on the grounds that Owen's ten books of epigrams were well known among seventeenth- and eighteenth-century literati, particularly German-speaking writers. He also attempts to show how the Latin text fits the opening lines of the rondo Finale of Symphony No. 64, a plausible suggestion in the light of the 'Lamentatione' and 'Alleluia' symphonies as well as the similar type of treatment in a later work, *The Seven Last Words*. Much later in his life, Haydn noted the following aphorism concerning change in his first London notebook: 'He who wisely observes how all things change cannot be made happy by good fortune or unhappy by bad' (*Cor.* 267). The recurrence of this theme suggests that it may have been of some importance to Haydn and that he may have wanted it to be understood in earlier works through the implied association with the text of a folksong. The use of folksong, then, appeared to have had much more potential than merely being a source of melodic material or as a means of creating a popular idiom.

Non-musical works for the stage were regularly performed at Eszterháza, including the plays of Shakespeare and the popular contemporary dramas of writers such as Lessing. Haydn could not have escaped these dramatic activities, and in fact a link can be seen between some of his symphonies and the theatre. On more than one occasion he was called upon to write incidental music for plays, and in some instances it appears that the music was intended to parallel the action on the stage.

The incidental music for Regnard's *Le Distrait*, which became Symphony No. 60, is a case in point. While all six movements of this work have been linked with various points of the play,[18] the fifth movement provides particularly interesting musical possibilities. This is a slow movement, marked 'adagio (di Lamentatione)', and begins with a richly sensuous, song-like melody. As the melody continues it becomes even more beautiful, finally moving into the minor. Upon the arrival of the dominant, instead of a return to the original melodic material, there is a loud and somewhat rude intrusion by a type of fanfare passage. The intrusive nature of the fanfare is confirmed ten bars later when the original theme finally does arrive in the dominant, as one had expected it should before the fanfare. The melody is now transformed even more beautifully, but this too must give way to another forte disruption. Towards the end, the first part of the melody returns in its original form, and on the eighth bar moves into a triplet figure which could provide a satisfactory conclusion. In the second and concluding phrase of this codetta, however, Haydn repeats the first phrase, but now in the new

---

[18] See Robert A. Green, '"Il Distratto" of Regnard and Haydn: A re-examination', *Haydn Yearbook*, 11 (1980), 183–95.

and wildly ridiculous allegro tempo. There could very well be a dramatic sequence in this movement based on the various events of the play.[19] In purely musical terms, a highly sensuous effect created by the melody is periodically disrupted by foreign material, or, in the case of the ending, a comical twist of given material.

No doubt it was this type of musical treatment of comic intrusion which Haydn's detractors found objectionable. However, for Haydn, the opportunity to realize musical contrast or manipulate expectation in the context of a dramatic work for the stage proved invaluable in cultivating his later symphonic language.

Opera and symphony

One of the most important musical factors in Haydn's development of a new symphonic language—which also takes vocal music, drama, and extramusical factors into account—was the cross-fertilization of opera and symphony during the 1770s. Haydn's involvement with opera (particularly from 1776 to 1790) has already been noted, and the influence of this on his symphonies has been argued by various writers, including Rosen and Landon. In fact, the larger issue of the bearing that opera and symphony had on each other during the eighteenth century has attracted the interest of a formidable group of scholars in this century. Rosen presents the issue in the following way:

> To say that the sonata style provided an ideal framework for the rendering of what was most dynamic on the stage is to oversimplify only insofar as it does not take account of the important role that opera itself played in the development of the sonata style. (*Clas.* 289)

Essentially the same point was argued by Edward J. Dent almost sixty years earlier:

> Just as Italian opera fertilized German instrumental music in the days of Metastasio, so it continued to do so in the days of Cherubini, Rossini and Bellini, as long in fact as German music maintained the classical tradition. This steady development of the operatic aria had a considerable influence on the development of the sonata and symphony.[20]

Dent found himself in general agreement with the German scholar Wilhelm Fischer, who traced a relationship between certain types of melodic writing in instrumental music and the operatic aria.[21] Numerous other writers have also addressed the issue, concluding as Philip

[19] Ibid., pp. 191–2.
[20] 'Italian Opera in the Eighteenth Century, and its Influence on the Music of the Classical Period', *Sammelbände der Internationalen Musikgesellschaft*, 13 (1912–13), pp. 504, 507.
[21] 'Zur Entwicklungsgeschichte des Wiener klassischen Stils', *Studien zur Musikwissenschaft*, 3 (1915), 24–84.

Radcliffe has, that 'it was hard for any composer of that period not to be affected by Italian opera'.[22] This view was also articulated in the eighteenth century, an example being the comments of Johann Adam Hiller in 1768: 'Comic opera is not precisely the best school for singers; but it has become much the best for today's composers. Symphonies, concertos, trios, sonatas—all, nowadays, borrow something of its style.'[23]

The interrelationship of opera and symphony is apparent at larger formal levels as well as in the treatment of phrases or motives. While the writers noted above have recognized a potential, few have actually pursued the analytical possibilities. This has in part been remedied by Mary Hunter's recent study which is an in-depth examination of the effect of sonata form on Haydn's operatic arias.[24] As for the principles and procedures of sonata form, it does not require a great leap of the imagination to see a parallel between them and the processes of theatrical drama. Distinctive themes could represent different characters, the development could carry out an exchange among them, and a recapitulation could bring about a resolution or simply place foregoing events into a new perspective. As early as the Neapolitan intermezzo, one can find ensembles which bear a strong likeness to sonata form, and which undoubtedly had a bearing on the formulation of this process. A well-known example is the duet which ends Part 1 of Pergolesi's *Serva padrona*, in which the two characters are separated tonally and thematically at the beginning, go through a lively exchange in the middle, and return by way of the tonic key and the original thematic material. A much more sophisticated sonata-form treatment of an ensemble half a century later is the sextet in Act III of Mozart's *Nozze di Figaro*.

The origin of many of the comic devices used by Haydn in his symphonies of the seventies can be traced directly to the intermezzi and full-length Neapolitan comic operas of the beginning of the century. These devices include disjunct or abruptly ending phrases (a process related to vocal argumentation in ensembles), bass repetition or patter, octave leaps, and the Lombardic rhythm.[25] The patter figures or octave

[22] *Beethoven's String Quartets* (New York, 1968), p. 13. See also Jens Peter Larsen, 'The Symphonies', in H. C. Robbins Landon and Donald Mitchell (eds.), *The Mozart Companion* (New York, 1969), p. 157; Alfred Einstein, *Mozart: His Character, His Work* (New York, 1945), p. 217; Joseph Kerman, *Opera as Drama* (New York, 1956), pp. 86–7; and Paul Henry Lang, *The Experience of Opera* (New York, 1973), p. 58.

[23] Quoted in Piero Weiss and Richard Taruskin (eds.), *Music in the Western World: A History in Documents* (New York, 1984), pp. 282–3.

[24] 'Haydn's Aria Forms: A Study of the Arias in the Italian Operas written at Eszterháza, 1766–1783', Ph.D. thesis (Cornell University, 1982).

[25] See Gordana Lazarevich, 'The Neapolitan Intermezzo and its Influence on the Symphonic Idiom', *Musical Quarterly*, 57 (1971), pp. 301–5.

leaps work especially well in a *buffa* sense when played by the bassoon, as can be seen in bars 23–9 of the first movement of Symphony No. 70. A theme based on the Lombardic rhythm (or Scotch snap) can have a particularly comic effect, as is the case with the second theme of the fourth movement of Symphony No. 62 (beginning at bar 54). This movement, in sonata form, begins with a very unusual effect for works of this time, which allows a strong contrast with the *buffa* theme at bar 54. The movement does not begin on the tonic, giving it a striking and somewhat unsettling opening which could not but engage the attention of the listener.

While the potential of opera as a means for creating a dramatic musical language was increasingly being realized in symphonies before 1781, Haydn took new steps in this direction in 1781 with the String Quartets, Op. 33. Aside from those features already discussed in Chapter 5, another important advancement in these quartets was the new treatment of pace (see *Clas.* 119–20). The action in the ensembles of comic opera is rapid and, in order to remain intelligible, had to have an underlying regularity. But the pace in comic opera can also change very quickly, and this can be brought about with devices such as shifts in harmonic rhythm or changes in phrase lengths. The nature of the action in the operatic ensemble, with its rapid changes and contrasts, was likely to produce music which was in perpetual danger of disintegration. But this aspect of the vocal writing—the irregular phrasing, interjections, and quick argumentative exchanges—was counterbalanced by stability in the orchestral accompaniment. Through the accompaniment it was possible to achieve a sense of dramatic clarity, and this quality was transferred to instrumental writing in a new way with Op. 33. The equality (or potential equality) of the parts allowed for a rapid and at times irregular exchange but, taken as a whole, the larger texture provided a vehicle for controlling the pace and allowing lucidity. Rosen suggests a new sense in which the music is literally impelled from within, unlike the unfolding of baroque music. 'He [Haydn] understood the possibilities of conflict in musical material within the tonal system, and the way it could be used to generate energy and to create drama' (*Clas.* 120).

The Frühromantiker

The peculiar relationship between Haydn and contemporary aesthetics took another curious turn in the last decade of the century. While Haydn the 'aesthetician' continued to argue the primacy of vocal music (or instrumental music with a vocal quality), contemporary aesthetics caught up with Haydn the symphonist, now seeing instrumental music as having surpassed vocal music. Those who took this new position were the *Frühromantiker*, including Jean Paul, Wackenroder, Tieck, A. W. Schlegel, and E. T. A. Hoffmann.[26] According to Hoffmann, instrumental music was the most romantic of all the arts.

This view of instrumental music, however, emanated from a school of thought which had rejected the Enlightenment; its adherents scorned the attempt to represent the passions or anything definite through music. It was, in fact, the indescribable or 'infinite' quality of instrumental music which appealed to them, which allowed music to supersede all other arts in capturing the essence of romanticism. Hoffmann's inclusion of Haydn in this outlook is not something which would have been of interest to Haydn, and this in part is confirmed by the fact that Haydn ceased to write symphonies at precisely the time that the symphony acquired its new aesthetic respectability. Haydn's idea of the symphony was shaped by the Enlightenment, and his goal was to achieve, not supersede, intelligibility. His extraordinary achievement was to devise procedures for instrumental music that would allow it an intelligibility previously thought possible only if words were present. In the process an entirely new dimension was realized which, one could argue, provided the standard for all subsequent symphonists.

[26] See Hosler, *Changing Aesthetic Views*, p. 189, and Neubauer, *The Emancipation of Music*, pp. 193–210.

7

Symphonic Ascent
Pre-Paris to the Loge Olympique

HAYDN wrote symphonies over a period of about forty years, and during that time theories about music as well as approaches to composition went through extraordinary changes. In the 1750s, the symphony was just beginning to emerge as a genre, and a concert public had scarcely become visible. By the end of the century, the symphony was considered by some to be the most significant of all artistic achievements, and there was a large public eagerly awaiting the arrival of new, highly individual works. Haydn was the composer most responsible for the high estimation in which the symphony was held in the 1790s, and it is useful to note some of the steps he took during these four decades. His ultimate arrival was not a haphazard or fortuitous achievement, since he appears to have had a singular, clearly envisaged goal from the very beginning which allowed him to reach the summit. While his changing approaches reflect new musical possibilities, they are also related to the larger changes through which thinking on aesthetics was moving as writers and theorists sought to illuminate more effective means of expression.

Haydn's relationship with his audience was a key factor throughout his four decades of writing symphonies. Even though his initial contract with the Eszterházy family was a highly restrictive one, his works being the property of his patron and written for his patron's use, it became apparent from a very early stage that these works were receiving a much wider dissemination. This dissemination (through publication and performance) his patron not only tolerated but no doubt encouraged as it became increasingly obvious that he had in his service someone who could enhance the international reputation of the Eszterházy name. In writing symphonies, then, Haydn wished to appeal both to the taste of the larger international audience and to the taste of his patron, and in fact there was probably very little difference if any between the two.

Haydn's apprenticeship as a composer included instruction with the distinguished Italian vocal master and composer Porpora, self-directed study of manuals by Fux and Mattheson, as well as the study of scores by composers such as Handel, Hasse, and Gluck. The musical and aesthetic perspective he gained was as fine as one could hope to receive in the middle of the century. He was exposed to the view that music should entertain as well as serve a moral purpose through affective means. Mattheson, for example, in *Der vollkommene Capellmeister*, which Haydn had studied carefully, postulated that 'if music was to serve "the glory of God and all virtues," and if the virtues were to be approached in the Cartesian manner by means of the passions, the arousal of the affects had to be the means and the end of music'.[1] Mattheson, of course, was not alone in this view as it was also advocated by Scheibe, Marpurg, Krause, and Sulzer, among others. And where affects were concerned, writers such as Mattheson, Scheibe, and Heinichen advocated the primacy of the single affect, which was not to be diluted by minor or secondary ones.[2] Lessing's view on this, already cited in the previous chapter, was that a symphony which expresses conflicting passions is a musical monstrosity. In the 1750s or even the 1760s, Haydn had no particular reason to quarrel with this. The best musical precedent for anything to the contrary lay in the ensembles of comic opera, and it was not until the late sixties and early seventies that Haydn began seriously to apply himself to this type of operatic composition.

In the early symphonies, Haydn subscribed to the prevailing aesthetic outlook. The single affect is emphasized, and through this means a moral purpose could be served. Throughout his career, Haydn never strayed far from the premise that a symphony should fulfil a moral purpose. Changes in his approach to the symphony reflect different means of achieving this, and these parallel the transformations in aesthetic thinking in general. The parallel, of course, is limited, primarily by the fact that Haydn ultimately built a symphonic language which far exceeded what theorists and aestheticians could envisage as being possible.

Pre-Paris symphonies

In his early symphonies, Haydn devised means which allow these works to engage in a rhetorical process and hence to carry out a moral purpose. Some of his quotations or other extramusical approaches have already been noted in the previous chapter. The same objectives are also served through purely musical means such as the treatment of thematic material, counterpoint, tonal movement, or a variety of smaller devices. At different points in his career there are marked differences in his approach to the treatment of these various devices, reflecting his changing approach (as well as that of his contemporaries) to the nature of the effect the symphony should have on an audience. Many of his early approaches were found to be very useful in later works and needed

[1] See John Neubauer, *The Emancipation of Music from Language* (New Haven, 1986), p. 51.
[2] Ibid., p. 158.

only to be adapted to his new purposes. The differences are not qualitative or even evolutionary. If Haydn had not written another symphony after 1772, his output could still be considered monumental and extraordinary.

One of the key factors allowing the affective approach in the early symphonies concerns the treatment of thematic material. First themes frequently take on a highly distinctive character, and often this is emphasized by a unison presentation of the theme. In support of the idea of the single affect, second themes tend not to be as distinctive and in fact are often derived from the initial theme. The emphasis on affect took on a new intensity in Haydn's so-called *Sturm und Drang* symphonies, those in minor keys from the late sixties and early seventies.[3] Some of these opening themes in minor keys are capable of generating considerable tension, such as the beginning of No. 52 with its persistent use of the leading tone and syncopation.

The type of theme which is crucial to the dramatic unfolding in certain later works (such as No. 83), embodying a combination of stability and ambiguity, can be seen in works of this period. The opening of No. 44 is a prime example of this type of dual or complex theme. The duality is first of all apparent in the dynamic marks which serve to emphasize the more important intervallic contrast (Ex. 5). The first three notes forcefully outline the tonic (although the mediant is absent). Against that, the move to the leading tone which follows is indicative of the next few bars which present the dominant in a less clearly defined way because of the semitone appoggiaturas. The theme itself, then, contains the kernel of a problem because of its two distinctly different parts, and this has clear implications for the unfolding of the movement and arrival at a conclusion. Unlike the complexity of late symphonies which can highlight the sense of conflict, the unfolding here tends to reflect more on the affective quality of the theme.

In symphonies up to about 1771, the importance of the single affect (which can be simple or complex) is reinforced by the treatment of tonality. In the exposition of the first movement of No. 44, for example, the motion to the new key is not the dramatic event which it can be in later works, but is enacted through sequential movement, defusing any sense of tension or duality which might arise at the tonal level. Once again in the development, modulatory ambiguity is largely absent. In works before this, it is even more likely that these will be the types of tonal procedures used.

One finds contrapuntal writing in both early and late instrumental

---

[3] The question concerning a possible connection with the literary *Sturm und Drang* movement will not be pursued here. This issue is treated by Landon in *Chron.* ii. 266–84, and in Neubauer, *The Emancipation of Music*, p. 159.

Ex. 5

works, although the types of counterpoint used can be very different. In earlier works Haydn was interested in the possibilities of applying the strict forms, as can be seen most clearly in the finales to the String Quartets Op. 20 Nos. 2, 5, and 6. The strict forms, which he had learned through his careful reading of Fux and study of eighteenth-century contrapuntal literature, were associated with rhetorical principles in music. This type of counterpoint tended to focus on a single subject which could be revealed in many ways through the various devices and procedures of counterpoint. In later works, and symphonic development sections in particular, counterpoint generally served a very different purpose, as it allowed contrasting or conflicting material to interact in simultaneous presentation. The model for this type of counterpoint was vocal rather than instrumental; it was the operatic ensemble which reached its peak with Mozart's great Italian operas of the eighties. The intense counterpoint which occurs in the development section of the first movement of No. 83 places three musical ideas in simultaneous interaction in much the same way that Mozart's characters engage in exchanges in operatic ensembles. The transference of this type of operatic counterpoint to instrumental music is not yet used in Haydn's early symphonies.

Beginning in the early 1770s, some fundamental changes occurred in Haydn's symphonic language. The apparent insistence on thematic unity of the earlier works is now replaced by a strong duality in a number of works. There are different possible explanations for the change occurring at this time. On the theoretical side, Haydn gradually came to discover that there was another body of opinion which not only condoned contrast but actively advocated it. Contrary to those who would not tolerate more than a single affect, Quantz recommended the use of striking dissonances to bring out 'the excitement of alternating passions'. C. P. E. Bach, whose influence Haydn so freely acknowledged, stated in his *Versuch über die wahre Art das Clavier zu spielen* that the musician 'has barely quieted down one [affect before] he arouses another, so that he constantly alternates the passions'.[4] The time of Haydn's earliest exposure to the written and musical works of Bach has been a matter of some controversy, but A. Peter Brown has argued convincingly that this did not happen before the 1760s for the *Versuch*,

---

[4] See Neubauer, *The Emancipation of Music*, p. 158.

and probably somewhat later for the sonatas.[5] It is not out of the question, then, that this acquaintance began to have an effect on Haydn's own writing at the beginning of the 1770s.

At the same time, his activities as a composer of comic opera very much increased. In 1768 and 1769, in fact, he wrote two operas in close succession with texts by Goldoni. It is entirely possible that this type of operatic activity, which involves dramatic interaction, should have a bearing on instrumental music written shortly thereafter. Considering the type of thematic contrast used in some instrumental works of the early seventies, the connection with opera becomes all the stronger. In some works in minor keys written at this time, Haydn introduces second themes or closing themes with a distinctly comic nature, in sharp contrast to unsettling or affective first themes. One of the best examples occurs in the exposition of the Piano Sonata in C minor (H. XVI: 20) of 1771, and a similar duality is found in the first movement of Symphony No. 52, also in C minor and written at about that time. Other types of duo-thematicism become fairly commonplace during the early seventies.

Along with the thematic contrast of the earlier seventies one finds a whole range of other procedures which transform Haydn's symphonic language into something decidedly dramatic. Some of these procedures can involve an interaction of stable musical material with that which is ambiguous. In No. 46, for example, a somewhat disjointed opening melody is set against a highly stable pattern (still in the tonic), and the interaction of these two passages is the focus of each section (including both tonal groups of the exposition) of the first movement. In the dominant section of the exposition, the roles in fact are reversed as the presence of a countermelody gives the first theme a stabilizing effect, while a shift to the minor and accompanying syncopation throws the previously stable passage into disarray (Ex. 6). This possibility of role reversal remains an issue for the remainder of the movement as tonal treatment continues to be a factor in the development and recapitulation. A highly unusual feature of this movement is a false recapitulation in the tonic key only eleven bars into the development.

The type of syncopation noted in No. 26 and now in No. 46 becomes more evident at this time as a feature of the dramatic language. In No. 26, the syncopation establishes a context for the drama of the Passion story, putting the listener in the right frame of mind through the disturbing effect which results from the displacement of the beat. Something similar happens in No. 45 where the syncopation accompanying the first theme is preparatory for the unusual events which follow in the first movement. In No. 46 the treatment of syncopation is

---

[5] 'Joseph Haydn and C. P. E. Bach: The Question of Influence', in Jens Peter Larsen, Howard Serwer, and James Webster (eds.), *Haydn Studies* (New York, 1981), p. 163.

Ex. 6

more concentrated as it helps to isolate a specific passage for reinterpretation. In this work it is used in a way similar to that of many later works in which the syncopation, through its blurring of the metre, can become a specific force set against that which is stable.

Other devices gaining new prominence at this time include those creating abrupt and unexpected results, effects which depend on timing. This could be a strategically placed dissonant chord, the use of silence, or the placement of expected material in unexpected situations. Rests can make an impact through both placement and length. Silence which seems too long can play havoc with the listener's expectations, or it can trick the listener about an arrival point, as happens in the joke at the end of the String Quartet, Op. 33 No. 2. In Symphony No. 39 in G minor, the phrases of the first theme are separated by rests, and the fact that these last more than a bar is unexpected. Symphony No. 45 is characterized by the unexpected, some notable examples being the tonal ambiguity at the end of the exposition, the appearance of a new theme in the development, and a recapitulation which is more developmental than conclusive. An important ingredient of that developmental character is an extended chromatic motion in the bass, starting at the beginning of the recapitulation and continuing in the same direction for about twenty-five bars. This type of chromaticism, with its potential for standing in contrast to stable harmony, becomes a fundamental aspect of the dramatic language of symphonies.

Haydn uses slow introductions in early works much less frequently than in symphonies after the mid-eighties, but once again his later approaches can be seen to be anticipated in the seventies. Perhaps the most striking example occurs in No. 57 (1774), which has a slow introduction longer than all but one of the late symphonies (No. 103). In the later symphonies Haydn uses slow introductions not only as a dramatic force against the lighter dance-like themes which follow, but the introductions can contain their own contrasting forces. These forces can be defined by opening passages which have stable melodies, harmony, and phrasing against ensuing passages in which that stability is broken down. That type of pattern can be found in No. 57, in which the first sixteen bars are strictly periodic while the last fifteen bars have no discernible phrasing pattern. An important feature of the late introductions is their thematic associations with subsequent allegro material, and at least one from the mid-seventies, No. 53, suggests this possibility. This particular introduction contains another possible quotation as well, that being the four-note motive associated with the 'Lucis Creator' plainchant used so strikingly by Mozart in the 'Jupiter' Symphony as well as other works such as Symphony No. 33 (1779).

It was noted in Chapter 1 that one of the devices used in later symphonies to draw attention near the end of the first movement to previously important material is a fermata which can stop the motion and introduce a coda. After the fermata the new treatment of the material in question is often the crucial point of arrival in the dramatic process. In Symphony No. 44, one finds a similar type of coda as the motion near the end of the first movement is brought to a halt with a fermata over a diminished chord at bar 140. The passage which is heard immediately after the fermata is from the first theme and receives special treatment here (Ex. 7). In its original appearance, the theme was seen to contain contrast (the tonic chord outline at a forte level and semitone appoggiaturas at a piano level). Now, beginning at a piano level, it is given in a canonic realization by the four string parts, allowing the stark fifths and octaves to coincide with the appogiaturas.

Even though Haydn's symphonies were disseminated internationally before the eighties, he nevertheless lacked control over this situation, having little or no recourse against unscrupulous publishers and not knowing under what circumstances the works were being performed. This changed to some extent in 1782 with the composition of a set of three symphonies, Nos. 76–8, which were intended for a specific foreign audience. In composing them as a set, which he had not done with symphonies since 1761, he was undoubtedly aiming to make them more desirable to a concert organization.[6] The intended audience was English, and Haydn, it seems, had hoped to go to England at this time.

Haydn used the minor key in a symphony for the first time since the early seventies in No. 78 (1782), and shortly thereafter he wrote No. 80

---

[6] See Landon, *Chron.* ii. 564. In *The Symphonies of Joseph Haydn* (London, 1955), p. 389, Landon suggests that they were written as a set for the purposes of publication.

Ex. 7

in a minor key as well, a work which also belongs to a set of three. Like No. 52 a decade earlier, Nos. 78 and 80 have a bearing on the language of No. 83, and it is in .the ability of the thematic material to define polarities that this occurs. In the case of No. 78, there is a strong division between the four-bar units which make up the eight-bar theme (Ex. 8). The disjointed, aggressive leaps of the first four bars stand in contrast to the smoother passage which follows with its cadential Neapolitan outline and expected harmonic resolution. The opening theme of No. 80 in D minor more strongly resembles those of the previous decade and, as in No. 52, he contrasts the opening minor theme (Ex. 9*a*) with a second theme which is of a distinctly comic nature (9*b*).

Haydn thus shifted to an approach which uses contrast or polarity rather than the presentation of a unified affect, and the process rapidly permeated all aspects of symphonic writing, including treatment of themes, tonality, and counterpoint. During this time a greater sense of intelligibility pervaded the sonata-form process, as the ideas presented in the exposition received a highly concentrated and comprehensible treatment in development and recapitulation sections. In spite of Haydn's remark to the publisher M. Boyer that these symphonies of the early eighties are 'easy', a new level of complexity is evident in some, particularly in the development sections of Nos. 77 and 78 in the way the counterpoint is used. Beginning at bar 90 of No. 77, one finds an intense contrapuntal exchange based on the first part of the opening theme,[7] a type of counterpoint which will be observed on a larger scale in the development section of No. 102. Another approach to counterpoint occurs in No. 78, as material from the first and second themes of the exposition is heard in simultaneous interaction beginning at bar 88 (Ex. 10). The greater accountability of recapitulations for foregoing events can be seen particularly well in No. 77. Here this is achieved by the use

---

[7] This passage is singled out for its importance by Karl Geiringer, who calls it a kind of *stretto maestrale*, in *Haydn: A Creative Life in Music* (Berkeley and Los Angeles, 1968), p. 321.

Ex. 8

Ex. 9

a.

b.

Ex. 10

of fermatas over the rests at bars 176, 178, and 179, giving the fragments which occur between these points a special significance (Ex. 11). As the interrelationships became more complex, the demands on the audience to listen reflectively became greater.

Paris: No. 83

The circumstances which surround the composition of the Paris Symphonies were special in relation to Haydn's prior symphonic

Ex. 11

activities. No longer was he in the position of trying to reach a foreign audience, but the outside audience, Le Concert de la Loge Olympique, now came to him with a commission. Unlike his previous symphonies which were reaching the international audience in a somewhat haphazard way, these were directed to a specific audience which Haydn could assume was sophisticated, and the performance was in the hands of first-rate musicians. That the performers were Freemasons and the performances were to be given by a Masonic concert society may very well have had a bearing on Haydn's approach to these works as well, as this was the time of his own Masonic initiation. One of the most striking works of this set of six symphonies is No. 83 in G minor, and it is possible that this is the first work of the set. Landon speculates that they may have been composed and sent to Paris in the order in which they appeared in Imbault's first edition which is: 83, 87, 85, 82, 86, and 84 (*Chron.* ii. 592).

While Haydn's means for the achievement of enlightened goals in symphonies appear to go through changes throughout his career, it is all but impossible to say that procedures used at one stage of his career are exclusive to that stage. Duality appears to distinguish works of and after the early seventies, but that is not to say that duality is absent in all works before that time. Similarly, the extraordinary musical process and the resulting intelligibility so evident in the first movement of No. 83 does not necessarily distance this work from all earlier symphonies. Every procedure or technique used in this movement has its basis in three decades of symphonic experience, and the aesthetic goal is not fundamentally different. Nevertheless, No. 83 does mark something new. Never before in a symphonic movement was the listener challenged as he is here to listen reflectively, to remember details at every step of the way, since every detail is crucial to the moral truth which will be revealed in the end. The commission showed great esteem on the part of the audience for the composer, and Haydn met this attitude in kind, showing great respect for the intelligence and virtue of his audience. What is new about No. 83 directly concerns the composer-audience relationship. Having some idea of the intelligence and values of his new audience, an idea which he could at least vaguely conceptualize since he could identify the audience through his correspondence with the Comte d'Ogny, he was now able to build his audience directly into the works themselves.

The intellectual challenge in No. 83 begins with the material of the first two bars, and a problem which is presented in these bars remains at issue throughout the entire movement. Haydn condenses the dramatic problem into four thematic notes, offering something epigrammatic upon which the listener can easily seize. The problem, very simply, is this: the first bar suggests a tonic triad figure, but on the strong beat of the second bar there is a raised fourth degree, delaying the arrival of the tonic frame note (Ex. 12). In symphonies both before and after 1785 a figure arpeggiating the tonic triad was a very normal way for the first theme of the first movement to begin. The effect is one of considerable stability, and the use of this type of figure in a newly heard work creates an expectation of the same type of pattern. It is less likely for Haydn's initial minor themes to be stable, and in the case of No. 83 he chooses to emphasize a tritone rather than a fifth. The result is a type of dissonance, a broken diminished chord emphasized by forzato marks. The expected fifth arrives on a weaker beat without forzato marks, and the arrival of consonance therefore takes a subordinate position to the dissonant figure. The dissonance and the consonance are, in a sense, superimposed upon each other in these four notes, setting up a duality or conflict within a very small thematic unit.

The dark character of this passage is abandoned with the first theme in the relative major at bar 33 (Ex. 13a). Haydn now focuses on simple triadic material and further emphasizes stability by giving this theme a dance character, as can be seen in the comparison with the *Rutscher* in Ex. 13b.[8] The next theme, at bar 45, is even lighter in character and gives this work its epithet 'La Poule' (Ex. 14). Before the exposition ends there is further reflection on the unstable nature of the first theme, as the figure at bar 59 outlines a tritone and can also be heard as an inversion of the first variant of the first theme (Ex. 15). The first and last themes of the relative major address the problem of the first epigrammatic theme.

In the development, Haydn used a contrapuntal approach which, in concentration and the amount of interaction, exceeded anything he had previously written in symphonies. The arrival of the counterpoint at bar 83 stands out as an important event, marked by an abrupt change to forte and a fuller texture (Ex. 16). Two of the previous themes are readily apparent: the initial theme is in the lower strings and bassoon while the inverted theme is in the first oboe. The violin part between these suggests the rhythm of the dance theme but strictly follows the contour of the first oboe part. The bright dance character (Ex. 13a) has now given way to darker thematic forces. The theme given in Ex. 14 is not present in the counterpoint, and thus does not participate in the

[8] The dance given for comparative purposes in Ex. 13b is a *Rutscher* found in Franz M. Böhme, *Geschichte des Tanzes in Deutschland*, ii (Leipzig, 1886), p. 164. See also Chapter 11, Ex. 20c.

Ex. 12

Ex. 13

a.

b.

Ex. 14

Ex. 15

Ex. 16

dramatic unfolding. Its role seems to have been that of comic relief, although it is integrated into the movement by the ubiquitous dotted rhythm that accompanies it. The treatment of the counterpoint here is similar to those points in the ensembles of comic opera where characters interact.

Emerging from the counterpoint at bar 97, the problem of the opening of the work is again presented, now with both the problem and its apparent solution given in two-bar units (Ex. 17). In dramatic works it is not unusual to find intransigent opposing forces, such as Don Giovanni and Donna Anna in Mozart's *Don Giovanni*, and some other character with the capacity for change, such as Donna Elvira. Capacity for change is found in this development section in the rhythmic violin part which gravitates towards the unstable thematic material ·at bar 83 but gradually returns to its original dance character towards the end of the development.

The recapitulation repeats the first sixteen bars of the work but then omits the second sixteen and proceeds with the dance theme, now in the tonic major. Some tension-generating material is therefore removed and the sense of stability is further emphasized by the fact that the dance theme at bar 146 outlines a root position triad instead of the first inversion found at bar 33. The particular treatment of the fermata at bar 181 (Ex. 18) demands the listener's attention, and the material which follows is of crucial dramatic significance to the preceding events. After the fermata Haydn states the problem twice in two-bar units and follows

Ex. 17

Ex. 18

this with the solution in the oboes at bars 186–7. The reference to bars 97–104 is clear and, as in various other later works, points to something earlier in the movement which may have escaped notice then but is in fact of central importance.

The conclusion of the movement (bars 182–7) presents a solution, but within that solution the forces which generated the initial conflict are placed side by side in a coexistent antecedent and consequent relationship. Haydn is therefore following an approach consistent with that of the writers of the Enlightenment. A work such as No. 83 demands both intellect and feeling from the audience, qualities with which Haydn knew his new audience was endowed. By following the events of the first movement carefully, the listener becomes engaged in a process of understanding, a process yielding a truth at the end. The forces used here are genuinely dramatic ones. In strictly musical terms, the opposition can be reduced to a conflict between stability and instability, a process not unlike that of any significant dramatic work. But instead of using characters or ideas or beliefs, the symphonist embodies his conflict in musical gestures which, in an archetypal way, parallel human conflicts. In the conclusion of the first movement of No. 83, Haydn can be seen to be demonstrating a very fundamental yet difficult truth: opposition is inevitable, and the highest form of unity is not the one which eliminates conflict. On the contrary, it is one in which opposing forces can coexist. The best minds of Haydn's age aspired to tolerance, not dogmatism. It is precisely this message that can be heard in many of Haydn's late symphonies.

PART 2

Audience Reception
and England

8

The Composer–Audience Relationship

IF Haydn's consistent objective in his symphonies was to achieve enlightened goals, then an issue of fundamental importance must be the composer's relationship with his audience. The nature of the effect that the works should have on an audience, however, is not something which the composer determines independently. It is determined within the context of larger social and philosophical aspirations of which the audience is an integral part, and hence the audience itself has a role in determining the nature of the works intended for it, in shaping the creative process of the artist.

For eighteenth-century composers and theorists, it was self-evident that the composer–audience relationship was of the greatest possible significance. This is apparent in theoretical writing on the connection between music and rhetoric (for example, Mattheson, *Der vollkommene Capellmeister*, 1739; Daube, *Der musikalische Dilettant*, 1770; and Forkel, *Allgemeine Geschichte der Musik*, 1788–1801) where music is, among other things, considered from the perspective of the principles of oratory. The importance of the composer–audience relationship is confirmed by major composers such as C. P. E. Bach, who spoke of avoiding 'the same error as orators who try to place an impressive accent on every word',[1] or Haydn himself who believed he had done his duty and been of use to the world through his works. In England, Abel and Burney agreed that C. P. E. Bach could have given his audience even more consideration, stating 'that the genius of Emanuel Bach would have been more expanded and of more general use' if he had been in a great European capital where he would have been 'obliged to study and respect the public taste' (*Mem.* iii. 309).

Reception

The past two decades have seen an enormous resurgence of interest in audiences or readers and their real or indirect effect on writers. This has primarily occurred in the field of literary criticism, led in Germany by the *Rezeptionsgeschichte* of Hans Robert Jauss and Wolfgang Iser, and also

---

[1] *Essays on the True Art of Playing Keyboard Instruments*, trans. and ed. William J. Mitchell (New York, 1949), p. 81.

practised in the English-speaking world by a large number of reader-response theorists. Musicology has recently been paying more attention to these activities, as can be seen from the studies on reception issues, examinations of specific audiences such as courts and concert societies, as well as the inclusion of 'reception' as a main theme at major international congresses.[2]

Since interest among musicologists in this subject is still fairly new, there remains some question as to how theories should be applied or devised. For the music scholar, a workable approach must clearly be devised from within the discipline of music, reflecting its particular nature as well as the distinctive character of the audience. The student of eighteenth-century music is at a distinct advantage in this regard since eighteenth-century composers, theorists, and other observers had much to say about the relationship between composers and audiences, the effect each could have on the other. The approach in this study is to return to the eighteenth-century commentary, and to focus particularly on Haydn's own remarks. The discussion in Part II does not move from a general theory to the particular application, but proceeds on the basis of the individual composer's experience as it is recognized by that composer and corroborated by his contemporaries. The issues raised by the eighteenth-century writers are, of course, often the same ones addressed by reception theorists today, and some of these parallels will be noted.

Haydn's letters and notebooks contain numerous direct and indirect comments on his relationship with his audience, and the impression these give is of a composer deeply concerned about the acceptance of his works and the effect his works should have on the audience. In 1782, not long after the issuing of the String Quartets Op. 33, he wrote to the publisher Artaria that van Swieten 'gave me distinctly to understand that in future I should dedicate my compositions directly to the public' (*Cor.* 37). The general practice had been to dedicate works to members of the aristocracy, and Haydn's comment suggests a shift to a new audience. The new audience, the 'public', incorporated a wider social spectrum, and Haydn on various occasions identified his own social orientation. Writing to Maria Anna von Genzinger during his first year in London, for example, he noted that his 'credit with the common people has been firmly established for a long time' (*Cor.* 120). And further, he made the following observation to Griesinger: 'I have associated with emperors, kings, and many great gentlemen and have heard many flattering things from them; but I do not wish to live on an intimate footing with such persons, and I prefer people of my own status' (*Not.* 55).

---

[2] For example, the 1987 meeting of the International Musicological Society in Bologna.

Haydn's desire to gain the approbation of his audience remained consistent throughout his career. On a number of occasions he observed that his works were universally loved with the exception of only a few regional critics. As early as 1776 he wrote: 'In the chamber-musical style I have been fortunate enough to please almost all nations except the Berliners' (*Cor.* 20). In London he was able to claim that, 'apart from the professors, I am respected and loved by everyone' (*Cor.* 120).[3] At the beginning of his second season in England he wrote the following to Luigia Polzelli: 'last year I made a great impression on the English and hope therefore to win their approval this year, too' (*Cor.* 126). Concerning the rivalry with Pleyel into which he had found himself thrust, he was able to face this with complete confidence because, as he put it, 'my reputation is so firmly established here' (*Cor.* 128).

A striking observation made by Haydn about his English audience concerns the apparent need to alter things for them. This could involve previously composed works such as Symphony No. 91, which, when he finally received the score sent through the post by Maria Anna von Genzinger, evoked the following comment to her: 'I have to change many things for the English public' (*Cor.* 131). This particular comment, however, seems somewhat inflated since it does not appear that any significant changes were made to the work.[4] Of greater interest, however, in the same letter of 1792, is a remark regarding the alteration of a work written for London (presumably No. 93) in response to the audience reception of that work: 'I intend to alter the last movement of it, and to improve it, since it is too weak compared with the first. I was convinced of this myself, and so was the public, when it was played the first time last Friday; notwithstanding which, it made the most profound impression on the audience' (*Cor.* 131). That there could be a direct audience intervention on a work has striking implications for the whole body of works written for that audience. There is also an implication here that if changes needed to be made to one work, this would also have a bearing on Haydn's approach to subsequent works as well. This important effect of reception on production has been put forward as a critical principle by Jauss, who states that 'the relationship of work to work must now be brought into this interaction between work and mankind, and the historical coherence of works among themselves must be seen in the interrelations of production and reception'.[5] This interaction is defined more precisely: 'The historicity of literature as well as its communicative character presupposes a dialogical and at once

---

[3] He appears to use the term 'professors' here specifically to apply to people involved with the Professional Concerts.

[4] See *Chron.* iii. 141–2, and László Somfai, 'The London Revision of Haydn's Instrumental Style', *Proceedings of the Royal Musical Association*, 100 (1973–4), pp. 159–63.

[5] *Toward an Aesthetic of Reception*, trans. Timothy Bahti (Minneapolis, 1982), p. 15.

processlike relationship between work, audience, and new work' (p. 19).

Haydn's final phrase in the sentence cited above, concerning 'the most profound impression on the audience', suggests an interest in something other than approbation alone. This other dimension has already been noted in various citations used in earlier chapters, concerning, for example, the profound impression made on the most inexperienced listener in *The Seven Last Words*, the rest and refreshment which music could give to the burdened, the fact that Haydn believed he could be of use to the world through his works, and his portrayal of moral characters in his symphonies. These views are supported by numerous others. Concerning *The Creation*, for example, 'music could . . . heighten these sacred emotions', so that the listeners could leave with their hearts uplifted (*Cor.* 187). He was able to thank God that he 'could render some little pleasure', and it gave him great satisfaction that through his music he was able to assist in 'efforts to comfort the unhappy' (*Cor.* 182, 248).

Musical background of the audience

Haydn found the English public most unlike the one he knew in Austria. In England he was able to say for himself that liberty is dear, and this may have been related to the social make-up of the audience and the visibility of·certain sectors of it. In his second London notebook he observed that 'the common people in the galleries of all the theatres are very impertinent; they set the fashion with all their unrestrained impetuosity, and whether something is repeated or not is determined by their yells' (*Cor.* 273). Given Haydn's own social orientation, he may very well have approved of this 'impertinence' and delighted in the fact that in England (unlike Austria) the common people could make such displays. At the same time, he doubted the ability of this segment of the audience to make sound judgements. In pointing out that 'the parterre and all the boxes sometimes have to applaud a great deal to have something repeated' (*Cor.* 273), he seemed to be implying that the occupants of the galleries might very well not recognize something special if they heard it. For this element of the audience there was much that needed to be done as far as refinement was concerned, and it was generally recognized that through education taste could be improved. Even after the appearance of *The Creation* and the negative reaction of some to the 'Representation of Chaos', Burney found it necessary to point out that 'the public in the cant of modern language, is *not up to it*, and must *learn to hear it*'.[6] Three decades later, William Crotch lamented that the taste of the English public 'still requires much cultivation', and

---

[6] MS Letter to Latrobe (appendix), undated [after 1800], Osborn Collection, Beinecke Library, Yale University.

noted that 'refined taste is the consequence of education and habit' (*Sub.* 13, 20).

Following the complexities of works such as the English Symphonies was no doubt beyond the capabilities of the inexperienced listeners referred to by Haydn. The part of the audience capable of listening reflectively was much more likely to occupy the parterre and the boxes. Many of these people were probably musicians themselves, in most cases amateurs and in some instances connoisseurs. With these (the connoisseurs in particular) Haydn felt a different type of affinity in that he was confident they would immediately understand his works and be sympathetic to his decisions. Concerning *The Creation*, he made the following observation: 'I would only wish, and hope, that the critics do not deal too severely with my Creation: . . . but the true connoisseur will see the reasons for them [treatment of certain passages] as readily as I do' (*Cor.* 154). Further, in the subscription announcement for *The Creation* in the *Allgemeine Musikalische Zeitung*, the purpose for the published score is that 'the public may have the work in its entirety, and so that the connoisseur may see it *in toto* and thus better judge it' (*Cor.* 155).

The members of various musical societies who gave Haydn honorary membership or medals of distinction were clearly regarded by the composer as connoisseurs. His letters of appreciation are interesting in a number of ways. In one such letter, to the 142 French Musicians, Paris, dated 1801, he addressed them as gentlemen 'who cultivate the arts from enthusiasm and not for gain' (*Cor.* 189). While his term 'Enthusiasmus' is not intended in the Shaftesburian sense of 'fanaticism', the comment as a whole echoes Shaftesbury's view of the idea of disinterestedness where art works are concerned. The good will which Haydn felt about French musicians and audiences was reciprocated by the Parisian Société Académique des Enfans d'Appollon, in a letter written to Haydn in 1807: 'artists consider it a sacred duty to pay the utmost attention to their [the symphonies'] performance, fully assured of the taste and sensibility of the listeners, who always share their just enthusiasm' (*Cor.* 244).

As for music journalists, Haydn doubted their ability to recognize quality, but he nevertheless took them very seriously. Reviewers can be taken as the reflection of the inclinations of an audience, so an artist concerned with approbation and effect will use them as a measuring-stick. Upon his arrival in London, Haydn informed Maria Anna von Genzinger that he 'went the round of all the newspapers for 3 successive days' (*Cor.* 112). He remained very much aware of what was in the newspapers, commenting that they were full of stories concerning his rivalry with Pleyel (*Cor.* 128). He was also prepared to use the papers himself, as in his open letters in the *Morning Herald* and the *Morning*

Chronicle. Haydn's friends kept him apprised of newspaper accounts concerning himself, as we learn from Dies (*Nach.* 127).

The composer hears the audience

Aside from the critics, Haydn had various other ways of discovering the inclinations of his audience, and the evidence points to the fact that this was very important to him. A particularly interesting although somewhat muddled observation of this was made in the diary of an interested English Haydn watcher, Charlotte Papendiek:

> Haydn, immediately on his arrival, told Salomon that he should stay the summer in England, and that as he heard there were to be twelve concerts and two benefits during the season there would be ample time for him to compose his first symphonies after he had had an opportunity of studying the taste of the English. He was determined that his first production should both amuse and please the musical public and rivet him in their favour.[7]

Unfortunately, she has her dates and the sequence of events confused, which should not be too surprising since these remarks were written a number of decades after the event. However, these errors need not detract from the validity of her sense of the relationship he had with his audience. His access to the taste of the audience, aside from the critics, was possible through the observation of works and audience reaction at the concerts he attended, reviews of the works of other composers, and commentary on his own previously composed works. His most direct access to an understanding of the taste of the English audience, however, came through his various friendships.

Haydn's own feelings about the English audience were made public in the pages of the *Morning Chronicle* on 18 May 1791. Here he made 'his most grateful Acknowledgements to the English Public in general, as well as to his particular Friends, for the zeal which they have manifested at his CONCERTS, which has been supported by such distinguished marks of favour and approbation, as will be remembered by him with infinite delight as long as he lives' (*Chron.* iii. 77). Through this relationship with the audience in general and friends in particular, it was evident to Haydn that he was able to share similar values with the English, and that his works therefore could fall upon receptive ears. Since reviews were not confined only to musical matters he was able to get some sense of audience values from the newspapers.

But much more important in this respect was his exposure to intellectuals and musicians in England who could give him a far more

---

[7] Charlotte Papendiek, *Court and Private Life in the Time of Queen Charlotte: Being the Journal of Mrs Papendiek*, ed. Mrs Vernon Delves Broughton, ii (London, 1887), p. 290. Also printed in *Chron.* iii. 51.

penetrating view of English taste. The list of such people is long, but some whom he saw frequently or whose company he particularly enjoyed include Johann Peter Salomon, Charles Burney, Thomas Holcroft, Thomas Twining, and Christian Ignatius Latrobe. Concerning Haydn's relationships with these individuals, documentation of actual exchanges is in some cases very limited. As was illustrated in the Introduction concerning Haydn and Burney, however, this in no way precluded the possibility that frequent exchanges occurred viva voce, and that Haydn tried when possible to save himself the trouble of writing letters. Not having the 'sheets of paper' which might have been or reports of the 'fine speeches innumerable' to Burney or anyone else in England, one has no choice but to speculate on what was said.

It can be assumed that the written works of the people in question or their correspondence with others will give some sense of the conversations they may have had with Haydn where matters of taste or values are concerned. The usefulness of this approach is borne out in the case of Burney since Haydn not only knew some of his works but also had discussions with him about at least one of Burney's major literary-biographical projects, namely the study on Metastasio. Also, as is readily apparent from his correspondence, Burney liked to discuss his thoughts in great detail with friends. The musical and aesthetic ideas of Burney and other English friends will be discussed in Chapter 9, with the assumption that at least some of this thought was known to Haydn and influenced or confirmed his own musical approaches.

There were basic assumptions that Haydn could share with English society at large. One was a sense of freedom and liberty. Writing to Maria Anna von Genzinger during his first year in England, he contrasted his present existence with that in Austria: 'Oh, my dear gracious lady! how sweet this bit of freedom really is! . . . I often sighed for release, and now I have it in some measure. . . . The realization that I am no bond-servant makes ample amends for all my toils' (*Cor.* 118). However, dear as this liberty was to him, he was determined to return to his patron's service again, an attitude which his more liberated English admirers found incomprehensible. That type of dependence on or responsibility to the aristocracy was no longer a part of the English consciousness.

Late in the eighteenth century, a wave of conservatism swept England in reaction to the disorder which followed the French Revolution, and in a sense this conservatism brought thinking among some in England more into line with the enlightened thought with which Haydn was familiar. Notions of morality, for example, which belonged to the early Enlightenment made a strong resurgence. In bitter reaction to the terror in France, Burney wrote that 'peace, tranquillity, content, benevolence, humility, politeness, and all religious & social Virtues, are not only neglected, but regarded as vices!!' Religion, morals, liberty, property, and life were in imminent danger.[8] Even Thomas Holcroft, whose radical political activities resulted in a charge of treason (of which he was acquitted but without a pardon), was a staunch defender of morality in the early eighteenth-century sense, and in fact disseminated works by writers such as Gellert and Lavater in translation. These observations, of course, are not intended as an argument for the presence of an English Enlightenment at the end of the eighteenth century. They simply indicate that among those with whom Haydn associated, his own attitudes concerning morality were reinforced.

Tolerance, that key manifestation of enlightened morality, had for over a century been official policy in England as a result of the Toleration Act of 1689. Shaftesbury had argued for intellectual as well as religious tolerance, and subsequent thought in England reinforced this view. The matter of Haydn's awareness of tolerance is raised by Griesinger in the context of a comment Haydn made in an old English abbey, apparently regretting that it was no longer Roman Catholic. Griesinger, to be fair, immediately presents an overview: 'This instance, however, does not indicate intolerant feelings. Haydn left every man to his own conviction and recognized all as brothers. In general, his devotion was not of the gloomy, always suffering sort, but rather cheerful and reconciled' (*Not.* 54). His view, along with that of his English hosts, was fundamentally optimistic: music was written in the belief that it could have a beneficial effect on the lives of people.

As the discussion of Symphony No. 83 has attempted to demonstrate, ideas such as tolerance could be embodied in purely instrumental works, and this is even more evident in some of the English Symphonies. The first movement of No. 83 could, of course, be interpreted differently by different listeners. For some, the most important part of the movement may be the humorous 'clucking' theme which is reinforced by the ubiquitous dotted rhythm. For others, the opening theme may be not so much a kernel of a dramatic problem as simply an affective theme which receives its distinctive character from the outline of a tritone. For these listeners, the 'clucking' theme may seem an unwarranted intrusion which diminishes the work. The listener who hears an elaborate working out of a dramatic problem does so as the result of a 'critical' listening process which requires not only reflection but also interpretation. How the composer 'intends' the listeners to hear is, of course, a fairly contentious issue. The entire issue of intention has been treated by most writers with considerable caution since the appearance of the article 'The Intentional Fallacy' by William K. Wimsatt and Monroe C. Beardsley in 1946.[9] This caution about intention appears, however, to be

---

[8] See Roger Lonsdale, *Dr Charles Burney: A Literary Biography* (Oxford, 1965), p. 369.
[9] Reprinted in William K. Wimsatt, *The Verbal Icon* (London, 1970), 3–18.

more a post-eighteenth-century issue than a concern of the Enlighten-ment. For writers who describe the arts as having rhetorical or didactic functions, it would be inconceivable that there should be any reservation about the revelation of intentions. In the case of Haydn, his biographers Griesinger and Dies were both interested in his intentions when writing symphonies, and Haydn was not in the least reluctant to provide an answer, suggesting that he often had portrayed moral characters (*Not.* 62). Even in 1823, the writer of the article on Haydn in the *Harmonicon* considered it crucial to be able to 'understand the meaning and main intention' of the symphonies (1/2, p. 17).

An apparent acceptance that 'intention' was a legitimate area of discussion, however, does not necessarily make it easier to define intentions. An issue related to intention arises in the assumption that the composer–audience relationship had a bearing on the nature of the works written for that particular audience. An interesting case concerns Haydn's Paris Symphonies. These works mark a new departure in that they were intended for a new, international audience. However, Haydn did not go to Paris and had to conduct his dealings with the concert society by correspondence. While his prince and some of his musicians had been to Paris, the second-hand knowledge gained from them is unlikely to have given him more than a vague sense of the new audience. Even in London, where he was able to attend concerts and see audience reaction at first hand, read reviews, and talk with knowledgeable individuals, there were still limits to his understanding of this foreign audience. The strongest sense of the audience which emerges, then, is in the symphonies themselves, in the manner Haydn correctly or incorrec-tly perceived his listeners and in the way the works are designed for them. It remains necessary to attempt to define his perception of his audience and to correlate that with the nature of the works.

Among literary theorists, the validity of this approach is by no means universally accepted. The problem arises in defining the audience or reader: can critics, or artists for that matter, speak with certainly about the 'real' audience? In literary theory, the construction of the idea of an 'implied' reader has redirected the focus away from the relationship of the author and his 'real' readers. With the implied reader, the critic is fundamentally concerned with the text itself. Following Wolfgand Iser, Daniel Wilson describes the implied reader as 'the behavior, attitudes, and background—presupposed or defined, usually indirectly, in the text itself—necessary for a proper understanding of the text'.[10] Or, stated in another way, by the implied or 'implicit' reader is meant 'the indications of how to read which are concealed within the text'.[11] As for the

---

[10] 'Readers in Texts', *Publications of the Modern Language Association*, 96 (1981), p. 848.
[11] Rien T. Segers, 'Readers, Text, and Author: Some Implications of Rezeptionsästhetik', *Yearbook of Comparative and General Literature*, 24 (1975), p. 17.

relationship of the implied and real reader, Iser and Jauss have argued that any understanding of the real reader can only become possible after an examination of the implied reader's role has taken place.

More recently, some critics have challenged this sequence and its resultant critical priorities. Gunter Grimm, for one, questions the possibility of constructing the implied reader's role in the text 'without prior knowledge of the real communicative relation between the author and the audience'.[12] Wilson, in support of Grimm, suggests the following: 'An analysis of the author's perception of his or her real public at the time the work was written will often aid interpretation of the author's relation to the implied reader of a text.' And, taking this even further, Wilson states: 'Indeed, it is difficult to imagine an author whose creation (including the implied reader) is not affected in *some* way by his or her perceptions of real readers.'[13] Following this line of thinking, it will be argued here that Haydn addresses his perceived audience in his symphonies in a way which allows his shared values with the audience to determine the nature of the works. A crucial part of that nature is a process which amounts to lessons in listening built directly into the works themselves.

Receptiveness of the listeners

Haydn appears to have had very definite expectations about what the listener could and should hear, and these expectations varied in relation to the sophistication of the listener. As has already been pointed out, Haydn uses the term 'inexperienced listener' and 'connoisseur' to identify the extremes in listening potential. Haydn's term 'inexperienced' sounds very much like Tovey's 'naïve' listener, although the two probably have very little in common. Tovey's naïve listener, as Joseph Kerman wryly observes, likely has at least a pass degree from Oxford,[14] and can probably not only hear chord progressions but modulations as well. Haydn's inexperienced listener is more likely to be in a church than a concert–hall, and his chances of recognizing or remembering salient musical features seem fairly slight. The same was probably true of the 'common' people in the galleries at theatres. He clearly believed it was possible to make a 'profound impression' on these listeners, but that was much more likely to happen through evoking the passions than following a complex process. In fact, the symphonic movements most likely to receive encores were slow movements, and it is in these movements, through melody, that affective writing could best be achieved.

The composer could expect much more of the listeners occupying the

---

[12] See Wilson, 'Readers in Texts', p. 859.
[13] Ibid.
[14] 'Tovey's Beethoven,' in Alan Tyson (ed.), *Beethoven Studies*, ii (London, 1977), p. 175.

parterre and boxes. It was this group which had the potential to follow dramatic processes in symphonies because of both musical sophistication and an understanding of enlightened principles. For this part of the audience, unlike the inexperienced listeners in the galleries, he could hope to go considerably further than nurturing refinement through a vague awareness of beauty. Here he could expect recognition of dramatic polarities, reflective listening, and the ability to draw conclusions. But even here listeners were at very different levels of sophistication. Since symphonies were intended for a general audience rather than the connoisseur musician (as had been true of string quartets), it remained necessary to allow each symphony in a sense to contain its own instructions in listening. In this way he could in fact take the listener by the hand and lead him to a particular point of discovery in musical and dramatic terms. Some works clearly do this more vividly than others. The most striking in this respect is Symphony No. 103 ('The Drum-roll') which puts forward an extraordinary integration of opposites in the exposition of the first movement and repeats it at the end of the movement in a way that cannot be missed or ignored. Symphony No. 102, on the other hand, is much more challenging, requiring that one follow every detail through the long and complex first movement. While the message is similar to that of No. 103, the process is very different as the listener is left much more to his own resources.

While one could say that Haydn was writing specifically for his audience, it seems equally true that the audience played a significant role in determining what the composer would write for it. An important side of this is the nature of the works which results from the shared values of the composer and audience. In this reciprocal relationship the composer or writer tended to write for an audience whose sense of values and taste was seen as being exemplary, while the audience had its values and taste reinforced by the works. The composer, then, would take into account the expectations of his audience, possibly including matters such as class, education, nationality, location, and the political climate. Having done that, however, he would not necessarily produce works which simply met the expectations of the audience.

The necessary balance that the artist must find is addressed by Shaftesbury, who mocked those who ignored or disdained the public. The only genuine approbation, however, came from what he believed the ancient poets had succeeded in accomplishing, which was in the way they formed, polished, and refined the audience (*Char.* i. 264). Those writers who simply followed 'the public relish and current humour of the times' would produce satires that are 'scurrilous, buffooning, and without morals or instruction' (i. 265). Over a century later, William Crotch raised the same issue, although in his case with a conservative axe to grind. 'Certainly', writes Crotch, 'it is the wish of the composer to please, if possible, all hearers—both the discerning few, and the unpretending multitude' (*Sub.* 21). In his view, however, this was not possible, and a composer should 'not, therefore, write for the majority of hearers; he must not be discouraged by the inattention or censures of the public' (p. 20).

While Crotch's reason for arguing this may have been misguided (he believed composers should return to the style of J. S. Bach), he nevertheless touches an important issue which recent critics have developed. This concerns the level of expectation of the 'multitude' and the aesthetic distance between the popular expectation and the actual achievement of the work. The smaller that distance, the closer the work comes to being considered 'light'.[15] The distance can be measured in a number of ways, such as in relation to previous works, in relation to works by other artists, or in relation to the thinking of an entire generation. And the distance may be near concerning certain aspects of a work, and much further concerning others.

For the successful writer or composer of the Enlightenment, a work would have at least two primary functions, combining Ruskin's dual images of the mirror and the lamp. On the one hand the work would reflect the society of the original audience and the author, while on the other hand the work would challenge the audience with new perceptions and contain visions which might well extend beyond the original audience. The common ground can be determined by the interaction of the composer with his audience, and his success can be measured by the amount of approbation the audience extends. However, approbation has a potentially negative value when considering the visionary or challenging aspect of the work, since that side of it is not as likely to have a popular appeal. If the works should receive universal approbation, one might have cause for concern as to their quality. Haydn, in this case to his credit, had his detractors, and those in England such as William Jackson and William Crotch are inadvertent testimony to the greatness of his symphonies. It is deviation from melodic and harmonic simplicity which these writers found objectionable, and, of course, it is very much in this complexity that Haydn's greatness lies.

The matter of aesthetic distance between existing works and newly composed works marks the English Symphonies in a distinctive way compared with earlier works. This is a two-dimensional matter in that one can see the distance being both shortened and lengthened at the same time. From his first observation of the need to bring pre-London symphonies into line with English taste to his final symphonic efforts,

---

[15] See Susan R. Suleiman, 'Introduction: Varieties of Audience-Oriented Criticism', in Susan R. Suleiman and Inge Crossman (eds.), *The Reader in the Text: Essays on Audience and Interpretation* (Princeton, 1980), pp. 36–7.

one sees Haydn endeavouring to present works which would please the audience, and in this his success continued to increase.

At the same time he made these symphonies progressively more complex, challenging the listener in unheard-of ways. In both sides of this equation the audience played a distinctive role. This is most obvious in his attempt to increase approbation from one work to the next. His remark concerning No. 93, that both he and the public were aware of the weakness of the Finale, confirms his concern about this. By attending concerts, he could measure the enthusiasm of response and note which movements were encored. There were, of course, other ways of measuring popularity. One concerns the fact that the symphonies were brought out in piano trio editions shortly after their original perform- ances, and Haydn undoubtedly had some idea of how sales were going. Our best indication of this two hundred years later is that the printing plates of the most popular works are worn very thin (*Chron.* iii. 516). In this respect Nos. 96 and 95, both of which were intended to gain audience approval through means that had been successful in the past, proved not to be as warmly accepted as he had hoped. The fact that he did not at any later point return to some of the approaches used in these works suggests that he may have moved in other directions as a result of reception.

An eighteenth-century composer such as Haydn clearly had no interest in alienating his audience. Gaining approbation or writing to please was a necessary first step, and eighteenth-century thought from Shaftesbury onward confirms that moral objectives cannot be achieved unless in the context of beauty or providing pleasure. Once approbation was secured, however, it was possible to increase the intellectual or moral demands. Support for this came from his literary and musical friends such as Burney and Holcroft who placed a very high premium on morality.

Haydn's twelve symphonies written for the Salomon concerts are naturally divided in half by his two visits to England, and each group of six can be further divided more or less on the basis of considerations concerning popularity and intellectual challenge. The first three of the first set show the composer's need to win audience approval. No. 96 uses stylistic features which had been popular in Paris, and No. 95 looks back to Nos. 78 and 80. No. 93 introduced new melodic charms and was a great success. With his reputation thoroughly established, Haydn could introduce more complex features into the next three symphonies (Nos. 94, 98, and 97) involving, for example, the heightened relationship between slow introductions and subsequent first-movement material. Upon his return to England in 1794, Haydn struck a balance in No. 99, 100, and 101 between complex and popular features, with the second movements of Nos. 100 and 101 winning particular approval. The first movement of No. 99, on the other hand, is one of Haydn's most complex symphonic movements. As for the final three, Haydn no longer needed to win approval (although he clearly did gain it). The level of complexity here is exceedingly high, and with this complexity, he introduced his audience to the highest intellectual and moral level that could be envisaged as being possible in symphonies.

9

Haydn and the English Audience

FOR writers of the eighteenth century, a necessary balance existed between approbation and a higher purpose in art. This balance, according to Shaftesbury, concerned orators, leaders, and practitioners of all the arts: 'where chief men and leaders had the strongest interest to persuade, there was the highest endeavour to please' (*Char.* i. 237). The artist could neither disdain his audience nor ingratiate himself with the public. His task was to 'polish the age' or refine the public so that his efforts would have consequences for the present as well as the future. While giving pleasure and providing moral instruction were seen to be inexorably linked, they nevertheless can be examined as separate phenomena, since each needed to be cultivated and nurtured on its own terms. In the case of Haydn, one can see him at times pursuing these separately in his own works, taking steps which have specific effects on either gaining audience approval or providing intellectual challenge. On the one hand, there is no doubt about his sense of business acumen, while on the other, he shared the values of the society which made up his audience and built these values into his works. Putting these into practice required the assistance and opinions of others, and in England these were readily forthcoming.

Haydn, like Shaftesbury, recognized the importance of critics, and for the most part took them fairly seriously. Shaftesbury had taken it upon himself 'absolutely to condemn the fashionable and prevailing custom of inveighing against critics as the common enemies, and pests and incendiaries of the commonwealth of Wit and Letters'. In fact, he went so far as to assert that they were 'the props and pillars of this building' (i. 235–6). As for Haydn, one of his first acts following his arrival in England was to spend three successive days visiting the various newspapers. As was observed in the previous chapter, he was aware of reviews of his works and undoubtedly valued these as a way of gaining greater familiarity with taste and measuring the response of his audience. Treating the critics with respect is, of course, sound business sense for the performing artist, and it is simply one among numerous steps taken by Haydn to secure audience approbation.

Gaining audience approval

Haydn's English business arrangements, of course, centred around Johann Peter Salomon. Salomon himself took a calculated risk in building a new concert series around Haydn in the face of existing and successful series, although Haydn's fame in England by the 1780s was such that the odds of success were very high. The financial terms offered by Salomon to Haydn made it very much worth the effort to come to England, and while negotiations between them were sometimes rigorous, the two remained on very amiable terms. In the 'Memoir of Johann Peter Salomon' in the *Harmonicon*, the financial arrangements are outlined:

The terms on which Haydn undertook so long a journey and so responsible a duty, were, three hundred pounds for composing six grand symphonies, two hundred for the copyright of them, and a benefit, the profits guaranteed at two hundred pounds. The latter produced three hundred and fifty pounds, and as Haydn refused to pay the band, the expense fell on his enterprising countryman.[1]

Elsewhere in this journal, the editor gives more details: 'His [Haydn's] next engagement was on the same terms, exclusive of the copyright of the six last symphonies; which, being left in the hands of a lady by the composer when he quitted England, were afterwards delivered to Salomon, on his paying the further sum of three hundred pounds.'[2] Haydn's reaction to making as much as £400 at a single benefit concert was that such things could only be done in England. While in England, Haydn amassed approximately four times as much per year (after travelling expenses) as his annual income with the Eszterházy family.

Salomon saw to it that Haydn and his works received the greatest possible exposure in England. As a person of intelligence and refinement, Salomon had access to many distinguished English families, and through him Haydn's social life became almost unbearably hectic. The symphonies were disseminated in various forms aside from their concert performances at the Hanover Square Rooms. Musical amateurs quickly gained access to the works through chamber-music arrangements, first as piano trios and later as quintets. When the rival Professional Concerts attempted to lure Haydn with offers of greater pecuniary reward, Haydn remained loyal to Salomon. On 13 August 1795 Haydn signed the agreement giving all future rights of the first six English Symphonies to Salomon, and on 27 February 1796 he signed a similar agreement for the last six.

---

[1] *Harmonicon*, 8 (1830), p. 45.
[2] 'Haydn's Diary while in England', *Harmonicon*, 5 (1827), p. 7.

While in London Haydn found himself in competition with his former pupil Ignaz Pleyel. The press clearly hoped for a musical war which would result in public displays of animosity, but Haydn was not about to provide the papers with such an event:

At present I am working for Salomon's concerts, and I am making every effort to do my best, because our rivals, the Professional Concert, have had my pupil Pleyel from Strassburg come here to conduct their concerts. So now a bloody harmonious war will commence between master and pupil. The newspapers are full of it, but it seems to me that there will soon be an armistice, because my reputation is so firmly established here. Pleyel behaved so modestly towards me upon his arrival that he won my affection again. We are very often together, and this does him credit, for he knows how to appreciate his father. We shall share our laurels equally and each go home satisfied. (*Cor.* 128)

In spite of the apparent congeniality, Haydn took steps which would prevent any chance of being defeated, involving both productivity and the quality of the works. The view of some writers was that while Pleyel had less 'science' than his teacher, he nevertheless was the more popular composer. For some writers a value judgement was intended here, that Pleyel's 'charm of simplicity and feeling' was to be preferred over Haydn's 'intricacies of science'.[3] Most critics eventually came to the view that Pleyel's works were imitations of Haydn's, and Haydn's resounding triumph led to the folding of the Professional Concerts in 1793.

Haydn's biographer Dies informs us of other aspects of the composer's sound business sense. Haydn's symphonies were always performed during the second half of the concert, and this was, according to Dies, intentional:

I must inform my readers of another arrangement which Haydn contracted that first year with the manager of the Musicians' Concert (Professional Concerts). These concerts were given once a week in the new concert hall in Hanover Square, and Haydn had committed himself to deliver a new work for each concert, in all twelve pieces of different kinds, adding the stipulation that his works should always be performed in the second half. On the one hand, Haydn thereby took upon himself a considerable obligation, for, to gain applause, he had to surpass in beauty the pieces presented in the first half. On the other hand, he had this advantage in return, that if he overshadowed the first half, his work remained in the memory all the longer and all the more glory would be his. (*Nach.* 126)

While Dies got some of the facts wrong (such as the name of the concerts and the number of works), he points out a shrewd strategy which in fact proved to be highly successful.

Another key to success was remaining on good terms with musicians

---

[3] *Gazetteer*, 5 Feb. 1791 and *Morning Herald*, 22 Nov. 1791, in *Chron.* iii. 44 and 108.

as well as management. Given the level of difficulty in his works, it
would have been courting disaster to perform them with inadequate
rehearsal time (as was the practice in London) or to incur any
displeasure from members of the orchestra. Since musicians were not
under the tyranny of virtuoso conductors at this time, they could if they
so desired sabotage the performance of a work. Dies informs us that
Haydn's attitude towards the orchestra was 'captivating and kind; he
won them over to his side at the first rehearsal' (p. 123). Although his
description may be somewhat embellished, Dies tells of a rehearsal in
which Haydn, not getting the desired sound, with great courtesy borrowed
a violin and demonstrated his intention with total clarity. According to Dies
he gained their respect and good will in other ways as well:

He often invited the most important players to dinner, so that they appeared
gladly for private rehearsals in his home. He praised them and interwove
reprimand, when it was necessary, with praise in the subtlest fashion. Such
behavior won him the affection of all musicians with whom he came into
contact, so that out of love for him they rose to the level of inspiration required
for performance of a Haydn work, and which generates the charm and grace we
are speaking of here. (p. 124)

An obvious sign of business acumen is the development of a good
relationship with the public itself. By thanking the public for its support,
as Haydn did in his open letter to the *Morning Chronicle* (18 May 1791),
he was in effect complimenting his audience on its good taste and
generating a spirit which would result in continued support.

The English public which Haydn encountered in 1791 was a social
and economic mixture. Concert announcements in London were
directed to the 'Nobility and Gentry', and the success of a concert series
clearly depended on the support of these groups. The middle class,
however, was also a part of the audience, and ticket prices reflected this.
The normal price for a single ticket to a concert in London in the late
eighteenth century was about 10 shillings,[4] and we learn from Haydn
himself that this was about the same price as a turkey or two plucked
ducks (*Cor.* 259)! While this price was within the means of the middle
class, it was far beyond the reach of the working class. Concert activity
was bustling in 1792, and the *Morning Chronicle* viewed it in the following
way:

There are no fewer than sixteen public Subscription Concerts at this moment
going forward in the metropolis, besides the various select parties with which it
abounds. Each of these has a distinguished leader and performers of great
eminence. This at least will prove to the world our musical *rage*, we wish it could
also shew our musical *knowledge* and *taste*.[5]

----

[4] See Thomas B. Milligan, *The Concerto and London's Musical Culture in the Late Eighteenth Century*
(Ann Arbor, 1983), pp. 13–14.
[5] Cited in Milligan, *The Concerto*, p. 17.

'Shakespeare of Music'

Haydn's arrival in England caused a very great stir, and Haydn himself was very much aware of this. Only a few days after his arrival he was able to write: 'My arrival caused a great sensation throughout the whole city.' Upon attending his first concert he was led up the centre of the hall 'amid universal applause' and was 'assured that such honours had not been conferred on anyone for 50 years' (*Cor.* 112). At the first Salomon concert he 'created a furor with a new Symphony, and they had to repeat the Adagio: this had never before occurred in London' (*Cor.* 116). That Haydn was genuinely revered by the English can be seen in the fact that he was consistently described as the 'Shakespeare of music' by both journalists and friends. The comparison was often made in reviews of his works, for example, in the review of his first concert: 'Like our own SHAKSPEARE [*sic*], he moves and governs the passions at his will.'[6] In Oxford a few months later he was referred to as 'this musical Shakespeare',[7] and at the beginning of the 1792 season he was again called the 'Shakespeare of Music' in the *Morning Chronicle* (*Chron.* iii. 128). Among his friends, Burney drew a somewhat oblique comparison with Shakespeare in his 'Verses on the Arrival of Haydn in England' (*Chron.* iii. 34), and Haydn was specifically called the 'Shakespeare of Music' by Thomas Holcroft (*Cor.* 145).

In Austria Haydn had been compared with Gellert, a great moralist but something less than an excellent poet or dramatist. The compliment given by the English was much higher, and it was highly unusual that a foreign musician should be compared to their beloved bard. While one could simply take the comparison as a high compliment, it is possible to see more in it since the eighteenth century had a distinctive view of Shakespeare. Possibly the most important circle of Shakespeare scholars was within the Literary Club, and some of these scholars included Samuel Johnson, George Steevens, and Edmund Malone. It is possible that some of the views of these writers could have reached Haydn through Charles Burney, who was an active member of the Club. A very notable critique on Shakespeare was Johnson's Preface to his own edition of Shakespeare's works (which Haydn had in his library). Burney was thoroughly familiar with this piece of Johnson's prose, and in correspondence with Johnson about it expressed his enthusiasm for the Preface, saying it had offered him 'more Pleasure, I had almost said Rapture, than any Production of equal length I have ever read'.[8]

In the Preface, Johnson dared to speak of Shakespeare's faults, and he

---

[6] *Morning Chronicle*, 12 Mar. 1791, in *Chron.* iii. 49.
[7] *European Magazine*, 15 July 1791, in *Chron.* iii. 93.
[8] See Roger Lonsdale, *Dr Charles Burney* (Oxford, 1965), p. 65.

justified this to Burney saying that 'we must confess the faults of our favourites, to gain credit to our praise of his excellencies. He that claims . . . the honours of perfection will surely injure the reputation which he designs to assist.'[9] The primary fault observed by Johnson undoubtedly has more to do with Johnson himself than with Shakespeare. This concerns the issue of morality. The presence of or emphasis on morality in literature was for Johnson a fundamental assumption, and in his opinion some of Shakespeare's works were weakened by the placing of entertainment before instruction. He cites examples, such as *As You Like It*, where Shakespeare's treatment of the text, in Johnson's view, actually forfeited the opportunity for exhibiting a moral lesson. In the end he was forced to conclude that morality in Shakespeare's plays was incidental rather than intentional, although he was able to admit that it was possible to identify 'systems of social duty and of civil and economical prudence' in Shakespeare.[10] His influence on other Shakespeare critics was strong, and the appearance of Elizabeth Griffith's *The Morality of Shakespeare's Drama Illustrated* (1775) attests to this.

While Johnson and Burney may have had reservations about Shakespeare, these were not shared by all writers or the general English public. Holcroft brought the same assumption about morality to Shakespeare, but unlike Johnson (whom he very much admired), he had no doubt that Shakespeare did in fact achieve moral instruction. In an essay entitled 'Of the Purpose for which Tragedies and Comedies Are or Ought to be Composed', Holcroft observed that 'the pleasure, given by a dramatic work, scarcely can be exquisite, unless the future happiness of man be kept in view: that is to say, unless some essential moral truth, or truths, are inculcated' (*Theat.* i. 140). Included in his list of works best able to achieve this are *Measure for Measure*, *Macbeth*, *King Lear*, and *Othello*. Both Holcroft and Johnson preferred Shakespeare's comedies over his tragedies although Johnson was particularly interested in the mixing of comedy and tragedy in the same play. The comparison of Haydn with Shakespeare by both friends and reviewers had at least two levels of significance. The unbridled enthusiasm which most of England felt for Shakespeare, it was agreed, could be bestowed on Haydn. At the same time, it seems possible that the assumptions about the function of dramatic works at the highest possible level could be transferred to music.

Music and morals

The values of Haydn's new audience were clearly demonstrated in the theatre and in the popularity and success of certain reading materials.

---

[9] A letter dated 16 Oct. 1765. See Herbert Spencer Robinson, *English Shakespearean Criticism in the Eighteenth Century* (New York, 1968), p. 126.

[10] Ibid., p. 134.

Like theatre audiences, they expected to be entertained, and Haydn, having studied the taste of the English and being 'determined that his first production should both amuse and please the musical public and rivet him in their favour' (*Chron.* iii. 51), found the means of succeeding. For the composer who wished to improve and refine his public, gaining its approbation was, of course, an important step in itself. Along with Shaftesbury, there were other voices at the beginning of the century arguing the possibility of moral or even religious improvement through pleasing or entertaining an audience. Cavendish Weedon, for one, as early as 1702, suggested that listeners of sacred music could be 'charmed into devotion by delight [since] composers of music of divine subjects are capable of being the most sublime and entertaining'.[11] 'Entertainment' for Weedon meant something more elevated than it signifies today. In music, the goal was by no means always achieved, provoking the complaint from Sir John Hawkins that it was necessary 'to reprobate the vulgar notion that its ultimate end is merely to excite mirth'.[12]

The possibility of a connection between music and morality was a long-established one, and English audiences were well aware of this through opera and oratorio. That the symphony could have a similar function seems to have occurred to both Haydn and at least some part of his audience. His symphonies were received with great approbation in London; however, pleasing his audience was as much a means as it was an end. In order to achieve enlightened goals it was necessary that a work should appeal to as large an audience as was possible. Holcroft, for one, spoke of a linkage between approbation and producing beneficial results. In his essay 'Of the Moral Nature of Tragedy', he states: 'It is scarcely possible to compose tragedy, so as to be received and applauded by the public, without more or less producing this beneficial result' (*Theat.* i. 141). By 'beneficial result', he is referring to moral influence, the effect of tragedy in which the 'heart is relieved, delighted, and imbued, by the purity and dignity of virtue, as well as by its comparative and everlasting tendency to happiness' (i. 141). The implication was that the audience expected some moral function to be present if works were to be well received.

Burney

In order to develop an understanding for this side of the English audience, Haydn was able to rely most heavily on the views of his friends. Indeed, his most direct access to an understanding of the taste of the English public came through his various friendships. With the

[11] Quoted in William Weber, 'The Contemporaneity of Eighteenth-Century Musical Taste', *Musical Quarterly*, 70 (1984), p. 191.

[12] *A General History of the Science and Practice of Music*, ed. Charles Cudworth, i (New York, 1963), p. xvix.

possible exception of Salomon, Haydn had no greater friend and admirer in England than Charles Burney, and no one in England was better qualified to make observations about matters of English taste than Burney. Burney's great charm and erudition had gained him access to many prominent families and had allowed him, to use Johnson's term, to become 'clubbable'. Burney's enthusiasm for Haydn is readily apparent in his 'Verses on the Arrival of Haydn in England' and his entry on Haydn in *A General History of Music*, which is prefaced by the remark: 'I am now happily arrived at the part of my narrative where it is necessary to speak of HAYDN! the admirable and matchless HAYDN!'[13] Burney was clearly a man of his age, and as a member of the Literary Club and the Johnson circle, subscribed to the view that works of art should have moral content. He also was able to counterbalance Johnson's sometimes scurrilous views on music, referring to music as 'a language as intelligible and durable as the Greek', and further, allowing this power to instrumental music which is capable of being sublime and having a stronger 'effect on our feelings than the finest opera air united with the most exquisite poetry'.[14]

During the years that Haydn was in England, Burney's literary efforts were concentrated on the Metastasio *Memoirs* which he started in 1789 and published in 1796. According to Roger Lonsdale in *Dr Charles Burney* (p. 371), Haydn's interest in the project made Burney work all the harder. Not only did Burney discuss this project with Haydn but in a limited way Haydn was a collaborator, bringing some prints of Metastasio to Burney from Vienna upon returning to England in 1794. Writing to J. C. Walker on 28 November 1794, Burney noted, 'the admirable composer & worthy man, Haydn, has brought me 2 or 3 of the best prints of Metastasio that have been engraved in Vienna; and I believe I shall have one of them engraved for the 1st vol. of my Memoirs'.[15] Haydn, of course, had met Metastasio some forty years earlier, having lived in his house and received some of the benefits of his generosity, and no doubt shared Burney's admiration for the poet and his works.

While the *Memoirs* is not one of Burney's better literary efforts, it nevertheless reveals much concerning Burney's attitude on the purpose of poetry and music. In his Preface to the three volumes, Burney makes the following statement:

However, as a POET of refined taste and sentiments, and a MAN possessed of every moral and social virtue that embellishes society, and exalts human nature, his conduct and opinions deserve display, as much as his literary

---

[13] *A General History of Music*, ed. Frank Mercer, ii (New York, 1957), p. 958.
[14] 'Haydn', in Abraham Rees (ed.), *The Cyclopaedia; or Universal Dictionary of Arts, Science, and Literature*, (London, 1819).
[15] MS letter in the Osborn Collection, Beinecke Library, Yale University.

abilities admiration. . . . but of Metastasio, whose writings are well known to breathe the most noble sentiments, and purest morality, we wished to know how his private life corresponded with his public principles'. (*Mem.* i. iv, vi)

The purpose for writing the *Memoirs* is finally stated in the following way: 'the present work is intended to convey to English readers some idea of the genius and moral worth of this extraordinary man' (i. vii).

Burney's great emphasis on morality stands out in the Preface along with the assumption that a strong correlation exists between the character of the writer and the moral impact of his works, and these themes are developed in the course of the work. With a convincing sense of subscribing to the view, Burney asserts that Metastasio believed the first duty of a writer of prose was to be understood (*Mem.* iii. 295), and that a true poet, as stated by Horace, 'unites the sweetness of verse with the utility of his precepts' (iii. 299). As a moral poet, Metastasio's utility was directed towards inspiring in mankind 'a love of virtue, and detestation of vice', and this in large measure could be achieved through the creation of virtuous or moral characters (iii. 303, 298–9). 'Virtue', according to Burney, 'cannot appear in more pleasing and alluring garb to humanity' than it does in Metastasio's works, and the result was the enjoyment of enormous public favour for the poet (iii. 299). The end result of morality is the happiness and tranquillity of mankind (iii. 298), a view which Burney shared with most writers of the Enlightenment.

Adding to the already didactic nature of the work, Burney attached to his list of Metastasio's works an explanation of 'the *moral object* which the poet had chiefly in view, while he was writing each piece' (iii. 315). This aspect of his work he took to be particularly important, informing a number of his friends in correspondence of his intention. He wrote to J. C. Walker that he intended 'to point out & illustrate the *moral tendency*, the utile as well as *dulci*, of his dramas; in both which qualities he seems to me to have surpassed all other dramatists, ancient as well as modern'.[16] The same view is expressed to William Mason, underlining the importance of Metastasio's moral tendency in relation to the happiness of mankind.[17]

Burney was unable to resist breaking into verse when his adulation went beyond a certain point of effusiveness, and here he concludes his work with verses entitled 'To the Shade of Metastasio'. Contained in it are the following lines:

> Lost must that mortal be, who hears in vain
> Thy moral lesson, or thy pious strain!
>
> . . . .

---

[16] MS letter dated 28 Nov. 1794, in the Osborn Collection.
[17] MS letter dated 11 May 1795, in the Fitzwilliam Museum, Cambridge.

> More sweet thy moral song, in virtue's praise,
> Than sporting sirens could to pleasure raise;
> Nor for the stage, was virtue ever drest,
> In such a pleasing, such alluring vest.
>
> (iii. 391–2)

Burney came to see his work on Metastasio as a gesture of protest against political forces (such as the French Revolution) which were eroding qualities such as 'peace, tranquillity, content, benevolence, humility, politeness, and all religious & social virtues', qualities he held as being fundamental to human existence.[18]

Out of this book Burney was able to draw some direct and indirect comparisons with composers. Among modern composers, C. P. E. Bach was held not far behind Haydn in Burney's estimation, and the two composers were closely linked in Burney's mind. He noted that Haydn had 'studied with particular attention, the pieces of Emanuel Bach, whom he made his model in writing for keyed instruments, as he candidly confessed to us when in England',[19] and he further noted that Bach probably provided Haydn's only genuine compositional model.[20] Burney, of course, admired the ability of Bach to move his listeners, but he agreed with Abel, as we have seen, that 'the genius of Emanuel Bach would have been more expanded and of more general use' if he had been in a great European capital where he would have been 'obliged to study and respect the public taste' (iii. 309). The employment of the word 'use' places the composer in the same category as the poet or playwright. Whatever reservations Burney may have had about Bach, he had none concerning Haydn, as he believed Haydn was successful in achieving those qualities in his works which Burney delineated in his Metastasio *Memoirs* as being important.

There was no doubt in Burney's mind that a work such as the *Memoirs* could be of immediate use to practising artists and writers. Writing to his daughter Fanny in 1795, he stated his position:

All the Critics—Warton, Twining, Nares, and Dr Charles—say that his [Metastasio's] *Estratto dell'Arte Poetica d'Aristotile*, which I am now translating, is the best piece of dramatic criticism that has ever been written. . . . before you write another play you must read Aristotle and Horace, as expounded by my dear Metastasio. . . . You know when I take up a favourite author, as a Johnson, a Haydn, or a Metastasio, I do not soon lay him down or let him be run down.[21]

---

[18] See Lonsdale, *Dr Charles Burney*, p. 370.

[19] 'Haydn', in Rees, *The Cyclopaedia*.

[20] *A General History of Music*, ii. p. 955.

[21] Letter dated 7 May 1795, in Fanny Burney, *Diary & Letters of Madame d'Arblay (1778–1840)*, ed. Charlotte Barrett, v (London, 1905), p. 254.

Burney's own view was in accord with those of Metastasio and Johnson, and he no doubt saw Haydn fitting in very well with these other favourites. Just as Fanny could profit from Metastasio, Haydn undoubtedly had in the past. Given that Haydn and Burney spent much time together, there can be little doubt that matters of audience, effect, and morality were discussed.

Twining

While the term 'moral' in fact refers to matters of ethics and virtue, it could have a more expanded meaning as well, a point which is elucidated by a close friend of Burney and great admirer of Haydn, the Revd. Thomas Twining. Upon Haydn's arrival in England, Twining could simply not wait to meet him, writing to his faithful correspondent Burney with the following entreaty:

I don't know anything . . . that would delight me so much as to meet him [Haydn] in a snug quartett party . . . If you can bring about such a thing . . . I care not where, if it were even in the black hole at Calcutta (if it is a good hole for music)—I say, if by hook or by crook you could manage such a thing, you should be my Magnus Apollo for the rest of your life.[22]

Twining had a rapacious appetite for every possible scrap of information concerning Haydn. The meeting between Twining and Haydn did ultimately take place.

In his dissertation 'On the Different Senses of the Word, Imitative, as Applied to Music by the Antients, and by the Moderns', he divided the power of music into three effects: 'upon the *ear*, the *passions*, and the *imagination*: in other words, it may be considered as simply delighting the *senses*, as raising *emotions*, or, as raising *ideas*' (*Aris.* 44). He explains that the two latter categories constitute that which is moral and expressive, and he clarifies the term 'moral' in this instance as that which is 'opposed to *physical*:—as affecting the mind' (p. 44). This expanded notion of 'moral' is taken further in his copious notes to his translation of *Aristotle's Treatise on Poetry*, in which he suggests that unlike modern writers such as Hume, the ancients included wisdom, courage, and eloquence along with ethical considerations in their understanding of virtue (p. 184). With Twining, then, morality is at the heart of all intellectual and aesthetic activity: 'unless we understand the *moral* language of any writer', we are not likely to be able to follow his higher purpose (p. 184). Matters of ethics are normally referred to with the

[22] Thomas Twining, *Recreations and Studies of a Country Clergyman of the Eighteenth Century* (London, 1882), p. 147.

term 'manners' in this dissertation, and Twining subscribes to Aristotle's view that 'music alone possesses this property of resemblance to human manners' (p. 54). Musical 'motions' [melody and rhythm] could be taken as 'analogous to the motions of human *actions*; and those *actions* are the index of the *manners*' (p. 56). Like Holcroft and others, Twining believed that comedy was a more effective vehicle for conveying moral principles than tragedy, and this is achieved through the creation of moral characters which can be emulated.

The correspondence and conversations of Twining and Burney were by no means limited to musical subjects. Burney had commented on Twining's enthusiasm for Metastasio, and he was also thoroughly familiar with Twining's work on Aristotle. Twining shared Burney's repugnance for the French Revolution, and, in the spirit of the Enlightenment, found acts of zealousness or extremism abhorrent. Underlying this was a sense of tolerance, although tolerance should not be extended in his view to those whose actions were intolerant. This he makes clear to Burney in a letter concerning the quelling of civil riots:

Good God!—what a scene!—and at *this* time of day! in a philosophic, *enlightened* age, as it is called!—what punishment is too much for those who endeavour to inflame a people with *religious* animosities? especially at such a time, when that kind of spirit has long been quietly laid, & mankind, in general, if left to themselves, have little or no propensity to that most horrid of all vices, called zeal.[23]

If zeal is the most abject of vices, it follows that tolerance is the most laudable of virtues. Haydn shared these notions concerning revolution and tolerance, as well as Twining's view that morality has a place in music.

Latrobe

Another close friend of Burney with a strong admiration for Haydn was Christian Ignatius Latrobe, a Moravian minister and professionally trained musician. Not a small amount of the correspondence between Latrobe and Burney concerned Haydn, in part because Burney knew very little German and Latrobe was able to provide him with translations. A friendly rapport developed between Haydn and Latrobe (who had received musical training in Germany), and in fact Haydn encouraged him to pursue a musical profession.[24] Latrobe for his part was a staunch defender of Haydn, regarding him as first among living and recent composers. Latrobe was both a man of the Enlightenment

[23] MS letter dated 15 June 1780, in the Osborn Collection.
[24] Christian Ignatius Latrobe, *Letters to My Children; Written at Sea During a Voyage to the Cape of Good Hope, in 1815*, ed. J. A. Latrobe (London, 1851), p. v.

and a profoundly religious person, and these qualities were carried over to his views on music. About Haydn he observed the following: 'He appeared to me to be a religious character, & not only attentive to the forms & usages of his own Church, but under the influence of a devotional spirit. This is felt by those, who understand the language of Music' (*Chron.* iii. 58). Latrobe had told Haydn that his acquisition and study of the *Stabat Mater* in 1779 had 'more than any other Work, helped to form my taste, & make me more zealous in the pursuit of this noble science' (*Chron.* iii. 58).

In the Introduction to the *Letters to My Children*, the editor (John A. Latrobe) noted that C. I. Latrobe's 'attention was constantly awake to the obligation that rested on him, to further the interests of sound religion and morality among the various classes of persons with whom he might be casually connected'.[25] Music could play a key role here and this is explained in the letter entitled 'The view I have of the religious influence of Music'. In his view, 'among the precious gifts which it has pleased God to bestow upon his creature man . . . I consider *music* as one of the most important and valuable, both as to its nature, its effects, its use, and its eternal duration' (p. 26). In assessing the affinity which his children had for music, he concluded that 'they have not only what is generally termed a taste for music, but they feel something of the secret and mysterious power which it possesses over the heart, and the rapturous delight which it conveys to the intellectual part of man, and which language cannot describe' (p. 27). Latrobe's 'Selection of Sacred Music', a collection designed to broaden awareness of composers other than Handel (there were six volumes covering about fifty composers over a span of twenty years), was intended, according to J. A. Latrobe, to 'fill up the hours of social recreation, especially where there are young people, so as to combine pleasure with profit' (p. xx).

Salomon

While Haydn was in England, probably no one was closer to him than Johann Peter Salomon. Aside from their professional collaboration they spent many hours together in social situations, both dining together privately and in larger social settings.[26] In spite of their business arrangements which were not without dispute, Haydn's esteem for Salomon did not diminish. This is evident in a letter to Salomon from Haydn in 1799 in which Haydn refers to Salomon as being honest and well-informed, and again affirms his esteem (*Cor.* 153). The fact that

[25] Ibid., p. viii.
[26] Upon arriving in England, Haydn reported back to Maria Anna von Genzinger that his habit was to dine nightly with Salomon. See *Cor.* 112.

Salomon was a Freemason may very well have made him even more acceptable in Haydn's eyes.

Salomon was not a man of letters, and available documentation leaves a very scant view of the personality and social, political, or religious views of the person who may very well have had the greatest influence in determining Haydn's understanding of the taste of the English audience. From John Taylor we discover that Salomon had a streak of sarcastic shrewdness,[27] but from the writer of the 'Memoir of Johann Peter Salomon' in the *Harmonicon*, we learn that 'he was honourable, generous, and sincere—his talent was always at command if appealed to by a case of distress, and his purse was so readily opened', that without the observation of a vigilant and trusted servant, all his worldly goods might soon have been given to charity.[28] As an artist he possessed, according to Burney, 'taste, refinement, and enthusiasm', and he moved freely in society as a result of his good sense, polished manners, and his intellectual abilities.[29] The fact that he was the person responsible for bringing Haydn to England particularly endeared him to the English public. His subscription concerts were recognized by George Dance (who drew portraits of both Salomon and Haydn) as a 'beneficial influence upon the taste and judgement of the rising generation'.[30] It seems highly probable that Haydn and Salomon were able to share views concerning the social function of music.

Holcroft

Through Salomon's wide circle of friends Haydn was brought into contact with various people of social or artistic importance. One of these was the writer, editor, translator, and political activist Thomas Holcroft. Holcroft was a talented amateur musician (violin and voice) and belonged to a musical club of which Salomon was also a member. Holcroft's association with Salomon was of a more intimate nature than simply belonging to the same club, as he informs us in his *Memoirs*: 'When I returned home, found Salomon . . . Spoke in raptures of Haydn, which well accorded with my own sentiments.'[31] The extent of Haydn's friendship with Holcroft is not entirely clear, although it appears from Haydn's one existing note to Holcroft that the writer played an advisory role to Haydn on literary matters similar to that of Greiner in Vienna.

---

[27] *Records of My Life*, i (London, 1832), p. 275.
[28] 'Memoir of Johann Peter Salomon', *Harmonicon*, 8 (1930), p. 47.
[29] Ibid.
[30] *A Collection of Portraits Sketched from the Life since the Year 1793*, ii (London, 1814), n. p.
[31] *Memoirs of Thomas Holcroft Written by Himself and Continued by William Hazlitt* (Oxford, 1926), p. 264.

This note, in delightfully fractured English, indicates that they knew each other well enough to meet or perhaps dine together occasionally: 'I tack me the liberty to Send you the Canon, and the 2 Songs and if is possible, I self will come to you to day, o[r] to morrow. I was oblieged to tack a Medicine to Day, perhaps I see you this Evening' (*Cor.* 144–5).

Aside from Holcroft's shared view with Salomon, there are other strong signs of his admiration for Haydn. Elsewhere in the *Memoirs* he chides friends at a chamber-music party who thought Mozart a better composer than Haydn (p. 267). In his personal library, which contained a fair collection of music (mostly chamber music), about half the items were works by Haydn.[32] A poem of tribute to Haydn by Holcroft appeared in the *Morning Chronicle* on 12 September 1794, and as Landon bluntly observes, is 'the only verse in connection with our composer which it is possible to read without cringing'. The final lines read: 'Then HAYDN stands, collecting Nature's tears, / And consonance sublime amid confusion hears' (*Chron.* iii. 272). Given Holcroft's rise to prominence from humble origins, the son of shoemaker, Haydn may have felt a special affinity here. This affinity receives some confirmation in the fact that they were both admirers of Gellert and Lavater. Holcroft had translated and published Lavater's *Physiognomische Fragmente* two years before Haydn came to England, and some years later did the same with Gellert's *Die zärtlichen Schwestern*.

Like the members of the Johnson circle, whose works he knew well, Holcroft set morality as his constant ideal, he wrote plays and books which were intended to 'do good in the world', and he regarded the stage as 'a very efficient school of morality'.[33] His views on morality extended to music as well, and opera in particular, an area in which he was experienced as both musician and librettist. In his essay 'Of the Moral Nature of the Comic-Opera' he observed that 'whatever contributes to the happiness of man is of a moral nature', and expands this by saying 'few indeed are the people who do not derive pleasure from music' (*Theat.* i. 214–15). Opera is then described as a 'means of moral instruction' and its moral utility (when it is well written) is not small (i. 215). His doctrine of moral function is clearly laid down in his preface to *The Adventures of Hugh Trevor*, a novel which Haydn acquired for his personal library. Similarly, in *Brian Perdue*, he explains his role as novelist in considerable detail: 'Whenever I have undertaken to write a novel, I have proposed to myself a specific moral purpose. . . . in *Hugh Trevor*, to induce youths (or their parents) to inquire into the morality of the profession which each might intend for himself.'[34]

---

[32] *A Catalogue of the Library of Books, of Mr Thomas Holcroft* (London, 1806), pp. 43–5.
[33] *The Life of Thomas Holcroft*, ed. Elbridge Colby, i (London, 1925), p. xx.
[34] Ibid., i. p. xxix.

Haydn's library

A further source of influence on Haydn in England was the books in his own personal library. Whether he acquired these himself or they were gifts from friends and admirers is of no great significance. The fact that the collection is both diverse and representative suggests that the acquisition was not entirely haphazard. Aside from dictionaries, historical, and travel books, his library of English books consisted of novels, poems, and plays as well as critical studies of aesthetics, social interaction, and man in general. Some of his books which fall into the latter category were by members of the Literary Club, including Adam Smith (*The Theory of Moral Sentiments*), Edmund Burke (*A Philosophical Inquiry into the Origin of Our Ideas of the Sublime and Beautiful*), and George Steevens and Samuel Johnson (*The Plays of William Shakespeare in ten Volumes . . . notes by S. Johnson and G. Steevens*). The fact that Burney was a prominent member of the Club probably accounted for Haydn's acquisition or receipt of these.[35]

The Literary Club was not without resembance to the Viennese Masonic lodge 'Zur wahren Eintracht' in that it was a collection of the best minds in the country covering letters, the arts, and social sciences. It was, however, much smaller and more exclusive, maintaining 'the high standard of intellectual gifts and personal qualities which made those unpretending suppers at the Turk's Head an honour eagerly contended for by the wisest, wittiest, and noblest of the eighteenth century'.[36] Opinions emanating from the Club were eagerly awaited and widely disseminated. The direction of the Club was largely determined by Johnson; according to Lord Macaulay, the 'overflowings of his full mind' pointed discussion towards 'questions of taste, of learning, of casuistry'.[37] Casuistry, to be more specific, is 'that part of Ethics which resolves cases of conscience, applying the general rules of religion and morality to particular instances which disclose special circumstances, or conflicting duties'.[38]

Morality, once again, is central to a significant number of the English books which Haydn owned. A prime example, by a member of the Club, is Adam Smith's *Theory of Moral Sentiments*. There can be little doubt that this work was strongly influenced by Shaftesbury's *Characteristics*. Morality is examined in the context of both private and public considerations and it is defined in the context of social and personal happiness. A further linkage is made between social duty or utility and

---

[35] For a complete list of the members of the Club, see M. E. Grant Duff, *The Club, 1764–1905* (London, 1905), pp. 133 ff.

[36] John Timbs, *Clubs and Club Life in London* (London, 1872), p. 184.

[37] Ibid., p. 185.

[38] *The Shorter Oxford English Dictionary*, 3rd edn. (1970), revised with addenda.

beauty, as Smith observes 'that utility is one of the principal sources of beauty', and by 'beauty' he is referring to 'the greatest elegance of expression' and 'the most lively eloquence'.[39] Furthermore, the matter of approbation is drawn into the equation: 'The characters of men, as well as the contrivances of art . . . may be fitted either to promote or to disturb the happiness both of the individual and of the society' (p. 187). The work of true utility promotes happiness, and this must be achieved through the presentation of works which will gain approbation.

Of the various novels in Haydn's library, Holcroft's *Hugh Trevor* has already been cited. Here, as in Gellert's *Schwedische Gräfin*, the theory of morality can be seen in practice in a novel. One other English novel owned by Haydn was *A Sentimental Journey through France and Italy* by Laurence Sterne. The epithetical use of 'sentimental' places this novel in the genre of works with a didactic function intended for a largely middle-class public. Of his various contemporaries, Sterne was one of the least likely to pursue a moral tack, preferring instead to indulge in wit and humour which would evoke simple laughter rather than a lesson through ridicule. With this work, however, a didactic posture was taken, in his own words, 'to teach us to love the world and our fellow creatures better than we do'.[40]

One other English writer represented in Haydn's library who is very much worthy of notice is Alexander Pope, whose *Essay on Man* Haydn owned in a German translation (*Bibl.* 191). In fact, it could be argued that a type of parallel exists between Pope's perception of the difference between his own early and late works, and the difference between the early and later works of Haydn which has thus far been observed in this study. Late in life Pope summarized his own works with the following verse in his *Epistle to Dr Arbuthnot*:

> . . . not in Fancy's Maze he wander'd long,
> But stoop'd to Truth, and moraliz'd his song.[41]

With the second line he is referring to *An Essay on Man*, the *Moral Essays*, the *Imitations of Horace*, and other works which place morality above all else. However, even in earlier works, morality is very much evident (as is also true of Haydn), and the use of the word 'fancy' appears not to exclude the possibility of moral considerations.

Since Haydn could have read *An Essay on Man* in German, there is a much greater probability that he did indeed read the work. If he read only the first few pages, he would have discovered the following in 'The Design': 'to prove any moral duty, to enforce any moral precept . . . it is

---

[39] *The Theory of Moral Sentiments*, ed. D. D. Raphael and A. L. MacFie (Oxford, 1976), p. 179.

[40] From a letter to his daughter, quoted by A. Alvarez in 'The Delinquent Aesthetic', *Hudson Review*, 19 (1966–7), p. 593.

[41] Quoted in Geoffrey Tillotson, *The Moral Poetry of Pope* (Newcastle upon Tyne, 1946), pp. 1–2.

necessary first to know what *condition* and *relation* it is placed in, and what is the proper *end* and *purpose* of its being'. The purpose of the *Essay* was to advance the theory of morality, and to form 'a *temperate* yet not *inconsistent*, and a *short* yet not *imperfect* system of Ethics'.[42]

Haydn's experience in England, and in particular his various friendships, appears to have reinforced in a strong way the ideas he had developed concerning the function of his works in the two decades before coming to England. The notion that the symphony had a primary aim of engaging the listener in a reflective or contemplative process was clearly not new. The symphonies written for London are not set apart from other symphonies in any qualitative way. The difference lies more in Haydn's relationship with his audience, the support he received for what he was attempting to accomplish, and the opportunity he had to observe the audience and hence measure his means of achieving intelligibility (or moral awareness) from one work to the next.

[42] Alexander Pope, *An Essay on Man*, ed. Maynard Mack, in John Butt (ed.), *The Twickenham Edition of the Poems of Alexander Pope*, iii. i (London, 1950), p. 7.

PART III

The Symphonies

10

Symphonic Intelligibility and Sonata Form

FOR Haydn's biographer G. A. Griesinger, a perfectly logical and appropriate question to put to the most celebrated symphonist of his time was 'to know from what motives Haydn wrote his compositions, as well as the feelings and ideas that he had in mind and that he strove to express through musical language' (*Not.* 62). There was no doubt for Haydn that it was appropriate to answer this question, although given his age, it would have been 'irksome' to elucidate each work in this way. Haydn's answer, which has already been cited in earlier chapters, should now be given in full:

But he said that he oftentimes had portrayed moral characters in his symphonies. In one of his oldest, which, however, he could not accurately identify, 'the dominant idea is of God speaking with an abandoned sinner, pleading with him to reform. But the sinner in his thoughtlessness pays no heed to the admonition'. (*Not.* 62)

For those who doubt the capacity of the symphony to do anything other than serve a purely musical function, Haydn's reply could be successfully dismissed in a number of ways. These could be the words of an elderly man whose thinking is no longer lucid. On the other hand, it could be yet another demonstration of Haydn's famous sense of humour. However, in the context of the eighteenth century, this reply is entirely lucid and genuine. As we have seen, his choice of the term 'moral characters' was borrowed from the practice of the moral weeklies, a tradition over a century old by this time. His reference to an abandoned sinner raises an interesting matter as well. Supporters of programmatic music may wish to take these remarks as evidence that Haydn attempted to represent specific objects, persons, or events in his symphonies. What seems more likely, however, is that Haydn was simply trying to find appropriate descriptive language for his symphonies, language which inevitably is inadequate. These words are probably intended metaphorically, pointing to general interpretive possibilities rather than anything specific. In this case, at least two important points emerge. In the first instance a situation of conflict is established, placing the symphony in a dramatic context. At the same time, morality lies at the heart of the drama.

The symphony and drama

Haydn's development of an instrumental language with referential and dramatic possibilities was recognized by various contemporary observers. Discussion of this was clearly most feasible in works where a particular function or association was specified by the composer. At issue in these cases was how successful Haydn was in achieving his stated goal, as well as whether or not his means were appropriate for the specific purpose in question or for music in general. One of Haydn's instrumental works which served an extramusical purpose, defined by textual associations, was *The Seven Last Words*, a work which Haydn himself was convinced would have a profound effect on even the most inexperienced listener. In England, during Haydn's stay and later, this work and others were much discussed. John Wall Callcott, an English pupil of Haydn, wrote about this work in the following way: 'In the final Section, the Time changes to four Crotchets, etc. As that Movement is termed *il Terremoto*, or *the Earthquake*, this confusion [resulting from metric changes] is particularly appropriate.'[1] Not everyone was so generous as to deem musical 'confusion' as having the possibility of being appropriate. To William Crotch, for example, the confusion in this movement is objectionable, making it 'deficient in dignity of style' (*Sub.* 143). For Callcott, however, specific musical means of generating confusion can be described, in this case metric instability, and can be identified as distinctive musical images.

Charles Burney, Haydn's most vocal and articulate enthusiast in England, made similar observations. In a letter to Latrobe just after the turn of the century, Burney rails against those who cannot understand that the introduction to *The Creation*, 'The Representation of Chaos', should indeed be confused:

and what should become again (may it be asked), but *Chaos*, when chaos is to be described? Were sounds to be arranged in harmonic & symmetric order before order was born? It struck me as the most sublime Idea in Haydn's work, his describing the birth of order by dissonance & broken phrases!—a whisper here—an effort there—a groan—an agonizing cry—personifying Nature—& supposing her in labour, how admirably has he expressed her throes! not by pure harmony & graceful melody, but by appropriate murmurs. . . . When dissonance is tuned, when order arises, & chaos is no more, what pleasing, ingenious and graceful melody & harmony ensue![2]

Burney's discussion of musical order and disorder in this letter has implications considerably beyond the boundaries of this one work.

[1] *A Musical Grammar*, 2nd edn. (London, 1809), p. 262.
[2] MS letter undated, in the Osborn Collection, Beinecke Library, Yale University.

Indeed, it is a recognition of the primary means of generating opposing images in any type of instrumental work, and hence the basis for an understanding of a dramatic process in instrumental works. In this case the representation of chaos is at issue, and Burney recognizes what should be self-evident, namely, that symmetry and order must give way to musical instability if chaos is to be represented. If, however, similar musical means are used in works which are entirely non-representational, such as most symphonies, then conflict can be generated by purely musical means. If this conflict is treated in such a way that it is at issue over an entire movement, and if it is brought to a conclusion where the foregoing events are taken into account, then it becomes more than mere 'variety' or 'contrast' but becomes dramatic in the truest sense of the word. The means for generating these primary musical images of stability and instability are of course numerous, and can involve anything from intervallic relationships, melody, phrasing, harmony, rhythm, or metre to large-scale treatments of tonality or other formal devices. At the heart of this musical duality is a primary sense of order and symmetry interacting with the opposite force. According to Shaftesbury and enlightened thought in general, there is a clear link between order and virtue and hence between disorder and evil. A symphony, then, which operates on the basis of an interplay between these forces, takes on the function of serving moral goals through purely musical means.

While contemporary critics appeared in general to be aware of Haydn's achievement, many were decidedly unwilling to express approval. Music which contains instability is also likely to be complex, a condition which, according to some, was inappropriate. Two English critics who particularly took Haydn to task for abandoning the simple style in favour of the complex were William Jackson and William Crotch. While Crotch was prepared to recognize Haydn as the greatest living composer of instrumentalal music, the compliment was greatly diminished in the light of Crotch's regard for instrument music. His enthusiasm for Handel made it difficult for him to be objective about the merits of any current or recent composer, and his censuring of Haydn was something to which Burney naturally took exception.[3]

While Crotch was somewhat reserved in his judgement of Haydn, Jackson's ignoble attack was completely without restraint. Before casting aspersions on modern music in general, he set up the conditions for his assault. In comparing melody and harmony he suggested that melody was better able to exist on its own, and that the pleasure given by a succession of chords was far inferior to the 'natural' quality of melody.[4] Melody which has a memorable quality is compared with

---

[3] See Kerry S. Grant, *Dr Burney as Critic and Historian of Music* (Ann Arbor, 1983), pp. 216–17.

[4] *Observations on the Present State of Music*, 2nd edn. (London, 1791), pp. 9–10.

music which has an 'unmeaning succession of sounds', and if 'the music of the present day be "weighed in the this balance" . . . the greater part will be found wanting' (p. 12) In case the point was not sufficiently made, he continues:

> But later Composers, to be grand and original, have poured in such floods of nonsense, under the sublime idea of *being inspired*, that the present Symphony bears the same relation to good Music, as the ravings of a Bedlamite do to sober sense. Sometimes the Key is perfectly lost, by wandering so from it, that there is no road to return. (16–7)

Comic opera is placed in a similar category although it fares slightly better, earning the epithet 'folly' instead of 'ravings'. Jackson was scrupulous to avoid names, although it was evident to all concerned that Haydn bore the brunt of this scurrilous attack. Burney for one could not let the matter pass without a response, and published a lengthy reply to Jackson in the *Monthly Review* (October 1791). He took great pleasure in pointing out some of the inconsistencies in Jackson's thinking, such as the fact that the assumption of melodic simplicity in 'ancient' music ignores the use of highly complex counterpoint, or the absurdity of the idea of melody existing without a sense of harmonic foundation.[5] In fact, Jackson's distaste for counterpoint was so complete that he actually complained about glees in three or more parts. While Jackson spoke disparagingly of the audience so lacking in taste as to rush to concerts of modern symphonies, Burney described the same public as being 'enlightened', and further, that 'a liberal and enlightened musician, and hearer of music, receives pleasure from various styles and effects, even when melody is not so vulgarly familiar as to be carried home from once hearing; or even when there is no predominant melody, if a compensation be made by harmony, contrivance, and the interesting combination of the whole' (p. 101).

Burney's response to Jackson's 'spleen and prejudice' is an important document in that it shows Burney to be one of the few critics in 1791 able to recognize the importance of the symphony as an independent entity in the context of the time. Burney too was an admirer of Handel and a lover of melody, but this did not obscure his awareness of the importance of complexity in the symphony and the role the symphony had with the new European audience. In fact, it is difficult to find a greater admirer of Handel than Haydn himself, and Haydn also had strong views about singing and vocal qualities in instrumental music. But he was able to balance the two approaches, either using them independently or intermingling them in the same movement. For writers of the period, the simple and the complex were procedures which could be used depending

---

[5] Burney's article is printed in full in *Chron.* iii. 100–4.

on what effect the writer wished to achieve, and there was no pejorative association with either one. In Germany, Gottsched had drawn a distinction between their relative functions, and this was accepted by Gellert and others. In dramatic works, plots could be, as John Van Cleve points out, 'termed "einfach und gemein" when they proceed in linear fashion from episode to episode without complication, "verworren" when events culminate in unexpected changes of fortune or in discoveries'.[6]

While a writer such as Jackson could be easily dismissed, as Burney took great pleasure in showing, his discussion of at least one matter requires greater consideration. Jackson's censuring of modern composers (such as Haydn) who have written 'floods of nonsense, under the sublime idea of *being inspired*', in using the word 'sublime', points to a much larger issue in eighteenth-century aesthetics. While Jackson does not define his terms, others, such as Crotch, were entirely prepared to do so. Crotch's definition of the sublime was the generally accepted one, involving 'vastness and incomprehensibility'; being lofty and elevated it excluded anything small, light, or comic (*Sub*. 32). Unlike Jackson, Crotch could accommodate the opposition of simplicity and complexity: 'Simplicity, and its opposite, intricacy, when on a large scale (such an intricacy as, from the number of its parts, becomes incomprehensible), are sublime' (p. 33). Crotch goes on to apply these ideas to orchestral music and define his images more precisely:

In music, the great compass of notes employed in a full orchestra conveys the idea of vastness undefined. A uniform succession of major chords, the most agreeable of all sounds, resembles a blaze of light; while the unintelligible combination of extraneous discords conveys a feeling like that caused by darkness. (p. 34)

While these comments, written over three decades after Haydn had left England, are very useful in defining musical images, they do not suggest that Crotch was prepared to see the interaction of the two forces within an intelligible whole. For Crotch, discordant material remains extraneous and unintelligible, and as such is not sublime but falls under the category of the ornamental style. 'The ornamental style is the the result of roughness, playful intricacy, and abrupt variations. . . . In music, eccentric and difficult melody; rapid, broken and varied rhythm; wild and unexpected modulation, indicate this third style' (pp. 35–6). Of his three styles (the beautiful is the second), the sublime takes precedence, and while it can be in combination with the others, it has no room for low styles such as comedy. He acknowledges Haydn as unrivalled among instrumental composers (who are inferior to vocal composers),

[6] *Harlequin Beseiged: The Reception of Comedy in Germany during the Early Enlightenment* (Berne, 1980), p. 19.

but will not go so far as to consider Haydn's works sublime. His distinction among the three styles is that 'it is sublime if it inspires veneration, beautiful if it pleases, ornamental if it amuses' (p. 43). Haydn's works, he declares, are pleasing and amusing (p. 143).

While Haydn's works did not rise to the level of the sublime for Crotch, they clearly did for Burney, who described them as such on numerous occasions. Burney's understanding of the sublime did not exclude intelligibility, but appears in fact to have depended on it. His discourse on *The Creation* already cited seems to bear this out: 'It struck me as the most sublime Idea in Haydn's work, his describing the birth of order by dissonance and broken phrases.' Both stability and instability or simplicity and complexity are included here, and both serve an intelligible function. In the same letter to Latrobe, Burney speaks of the requirement that the listener engage in an imaginative process which will allow the composer's designs and conceptions to be understood.[7] For Burney there was no question that music should be understood and that its highest achievement lay here rather than in some vague sense of vastness or incomprehensibility.

Few eighteenth-century theorists, of course, were prepared to give serious acknowledgement to the merit of instrumental music when compared to vocal music. Vocal music, because of opera, was capable of being dramatic, but no such possibility was generally accepted for the symphony. Burney was an exception in this regard although his views did begin to receive some support after the turn of the century. One such subscriber was A. Burgh, who, by 1814, went so far as to place instrumental music above vocal music:

There is a general cheerfulness and good humour in Haydn's allegros, which exhilarate every hearer. But his adagios are frequently so sublime in ideas, and the harmony in which they are clad, that though played by instruments, they have a more pathetic effect on the feelings, than the finest opera air, united with the most exquisite poetry.[8]

Burgh also saw Haydn's symphonic complexity as an asset, calling Haydn an 'astonishing and inexhaustible genius' whose instrumental pieces 'are so original and so difficult' (pp. 301, 303–4). His admiration for Haydn went much further and included a supportive view of another aspect of duality in the symphonies: 'The genius and fancy of Haydn were acknowledged, but his mixture of serious and comic were disliked; and as to rules, he was supposed to know but little of them. This censure he long since disproved' (p. 304).

The nature of the duality or drama possible in Haydn's symphonies is

---

[7] MS letter undated, in the Osborn Collection.
[8] *Anecdotes of Music, Historical and Biographical*, iii (London, 1814), p. 304.

not unlike the type of duality described by Shaftesbury at the beginning of the century. Order and proportion provide the standard for measuring beauty in music as well as morality. But the opposite— deformity, the odious, or dissonance—also exists, and dissonance or disproportion can be associated with knavery or evil. These opposing forces can be seen within the context of something larger which in the end is optimistic. From testing order or virtue, an ultimate harmony emerges which will be all the more satisfying. Similarly, the coexistence of these forces promotes an attitude of tolerance. Since music can, without the aid of words or any extramusical association, generate proportion, disproportion, or an interaction of the two, it is entirely possible in Shaftesbury's scheme of things for purely instrumental music to engage in dramatic discourse, the goal of which is moral represent-ation. In the hands of Haydn, not only is this possible, but the symphonic language is such that the listener can in effect be instructed in listening by the work itself and hence be led to a particular point of discovery.

By 1770 Haydn had accepted an aesthetic which involves duality, and he subsequently shifted his emphasis to the refinement of musical procedures which could accommodate this new process. Sonata form, with both flexibility and formal possibilities, emerged as Haydn's chosen vehicle for the achievement of the new type of intelligibility which was possible in instrumental music. Consequently, first movements increas-ingly took on additional weight and importance, and it is these movements which are the focus of this study. Clearly there is no intention here to diminish the importance of other movements. Indeed, contemporary audiences often reacted most strongly to second move-ments, and some of these, such as the one in Symphony No. 102, are highly complex and dramatic, not lacking in conflict. Similarly, in anticipation of Beethoven's shift of emphasis in later works to the finale, Haydn does the same in certain instances, No. 101 being an extraordin-ary example of that. The process which gives rise to intelligibility in Haydn's sonata-form movements, however, is nothing short of astonish-ing, making these the logical focus for a study concerned with the ability of instrumental music to reveal moral principles in the late eighteenth-century sense.

In spite of the enormous amount already written on sonata form and its application to Haydn's symphonies in particular, much more needs to be said. While sonata form has been recognized as a dramatic process, using the forces of stability and instability, the specific late eighteenth-century aesthetic implications of this have not received an adequate airing. Some critics have, of course, addressed sonata form within an eighteenth-century context, attempting to come to terms with it in the light of the commentary by theorists of the time. This has in some cases simply muddied the waters. If a theorist such as Koch is invoked, one encounters, as late as 1802, continued emphasis on the single affect. Secondary themes, according to Koch, may provide contrast which reinforces the main thought, but must 'not disturb the prevailing sentiment and hence damage the unity of the whole'.[9] In Chapter 6 it was noted that the activities of theorists do not necessarily parallel those of current musical practice, but may be determined by other factors such as earlier practices. Koch's conservatism seems almost a half century out of step with compositional practice, and his remark about 'accessory ideas' which 'do not disturb the prevailing sentiment' may very well have been intended to censure composers like Haydn who violated his notion of unity. It is not without significance that Koch, writing near the end of the century in his *Versuch einer Anleitung zur Composition*, tends to select, in support of his discussions, musical examples (including his own music) from before 1770.[10]

There is a notable gap between theory and practice here which must be addressed critically. There is no question that much can be learned from theorists, although it is naïve to think that these persons did not have axes to grind. The now fashionable position that tonality provides the structural basis for sonata form owes more to the views of theorists than the works themselves. The use of eighteenth-century views to narrow the range of possibilities, for example to diminish the importance of thematic material in relation to tonal procedures, seems particularly counter-productive. The means of discourse, development, or drama in sonata-form movements depend on an equipoise of tonal, motivic, thematic, rhythmic, or metric procedures, and an analysis prejudiced by a hierarchical approach to the various musical elements will be greatly impoverished.

The singling out of tonality, and particularly an emphasis on the tonic-dominant relationship by some commentators, has not gone unchallenged. The idea of an opposition between tonic and dominant is by no means self-evident. The dominant is the key most strongly related to the tonic, and its confirmation is a point of stability rather than tension. Rosen goes further on this, addressing the issue in the following perplexed way:

I cannot believe that a contemporary audience listened for the change to the dominant and experienced a pleasant feeling of satisfaction when it came. The movement to the dominant was part of musical grammar, not an element of form. Almost all music in the eighteenth century went to the dominant: before 1750 it was not something to be emphasized; afterward, it was something that

---

[9] Quoted in Leonard G. Ratner, *Classic Music: Expression, Form, and Style* (New York, 1980), p. 218.

[10] See Koch, *Introductory Essays on Composition*, trans. Nancy Kovaleff Baker (New Haven, 1983), p. xx.

the composer could take advantage of. This means that every eighteenth-century listener expected the movement to the dominant in the sense that he would have been puzzled if he did not get it; it was a necessary condition of intelligibility. (*Clas.* 33)

This leads Rosen to the conclusion that 'the isolation of the harmonic structure, while an advance over a basically thematic definition of "sonata form," is therefore generally unsatisfactory', and, 'an account of the sonata in purely tonal terms does not falsify the way a classical sonata moves, but it obscures the significance of the form' (p. 33).

If tonal opposition is not to be found in fundamental key relationships, then it must lie in the relationship of points of tonal stability and material which is not stable. Rosen looks at this type of opposition in the following way: 'The stability and clarity of the opening and closing pages of a classical sonata are essential to its form, and they make the increased tension of the middle sections possible' (p. 70). And further, 'the emotional force of the classical style is clearly bound up with this contrast between dramatic tension and stability' (p. 74). And finally, Rosen makes his position entirely clear: 'I do not want to turn Haydn, Mozart, and Beethoven into Hegelians, but the simplest way to summarize classical form is as the symmetrical resolution of opposing forces' (p. 83). Rosen's general disregard of eighteenth-century opinion has annoyed some commentators, but it is difficult to take issue with his ability to hear. Like Tovey, who was also prepared to use his ear as the final arbiter, Rosen has presented a convincing demonstration of musical judgement. What his approach shows perhaps most sagaciously is that the music of the composers in question, on its own terms and without reference to contemporary opinion, can speak to audiences of the present at the deepest possible level.

SONATA FORM IN THE LATE SYMPHONIES

Before proceeding with specific analyses and discussions of Haydn's English Symphonies which demonstrate dramatic activity and moral purposes, it may be useful to outline certain features of his approach to sonata form in late symphonies which appear with some consistency. This will be done by isolating the various components of these movements for discussion while at the same time recognizing that the overall effect is that of a process rather than a form.

Slow introductions

A principal difference between works before and after 1785 concerns the use of slow introductions. They are used sparingly in the large body of earlier symphonies whereas only five of the last twenty-three are lacking them. The slow introduction, then, became an indispensable part of Haydn's later symphonic language. Throughout the late symphonies, one sees its role becoming progressively stronger. Only one of the English Symphonies is without one, and the introduction is seen in the final symphonies to take on larger dimensions and to become more self-contained as a formal unit. But in spite of the self-containment, this material also develops a more integral link with first themes or with later sections of the movement.

Various writers have not been prepared, however, to grant equal status to introductions compared with other first-movement material. Some have argued that the introduction has the subordinate purpose of preparing 'the listener for the main part of the movement',[11] or of 'being only a stepping-stone to a movement of more pronounced character' (*Clas.* 346). Had Haydn wished only to establish a context in a work such as No. 103, he could have successfully accomplished that in much fewer than thirty-nine bars and it is unlikely that he would have ended the introduction in the wrong key (a key relationship which returns at bars 68–71). Rosen rightly points out that the introductions have a nebulous character, but suggests that if this feature were not retained, they would run the risk of sounding like real openings (p. 347). It seems curious, however, that Rosen should wish to subordinate this to the well-defined passages that follow. The character of the material seems much more than a ride through the forest before one comes upon a magnificent château. Burney's observations concerning the function of the introduction to *The Creation* have important implications for the symphonic introductions, a comparison which has been recognized by various writers.[12]

In the introductions of the English Symphonies, the harmony is often fairly unpredictable. In these cases, the introductions often begin with a periodic phrase pattern in which the harmony is stable and there is definable melodic or thematic material. Following this, the thematic character disappears, the phrase structure becomes irregular, and the harmony digresses, often by way of the tonic minor. In some, the digressions are very sudden, and abrupt or unorthodox changes are occasionally emphasized by contrasting dynamics, as in Nos. 98 and 99. As well as irregular phrasing, there can also be some mild metric displacement through the use of syncopation, as in No. 102 (although this is not disruptive in the way that it could be in a faster tempo), or the placement of forzato markings on off-beats as in No. 101.

[11] H. C. Robbins Landon, *The Symphonies of Joseph Haydn* (London, 1955), p. 572.
[12] See particularly *Clas.* 348; László Somfai, 'The London Revision of Haydn's Instrumental Style', *Proceedings of the Royal Musical Association*, 100 (1973–4), p. 166; and *Chron.* iii. 583.

While most introductions prepare the tonic of the first theme, there are a few notable exceptions. These are Nos. 99 and 103, and in both cases the work is in E flat and the introduction ends on G (although in No. 99 the final chord provides a sudden preparation). In No. 103, with the return of G in the transition, the introduction foreshadows subsequent important events in more ways than one. The relationship of introductions with subsequent parts of first movements is one of both contrast and affinity. The case to be argued here is that the slow introduction is a primary force in the dramatic language of the late symphonies and plays an essential role in the process which provides intelligibility in first movements.

Themes

There are, broadly speaking, two main types of theme in Haydn's late symphonies. The first is a simple theme which is stable and exemplifies the balanced phrasing of the dance. As a dramatic force, the simple theme stands as one of the dramatic polarities, and contrast can take place as a result of the relationship of this theme to some outside force. This other force may first of all be apparent in the slow introduction if the work in question has an introduction, and also can be found in the less stable material which occurs after the theme has been stated. The interaction begins in the exposition and is expanded in the development section. Examples of simple first themes can be found in Nos. 93 and 104 in which melodic shape is the predominant characteristic; Nos. 88, 99, 100, and 103 which have a dance-like character; and Nos. 82, 87, 89, and 97 which strongly outline the tonic chord.

The other main type of theme is the complex one which has ambiguity already built in. Stability is still very important in the complex theme, but the stability here must be considered in the context of the internal ambiguity which is set against it. The dramatic problem of the work in this case may be built into the theme itself, as in No. 83, and subsequent thematic permutations will show the tension generated by the internal conflict. Examples of this type, which generally involve beginning with an off-tonic passage that moves to the tonic, are found in Nos. 86 and 94. Others, such as the opening vivace theme of No. 102, are also complex, although the nature of the complexity does not become evident until most of the first movement has been heard.

Transitions

Transitions have a primary tonal function of modulating to the dominant or relative major, but their length and treatment of material generally make them much more than 'bridges' between important events, suggesting that they are as important as stable tonal areas or themes. In contrast to the stability and memorability of themes, transitions engage in a discursive process in which there is motion and unfolding, and this may be done through the expansion of existing material or the presentation of contrasting material. However, even if the material is contrasting, it is usually possible to find some motivic or rhythmic links with prior material. Because of the more stable or self-contained nature of the theme, a type of contrast is therefore established between the theme and the motion of the transition. The unstable aspect of transitions in Haydn's late symphonies can be apparent in a number of ways, including the treatment of phrasing, harmony, a lack of melodic shape, metric ambiguity, and thwarted expectation of the arrival of the second group.

Haydn's delineation of themes and transitional material is much stronger in the later than in the earlier works. In later works, Haydn preferred well-defined eight-bar themes which are repeated in full, either verbatim or with a return to the tonic if the opening phrase had moved to the dominant. With its repetition and clarity, the theme is separated from the transition in spite of the fact that the material of the transition normally grows from the theme. At the level of phrasing, then, the transition contributes to the dramatic relationship of stability and ambiguity by departing from the regularity of the theme. It is not possible in all cases to trace a motivic connection between transitions and themes. In some instances, there may be a relationship with the introduction rather than the theme. A particularly interesting example of this occurs in No. 99, a work with an especially ambiguous harmonic unfolding in the introduction. In this case the specific chromatic movement of the introduction is duplicated in the transition. In other works as well, it is possible to draw parallels between slow introductions and transitions, suggesting that a dramatic link may exist between these sections.

The harmonic movement in transitions in both early and late works is characterized by the sense of propulsion towards the new key, and this sense of direction is an important part of the discursiveness of this section. Harmonic instability is normally not a major factor here although in some works such as Nos. 89, 97, 102, and 103 some digression occurs before the arrival of the dominant preparation. The sense of direction here establishes the expectation of stability in the new key area. The relative stability of harmony in the transition, then, places harmony in contrast to other elements such as irregular phrasing and the lack of thematic definition.

A sense of irregularity or instability in transitions can be heightened by the use of various devices, one of which is syncopation. The disruptive function of syncopation is confirmed by its use as a device in eighteenth-century opera to emphasize points of intense conflict or confusion. In *Don Giovanni*, for example, a prominent use of syncopation in Act I occurs just before Donna Anna's cry for help while she is pursuing the Don near the beginning of the work ('Introduzione', bars 87–8), and another instance accompanies Zerlina's cry for help in the finale to Act I immediately after she has been attacked by Don Giovanni (bars 477–8). These are probably the two points of greatest confusion on stage in the first act, and the syncopation aptly heightens that effect. In both cases, the syncopation occurs in ensembles and while the tempo is very fast. As a disruptive device in the symphony, syncopation can be particularly effective if it is set against something which is stable, with a rhythmic and metric stability such as one finds in dance-related passages. In some transitions, syncopation enters into a direct confrontation with this type of material, two examples being in Nos. 86 and 82.

Transitions, then, carry the drama forward and also stand in contrast to the stability of opening themes. They may have thematic links with themes and introductions and may contain their own dualities. In some late works, such as Nos. 102 and 103, passages occur in transitions which may seem inconsequential but are later revealed to be the crux of the drama. These passages are fusions of the dramatic polarities, and the fact that Haydn introduces them in transitions in these works is of some significance. Not only is a fusion of opposites central to the dramatic process but the musical passages containing it appear in a section which is characterized by motion. The coexistence of opposites is therefore placed in the context of that which is ongoing.

New key sections

Dramatic opposition between harmonic or tonal forces seems most likely to result from the interaction of stable keys with less stable modulatory passages, rather than from a polarity of tonic and dominant. Taking other musical elements into account, this opposition is strengthened by the fact that the stable key areas are associated with themes, periodic phrasing and steady rhythms while the modulatory material is non-thematic, the phrasing is irregular, and the pace is accelerated. The stable tonal points, then, are points of departure and arrival, and the contrasting material is that which is in motion. In the stable areas, one is able to listen reflectively since a strong image has been imprinted on the memory, while in the transitional sections one must respond to a state of transformation, exercising expectation rather than holding on to something firm. The distinction, of course, is not as simple as that, since the expectation of arrival may be thwarted by forces which give the appearance of arrival but in fact lead to further disorientation. Second groups (or new key sections) may, therefore, stand in contrast to transitions if they are stable, or they may contain their own duality if they begin ambiguously and gradually achieve tonal stability.

The possible ambiguity at the beginning of the second group involves themes, phrasing, and harmony. The expectation of the arrival of the new key is something with which Haydn enjoys playing, and here one can consider Tovey's distinction between 'in' and 'on' the dominant. In Haydn's symphonies, the shades of difference between 'in' and 'on' are subtle and numerous, and in some cases it is all but impossible to say at what point the new key arrived, even though one does not doubt that it did.

In the case of those works which have a return of the first allegro theme at the beginning of the new key, it is not unusual for the theme to dissipate well before it has gone eight bars, and the interruption is followed by material which casts the key into considerable doubt. Here is a combination of similarity and contrast, bringing the memory and reflection into play but also causing distortion by turning the familiar material into something different. Once the digression has occurred, that theme does not reappear later in the exposition, and the real stability comes with a new closing theme (which may be related to the first theme) and an unmistakable preparation and arrival of the dominant. The function of the ambiguous passages in second groups is different from that of transitions. Transitions are directed towards a goal, and the type of harmonic digression which occurs in Nos. 89, 97, 102, and 103 is merely a delay. The possible ambiguity at the beginning of the second group may be in response to the preparation of the previous section. The preparation may not have been sufficiently strong to establish the new key and the subsequent ambiguity is a confirmation of the lack of stability. The function is more genuinely ambiguous, and in works in which this happens to a returning first theme, a duality concerning that theme is presented through an association of both stability and ambiguity.

Developments

While expositions are combinations of statements and discursive expansions, developments are almost completely discursive. All the dramatic forces are usually presented in the exposition, and the development, like the central part of a theatrical play, carries forward the interaction between the opposing forces. The important activities here are harmonic expansion and counterpoint, and within these, other musical elements such as phrasing are also placed in new contexts. In Tovey's view, the 'essential idea of sonata development is the break-up of the themes as originally phrased, and the rebuilding and recombining of their figures into sentences and sequences of a different kind'.[13] The implication here is that the initial material, because of its treatment in the development, is transformed into something new and different, something which can never again be as it was. Here is a fundamental dramatic principle: in a theatrical work for the stage, a character is not the same at the end as he was at the beginning, but is changed in response to internal and external forces. In the symphony, those parts of the opposition which are able to be imprinted on the memory are taken through a process of change, a change which normally begins in the exposition and is taken to great lengths in the development.

Haydn's intimate knowledge of opera had a fundamental bearing on his formulation of a new symphonic language. One of the primary requisites of this new language was an understanding and application of counterpoint, not that of the sixteenth-century or the early eighteenth-century fugue, but rather a type of counterpoint which was born in comic opera. The raison d'être of this counterpoint is opposition in that it permits characters in an opera to engage in simultaneous argument-ation, allowing the action and conflict of the work to occur in the music. Unlike strict counterpoint (known to every eighteenth-century composer through the study of Fux's *Gradus ad Parnassum*) which generally had an extended and continuous flow, the counterpoint found in ensembles such as those of the Neapolitan intermezzi was characterized by its abrupt punctuation, related to the disjointedness of the text. In the case of the intermezzo ensemble, this musical characteristic was related to the free improvisatory quality of the *commedia dell'arte*, which was the dramatic source of the librettos used in these works by composers such as Alessandro Scarlatti, Leonardo Vinci, Domenico Sarro, and G. B. Pergolesi.[14] Dialogue in the ensembles could be rapid and disruptive, or exchanges could be separated by rests, sometimes placed incongruously so the expectation of a reply is thwarted. Haydn undoubtedly knew Pergolesi's *Serva padrona*, and in the duet which concludes Part I one finds a fine example of this type of counterpoint.

The achievement of Mozart, of course, is unsurpassed in the writing of complex operatic ensembles, as some of his finales are as long as symphonies with never a weak or dull moment. The complexity is often achieved in vocal counterpoint, in the argumentative exchanges between individuals or groups of characters, and one of the clearest examples of this occurs in the finale to Act I of *Don Giovanni*. This finale contains the famous scene in three separate but simultaneous metres, very consider-able tonal ambiguity, and a final section in which Don Giovanni and

[13] *Essays in Musical Analysis*, i. *Symphonies* (London, 1935), p. 13.

[14] See Gordana Lazarevich, 'The Role of the Neapolitan Intermezzo in the Evolution of Eighteenth-Century Musical Style: Literary, Symphonic and Dramatic Aspects, 1685–1735', Ph.D. thesis (Columbia University, 1970), and Charles E. Troy, *The Comic Intermezzo: A Study in the History of Eighteenth-Century Italian Opera* (Ann Arbor, 1979).

Leporello are pitted against the group of pursuers (Donna Anna *et al.*) in some very lively and disruptive counterpoint. In this section the group maintains a type of threatening stability on the words 'Trema, trema, o scellerato', to which the Don and Leporello mockingly respond. Their word 'confusa' aptly describes the effect of the rhythm of their interjections at a fast tempo. And further, while the group continues to emphasize the beat of the bar, the Don and Leporello embark on a new type of disruptive counterpoint which gives more a sense of disorderly speech than singing.

Haydn's increased use of counterpoint in his symphonic developments can be seen to run parallel with his own operatic activities. The type of counterpoint in ensembles frequently makes use of motivic material. In developments the motivic material may be derived from a variety of sources in the exposition, including the main themes, the two parts of a complex theme, transitional material which may or may not have been related to a theme, or the introduction. The material which is emphasized may have seemed insignificant in the exposition, and the treatment in the development can reveal a new importance. Like the operatic ensemble, the development propels the action forward and may have different types of articulation including extended passages without breaks, or frequent halts with short or long silences. Phrasing conforms to the needs of driving the motivic material forward, and is therefore generally irregular. Also, regular phrase lengths can be placed in the counterpoint in such a way that regularity gives way to the forward motion.

The harmonic motion is clearly of vital importance to the forward drive, and once again parallels with the operatic ensemble can be found. Here, in fact, the cross-influences and similar dramatic intentions make it difficult to say if the type of harmonic treatment of the symphonic development was derived from the operatic ensemble, or if the ensemble gained its power through a symphonic conception. In the Mozart finale already cited, the tonal and harmonic ambiguity of the section following the complex dance scene corroborates the confused action on stage at that point. Hearing Zerlina's scream, people rush to her rescue, and the harmony of that scene moves by tritones or chromatically, ending a tritone lower than it began. Moving to the next section in which Don Giovanni tries to shift the blame to Leporello, there is no preparation for the new key of F.

The use of harmonic instability to parallel confused action in an ensemble was, of course, not Mozart's invention but can be found in operas with which Haydn was very familiar by the 1770s. One of these, *L'amore artigiano* by Florian Gassmann, a particular favourite which Haydn first directed in 1777 and revived for special occasions in 1780 and 1790, has exceptionally rich ensembles, the most substantial being the finale to Act I. This ensemble is in four sections and begins in a stable manner. In the second section, different rivalries surface, creating very considerable antagonism and confusion. The third section is tonally ambiguous, as it begins on an unprepared E flat and ends on F, failing to prepare the fourth section which begins in B.

Just as transitions in expositions can combine the stable and irregular treatment of elements, it is also possible for this to occur in developments. The appearance of a remote key, even in an unprepared context, can be placed in a way that it occurs on relatively stable material. The most obvious example of this is the false recapitulation, but it may also occur in other types of familiar thematic material such as a second or closing theme. It is not unusual for harmonic activities and counterpoint to be related, as the passages of intense counterpoint may expand in such a way that harmonic stability and direction are in question.

Recapitulations and codas

The means of achieving the formal and dramatic results in recapitulations are as varied as the number of works in which they occur. Stability is desired at the beginning of the recapitulation, and it is not unusual to find it prolonged through the removal of the irregular transitional material which had followed in the exposition. In this truncated version of the exposition, Haydn arrives at the second theme or closing theme without complexity, now in the tonic as well. In those works which had the original theme begin the new key section of the exposition, that repetition of the theme is normally omitted in the recapitulation. The ambiguity which tended to occur between what one assumed was the beginning of the new key and its firm arrival at the closing theme is therefore removed from the recapitulation. The stability is also apparent at the end of the movement, either as a cadential emphasis on the tonic or as a new interpretation of earlier material which had been unstable, now giving it tonal and rhythmic solidity.

Against this stability is a new dramatic treatment, one which offers more expansion and arrives at the dramatic conclusion, a combination Tovey describes in reference to No. 92 in the following way: 'Thus the prevailing impression [of the recapitulation] is one of perpetual expansion as regards themes and phrases and developments, while the perfect balance of keys and harmonies provides that sense of underlying symmetry which makes the expansion so exhilarating'.[15] the expansion or possible new ambiguity in recapitulations may occur in any single musical element or a combination of different ones, and can happen at any point in the section. Near the beginning of the section it could be the

[15] *Essays*, i. p. 145.

failure of the tonic to be firmly established or a new treatment of the first theme. Further into the section, some works introduce another key which comes as a surprise even if it is not remote, since one does not expect anything other than the tonic. In these cases, it is usually possible to find a basis for the unexpected key in the tonal relationships of the development.

In the late symphonies, the final section of the first movement places the foregoing events in a new context, one which demands assimilative listening. In a number of cases, this new context or reinterpretation is achieved in a coda. In some late works, the coda reintroduces the polarities which generated the conflict in the movement, placing them in a proximity to each other that suggests a fusion or coexistence of opposites, as occurs in Nos. 83 and 103. It is also possible that the material which the coda emphasizes may have seemed insignificant or have gone by unnoticed in its first appearance, but now takes on an importance which places it at the centre of the dramatic realization, No. 103 being the most extreme example of this. In other cases as well, the reinterpretation may reveal a deeper significance to an idea which previously seemed straightforward, as happens in No. 102. The coda may also provide stability, but this stability may be a new presentation of material which was previously unstable, as is the case in No. 94, thereby bringing about something new through dispelling of prior tension. In some works, the coda or the end of the recapitulation brings a clear return of material from the introduction, as in Nos. 97 and 103, leaving no doubt about the involvement of the introduction in the overall dramatic process. Aside from these two, it is possible to see an indirect involvement in others because of the thematic relationships of material from the introduction with that which is ultimately considered in the coda.

Sonata form as Haydn conceived it was not the natural outcome of an evolutionary process or stylistic development. While some of the grammar was available, the form itself did not assume a position of ascendancy until composers such as Haydn recognized an extraordinary potential here for their compositional and aesthetic purposes. Largely through Haydn's brilliant contrivance, an intelligibility of the highest order was achieved in instrumental music.

I I

Melodic Sources and Musical Images

THE interaction of opposing forces near the beginning of first movements is fundamental to Haydn's symphonic language in the late symphonies, and a primary facet of this interaction is to be found in the relationship of the slow introduction and the initial 'allegro' theme. The importance of the introduction to Haydn's late symphonic language is evident not only in its frequent use but also in that there is a thematic relationship of this material to the first theme in the fast tempo (or some other part of the first movement). The fact that this material is both contrasted and thematically related seems to suggest the possibility that the relationship may be of critical dramatic importance, and in numerous examples this relationship is indeed crucial to the dramatic unfolding of the movement. In works such as Nos. 97 and 103, in which the introductory material appears at some other point or points in the movement, one cannot doubt that this is of the greatest dramatic significance. In others as well the affective contrast and thematic similarity may also have a strong bearing on subsequent events of the first movement.

While the polarity between introductions and themes is defined by purely musical means such as contrasts in tempo, harmony, rhythm, melody, or distinctions between ambiguous and clearly defined passages, Haydn has reinforced this dramatic delineation by using melodic source material which strengthens a sense of archetypal opposition through association with particular events or states of being. An awareness of these sources is not essential to an understanding of the works, but nevertheless can add an interesting and enriching dimension. If the sources with their specific references are identified, it is not to be concluded that they necessarily transform the symphonies in question into programmatic works. It is entirely possible that the sources, with their potential to be images, are not used consciously by Haydn, but rather arise naturally from his storehouse of material in order to create certain effects or impressions. Some of these possible sources will be isolated in this chapter in order to show how their specific associations confirm the more general aim of Haydn's treatment of opposition.

Identifying the sources

The search for Haydn's melodic sources is a well-established endeavour, and attempts to isolate specific sources have met with varying degrees of success. There are also studies which demonstrate affinities with general types of sources. Some of the most successful attempts at identifying specific sources have concerned earlier works, and in some of these cases, as was seen in Chapter 6, extramusical associations have been made. The search for Haydn's melodic sources began in earnest at the end of the nineteenth century with the work of Franjo S. Kuhač and his English popularizer, W. H. Hadow.[1] As one can see from these works, the reasons for pursuing this type of study can be at least as interesting as the results, but in the light of the genealogical work of E. F. Schmid, the question of Haydn's national origin can be considered a dead issue.[2]

In the twentieth century, with the increased activity in the study of Austrian folk-music, certain melodies of folksongs or folk-dances have come to light which seem to have genuine similarities to some of Haydn's themes.[3] These examples appeared randomly and the nature of the affinities was sometimes in doubt, which prompted Karl M. Klier to conclude that a more systematic approach to collecting source material was necessary. Such a study was offered in the form of a large catalogue by David Stephen Cushman, and in this work one can see how thorny the problem actually is.[4] The sources are categorized by Cushman according to the degree of similarity with Haydn's melodic material, but often in the final category one perceives very little resemblance at all. A difficulty arises when one attempts to separate the possible sources from their role in the composer's creative process, making it all but impossible to demonstrate that vague similarities are anything more than coincidental.

The specific types of material which appear in Haydn's introductions and 'allegro' themes are drawn from a variety of sources including plainchant, hymns, folksongs, folk-dances, other dances, and possibly opera. Some possibilities have been recognized by various writers, and the first point to become apparent concerning sources was that Haydn's

[1] Kuhač, *Josip Haydn i hrvatske narodne popievke* (Zagreb, 1880), and Hadow, *A Croatian Composer: Notes Toward the Study of Haydn* (London, 1897).
[2] *Joseph Haydn. Ein Buch von Vorfahren und Heimat des Meisters* (Kassel, 1934).
[3] Some of these can be found in the following: Walter Deutsch, ' "Volkstümliche" Wirkungen in der Musik Joseph Haydns', *Musikerziehung*, 14 (1960), 88–92; Karl M. Klier, 'Haydns Thema aus dem Andante der "Symphonie mit dem Paukenschlag"', *Völkische Musikerziehung*, 6 (1940), 55–8; and Raimund Zoder, 'Haydn-Menuett und ein Steyrischer', *Volkslied, Volkstanz, Volksmusik*, 48 (1947), 28–9.
[4] 'Joseph Haydn's Melodic Material: An Exploratory Introduction to the Primary and Secondary Sources together with an Analytical Catalogue and Tables of Proposed Melodic Correspondence and/or Variance', Ph.D. thesis (Boston University, 1972).

first-movement 'allegro' themes are related to dance music. It has become commonplace to think of minuets and trios or finales in relation to dance music, particularly the affinity to the ländler in the former[5] and the contredanse in the latter,[6] but the possibility concerning first movements has drawn considerably less notice. A germinal study which considered the general issue of dance-related themes was that of Wilhelm Fischer, in which melody is divided into two basic types that stem from the aria or dance.[7] Fischer saw the dance type as having the potential for expansion or development, and this clearly applied to Haydn.

More recent research has suggested connections between dance types and Haydn's first-movement themes, an example being Jürgen Beythien's study which draws a connection between the contredanse and themes of some of Haydn's late symphonies.[8] One use of plainchant in a late symphonic slow movement has been suggested by Landon. This concerns No. 103 and the possible although somewhat remote association of the first few notes with the familiar melody of the 'Dies Irae' plainchant. He goes so far as to suggest that this oblique reference would have been evident to Catholic listeners, even though it may have escaped English audiences (*Chron.* iii. 595).

When considering Haydn's use of source material, the element of conjecture cannot be completely eliminated since his melodies are never exactly the same as the specific sources. No attempt will be made here to show that specific passages in Haydn's music could have been drawn from particular sources; instead, the discussion will focus on general types that help to define the forces or polarities of dramatic interaction. In the case of 'allegro' themes, it seems probable that Haydn intended to establish a sense of stability and naturally drew his material from a type of source which would provide the desired clarity. While these themes may display some disruptive characteristics as well, the overall effect is nevertheless one of stability. Even though specific dance types can be identified and have the potential to be musical *topoi* (as Leonard Ratner has shown in *Classic Music*), the discussion here will not go beyond the observation of general dance-like features. In the case of folk-music as a possible source for symphonic themes, sound advice is offered by

---

[5] Eugene L. Beenk, 'Laendler Elements in the Symphonic Minuets of Joseph Haydn', Ph.D. thesis (University of Iowa, 1969).

[6] Dénes Bartha, 'Volkstanz-Stilisierung in Joseph Haydns Finale-Themen', in Finscher and Mahling (eds.), *Festschrift für Walter Wiora* (Kassel, 1967), 375–84, and Heinrich Besseler, 'Einflüsse der Kontratanzmusik auf Joseph Haydn', in *Bericht über die Internationale Konferenz zum Andenken Joseph Haydns* (Budapest, 1961), 25–40.

[7] 'Zur Entwicklungsgeschichte der Wiener klassischen Stils', *Studien zur Musikwissenschaft*, 3 (1915), 24–84.

[8] 'Der Einfluß des Kontretanzes auf die Orchestermusik der Deutschen Frühklassik', D.Phil. thesis (University of Jena, 1957), p. 395.

another central European composer with a profound interest in his own musical heritage, Gustav Mahler:

The music which the masters have assimilated in their childhood forms the texture of their mature musical development. . . . The music is absorbed and goes through a process of mental digestion until it becomes a part of the person. . . . It is stored away in their brain-cells and will come forth again in the minds of creative musicians, not in the same or even similar form, but often in entirely new and wonderful conceptions. . . . When he [Haydn] came to produce his great works, he was so thoroughly imbued with the musical language of the people that the folk-song character and influence keeps cropping up all the time.[9]

The identification of sources, then, must be done with this process of abstraction in mind. The consideration of the general rather than the specific determines that any possible extramusical association will also be of a general nature. Therefore, folk-dances will not be considered from the point of view of the implications of specific types. It is the more general nature of musical stability in folk-dances which is of interest to this study, and the possibility of relating that musical character to social stability. Similarly, the dramatic importance of the slow introduction is to be found in its sense of ambiguity, and the melodic sources here are drawn from plainchant, folksongs, and hymns which have a darker association, such as with death, sin, or sorrow.

The dance and 'Allegro' themes

The body of material on which one can draw in considering possible dance sources for Haydn's themes is extremely large and varied. Studies in European folk-music indicate a high degree of uniformity covering different nations and different periods of time. In pointing to the interconnections in time and locations in European folk-music, Walter Wiora suggests that many melodies are not only variants of one tune but that numerous tunes can be seen as modifications of a single type.[10] This type of conclusion is no longer to be seen as the result of speculative optimism: researchers in melodic comparison such as Wiora believe their methodological foundation is sufficiently solid to distinguish between accidental and genuine similarities.[11] The research into possible Haydn sources, then, need not be limited to a brief period of the eighteenth century, but is in fact strengthened by a wide historical range

---

[9] 'The Influence of the Folk-Song on German Musical Art', *Etude*, 29 (1911), pp. 301–2.

[10] K. G. Fellerer (ed.), *Anthology of Music*, iv. W. Wiora, *European Folk Song*, trans. R. Kolben (Cologne, 1966), pp. 5–6.

[11] Ibid. See also Wiora, 'On the Methods of Comparative Melodic Research', *Journal of the International Folk Music Council*, 9 (1957), 55–8, and Oskar Elschek (ed.), *Methoden der Klassifikation von Volksliedweisen* (Bratislava, 1969).

of similar material. The fact that printed or manuscript copies of music appeared at a particular date suggests neither the beginning nor ending of a phase so far as folk-music is concerned. As for location, it must be kept in mind that while Haydn's earliest exposure was to the folk-music of Lower Austria, he spent most of his working life on the border of Hungary and Austria.[12] The sources, then, will be drawn from an area of Central Europe which includes Austria and various surrounding countries.

The most valuable collection of pre-nineteenth- and early nineteenth-century Austrian folk-dances (and Austrian folk-music in general from that period) is the Sonnleithner-Sammlung, held in the archives of the Gesellschaft der Musikfreunde in Vienna.[13] It was assembled in 1819 by Joseph Sonnleithner and is made up entirely of manuscript copies. In 1969, the sesquicentenary of the collection, new research and discussion brought it very much into notice. This included a detailed catalogue of all items,[14] a seminar at the Institut für Volksmusikforschung in Vienna, and a series of articles in the *Österreichische Musikzeitschrift* (vol. 24, 1969). The collection is arranged according to geographical areas and on the basis of musical function. The main category divisions are the provinces of Austria, with the exception of one section which is made up of death songs from all parts of the country. The subdivisions distinguish localities within the provinces and the type of musical function. The province of Haydn's birth, Lower Austria, is one of the largest sections, containing about three hundred musical items.

Dating is less defined than geography and function, but it seems fairly safe to assume that in this collection, assembled ten years after the death of Haydn, most of the folk-music or types of folk-music could have been known to Haydn. The dance music of the Sonnleithner-Sammlung includes both folk-dance transcriptions and composed dances, thereby making it at least one step removed from a genuine folk-dance tradition. This type of transciption results in what Wiora refers to as a folk-tune which is preserved but not fossilized.[15] In the process, something of the power of imagery of the folk-dance may be lost, but in contrast to this, Wiora argues that composers such as Haydn came very close to preserving the genuine character of folk-music in their works.[16] While

---

[12] Regarding Hungarian influences, see Erwin Major, 'Ungarische Tanzmelodien in Haydns Bearbeitung', *Zeitschrift für Musikwissenschaft*, 11 (1928–9), 601–4, and Bence Szabolcsi, 'Haydn und die Ungarische Musik', in *Bericht über die Internationale Konferenz zum Andenken Joseph Haydns* (Budapest, 1961), 159–75.

[13] The abbreviation used in musical examples will be S-S/GdMf.

[14] Walter Deutsch and Gerlinda Hofer, *Die Volksmusiksammlung der Gesellschaft der Musikfreunde in Wien (Sonnleithner-Sammlung)* (Vienna, 1969).

[15] *European Folk Song*, p. 10.

[16] 'Ethnomusicology and the History of Music', *Studia Musicologica Academiae Scientiarum Hungaricae*, 7 (1965), p. 191.

transcriptions do not reflect the same process which is used by a composer such as Haydn, they are nevertheless invaluable as approximations of the genuine sources for comparative purposes.

An early printed collection of Austrian folk-music dates from the same year as the Sonnleithner-Sammlung and is very thorough in its scholarly presentation.[17] Moving beyond Austria, two Hungarian manuscripts of eighteenth-century folk and dance-music of particular value are MSS Linus and Vietoris.[18] A number of late nineteenth- and twentieth-century published collections of dance music from Austria, Hungary, and Germany are also very useful for their abundance of examples and scholarly thoroughness as to dates and locations.[19] At least one of these, a collection of German dances in tablature, draws from sources much earlier than the eighteenth century, but examples are frequently similar to those in eighteenth-century collections, again suggesting a consistency in certain types of non-art music.

Music which is intended for dancing is distinctly set apart from other music because of its need to conform to the motion or gestures of the dance. This involves rhythm, melodic shape (or the two of these in combination), metre, and above all symmetrical phrasing. Also, the function of the phrase in relation to the dance is musically defined by rhythm, shape, and tonality, all of which create gesture. Haydn's indebtedness to dance as a source is clearly apparent in his symphonic writing, and in the late symphonies this applies to first movements as well as later ones. This general indebtedness of Haydn and others is substantiated by a wealth of writing by eighteenth-century theorists.[20] It is the sense of vitality of the dance and its unifying or stabilizing power which is relevant to the symphony. For the purposes of comparison, thematic material other than first themes in first movements will also be considered, as well as material from works which do not have slow introductions.

In the examples which follow, there is no intention to suggest that the folk-dances quoted are the actual sources of Haydn's themes. The

---

[17] *Oesterreichische Volkslieder mit ihren Singweisen*, Franz Ziska and J. M. Schottky, eds. (Budapest, 1819).

[18] MS Linus, 1786, National Széchényi Library, Budapest, and MS Vietoris. See Charlotte Abelmann, 'Der Codex Vietoris. Ein Beitrag zur Musikgeschichte des ungarisch-tschechoslowakischen Grenzgebietes', D.Phil. thesis (University of Vienna, 1946). The collection is also known as the 'Eszterháza Songbook' although there is no evidence that it ever was in the possession of the Eszterházy family.

[19] The following are but a few of a very wide choice: Franz M. Böhme, *Geschichte des Tanzes in Deutschland* (Leipzig, 1886); Robert Lach, *Zur Geschichte des Gesellschaftstanzes im 18. Jahrhundert* (Vienna, 1920); Wilhelm Merian, *Der Tanz in den deutschen Tabulaturbüchern* (Leipzig, 1927); Raimund Zoder, *Altösterreichische Volkstänze* (Vienna, 1937); and Pál Péter Domokos, 'Magyar Táncdallamok a XVIII. Századból' (Hungarian Dance Melodies from the Eighteenth Century)', *Zenetudomány: Tanulmányok*, 9 (1961) 269–94.

[20] See Leonard G. Ratner, 'Eighteenth-Century Theories of Musical Period Structure', *Musical Quarterly*, 42 (1956), pp. 446–7.

comparison here does not go beyond the relating of general gestures which suggest a dance character in Haydn's themes. The comparison in Ex. 19 is strictly concerned with rhythm, and other musical elements are not taken into account. One of the most familiar rhythmic character-istics of the folk-dance is that of an eighth-note followed by two sixteenths (or a quarter-note followed by two eighths) in sequence, a feature which pervades dances such as the *Polonaise*, the *Deutscher*, *Anglaise*, or *Dreher*. This figure is frequently used by Haydn in his themes, and the ways in which he uses it can be seen to correspond with various types of dance (Ex. 19). Along with rhythm, melodic shape can also be a factor. Again the melodic shape in question is not such that one could say that the particular composed melody is taken from a specific dance. In the case of Ex. 20*a*, the motion of the second bar in Haydn's theme is in the opposite direction of that of the minuet from the Tyrol; however, Haydn's theme exemplifies the smooth shape which is characteristic of the minuet.

The most crucial element of the dance, however, is the sense of symmetrical phrasing, and the periodicity of Haydn's themes as well as the sense of gesture within a specific phrase are directly related to this aspect of the dance. Eighteenth-century theorists took special notice of the strict phrasing in dance music, observing that the dance was the only type of music in which definite numbers of bars were a requirement.[21] The same sense of periodicity can be found in many eighteenth-century folksongs, but frequently there is also a connection between folksinging and folk-dancing.[22] The regularity and balance of phrasing are directly related to the motion of the dance, and the sense of direction within the phrase at the smallest and largest levels corresponds to the directional gestures of the dance steps. Here the divisions of phrasing, rhythmic impetus, melodic shape, and harmonic direction are all called into play.

The prominent dance character found in many of Haydn's first-movement themes may be more than a simple source for melodic material or the creation of a popular spirit through the evocation of rusticity. While dancing may appear to be nothing more than a recreational activity, dances of both folk and courtly origins were seen by those who practised them as having certain types of ritual or moral significance. Dance masters regarded their art as playing a germinal role in the moral education of the young, and classified dances according to their ethical merit.[23] Folk-dance can be a ritual expression and be of primary importance to community life. In order to link the significance of this with symphonies, it is not necessary to identify the specific dance

---

[21] Ibid., p. 443.

[22] Many of the examples in Ziska and Schottky, *Oesterreichische Volkslieder* belong to this category.

[23] See Wye Jamison Allanbrook, *Rhythmic Gesture in Mozart:* Le nozze di Figaro *and* Don Giovanni (Chicago, 1983), p. 69.

Ex. 19

a. No. 87/1   S–S/GdMf, Tirol, XXI/9, *Saltarello*

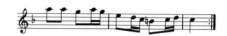

b. No. 103/1   Lach. p. 3, *Passepied*

c. No. 100/1   From MS Linus

Ex. 20

a. No. 90/1   S–S/GdMf, Tirol, XV/3, *Minuet*

b. No. 93/1   S–S/GdMf, Niederösterreich, VII/13.5

c. No. 83/1   Böhme, ii, p. 164, *Rutscher*

d. No. 89/1   Zoder, No. 1, 'Der Strohschneider'

types. In the symphonies there are general associations which can be made, and these concern the life-reinforcing characteristic of folk-dancing. This is apparent from the occasions at which folk-dancing occurs such as springtime festivals and weddings, and the celebration of birth, growth, stability, and unity.

Folk songs, hymns, and slow introductions

In the case of Symphony No. 103 and possible reference to the 'Dies Irae' plainchant, the fact that the association only consists of four notes makes the connection very speculative. There is even less evidence than with the dance and 'allegro' themes to suggest that Haydn knowingly drew his material from a given source. It is entirely possible that the relationship is coincidental and inadvertent, but the coincidence, in the sense of Mahler's understanding of the process by which folk material is assimilated and used by Haydn, may not be surprising. Similar types of fragmentary associations occur in the slow introductions of other late symphonies, and one of these, which appears with some consistency, will be examined.

In the case of many of Haydn's 'allegro' themes, it was possible to observe general features in common with dance music rather than specific melodic associations. In the slow introductions, one can find a particular melodic feature and variants of it which a significant number of late works have in common. The prototype of this melodic fragment is to be found at the beginning of Symphony No. 102, consisting of a rising fourth and a stepwise return to the original note. In order to be included in this group, the figure must appear prominently at the beginning of the work, either starting on the first note of the work as happens in No. 94, or immediately after an introductory chord or set of octaves, as in No. 102 (Ex. 21). Because of the brevity of this figure, it does not constitute an actual melody but rather is the strongest melodic feature of an overall melodic line. It is important to the line because it provides the beginning and in almost all cases reappears in some form later in the line, either as an inversion, as some kind of variant, or in a fairly identical form. The basic figure, as stated, is the opening of Ex. 21*a*, 1–4–3–2–1 (1 does not necessarily represent the tonic). Ex. 21*b* is the variant closest to the prototype, simply omitting 3 in the descending line. In Ex. 21*c*, the descending line is omitted entirely, leaving the interval 1–4–1, but an interesting feature here is that the recurrence in bars 3–4 completes the descending line, thereby strengthening the tie with Ex. 21*a*. One also finds variants of this melodic fragment at the beginning of other works. In contrast to the open fourth of No. 100, No. 91 presents a shape in which the fourth is almost completely filled out in both directions. Nos. 84, 90, and 99 provide a different type of variant, with an opening

Ex. 21

a. No. 102/1

b. No. 94/1

c. No. 100/1

interval of a third (or tenth in Nos. 90 and 99) rather than a fourth. But as with Ex. 21*c*, other factors may help to strengthen the association with the prototype. In No. 99, a very close variant appears in the flute part in bars 8–9.

This figure, to be sure, is a very common one and appears in many types of folk-music. The rising fourth can provide a very vigorous start, particularly if the first note is an anacrusis, and one finds the rising fourth at the beginning of many lively folksongs and dances. However, the rising fourth followed by the descending stepwise pattern tends to have a different context, especially if the tempo is slow, making the descending tetrachord the crucial factor in the figure. One of the best-known examples of this (although Haydn is unlikely to have known it) is the chorale setting of 'O Haupt voll Blut und Wunden' in Bach's *St Matthew Passion* (or the same melody in the chorale of Cantata 161, 'Komm, du süsse Todesstunde'). Here the melodic figure found in Symphony No. 102 appears in the first five notes, and, while it is extended one note lower by Bach, it comes to rest on the starting pitch. Again one is dealing with an opening melodic fragment, a type of *incipit* rather than an overall melody, but it is a fragment from which the melody gets its shape.

Bach uses this melody in connection with the subject of death.[24] An investigation of seventeenth- and eighteenth- century collections of hymns and religious folksongs from Austria, Hungary, and Germany

[24] The source for Bach's melody was a lovesong, although by no means a happy one. See David P. Schroeder, 'Melodic Source Material and Haydn's Creative Process', *Musical Quarterly*, 68 (1982), pp. 510–11.

reveals that this melodic figure in association with similar types of texts is by no means an isolated phenomenon. Many examples can be found in these collections, and, in contrast, it appears less often in nineteenth-century collections, all but disappearing by the end of the century. The most important collection of folksongs in this regard is once again the Sonnleithner-Sammlung. As was indicated above, the main divisions here are geographical, with the exception of one section which bears the title 'Totenlieder aus Österreich'. The songs in this section are composed works for performance by skilled musicians, written for one voice or four parts, and occasionally with designated instruments. As well as a separate section for *Totenlieder*, individual examples appear in the geographical sections, and the group of *Totenlieder* from Lower Austria is particularly rich. These are generally strophic songs and reflect the oral tradition more directly.

The pertinent seventeenth- and eighteenth-century Roman Catholic hymn-books are numerous.[25] The study of those from Austria can be augmented by hymn-books from Germany, and examples from a vast number of these can be found in the excellent collection of hymns by Wilhelm Bäumker.[26] Bäumker's attention to sources, dates, and locations makes his large work extremely valuable. The various items in Ex. 22 are but a small sampling of *Totenlieder* from a variety of printed and manuscript sources.

In the items of Ex. 22, it is possible to see a characteristic *incipit* of which there is a prototype and a number of variants. The prototype is a rising fourth and stepwise descent to the starting note, a figure identical to the opening of Symphony No. 102, and the variants in a number of cases correspond with the related figures which open some of Haydn's other slow introductions. Similarities can be seen between Ex. 22*a* and Symphony No. 91, 22*c* and No. 100, and 22*d* and No. 94. As well as being prominently displayed at the beginning of the song, this figure usually has a strong bearing on the melodic shape of what follows, either in the form of direct repetition or as a type of variant, a process which was also apparent in Haydn's introductions.

While the 'Dies Irae' is most commonly associated with the familiar plainchant melody, one can also find examples of it in seventeenth- and

[25] Some collections of particular interest from Vienna include *Davidische Harmonia. Das ist Christlich Catholische Gesänge* (1659); David Gregor Corner (ed.), *Geistliche Nachtigal. Das ist ausserlesene Catholische Gesänge* (1674); *Gott-Lob singendes Jahr. Das ist geistliche Gesänger* (1737); *Katholisches Gesangbuch auf allerhöchsten Befehl Ihrer k. k. Majestät Marien Theresiens* (1750); and *Cantus Ecclesiasticus* (1761). Some valuable hymn-books from other Austrian and Hungarian locations are Nicolaum Beuttner's *Catholisch Gesang-Buch* (Graz, 1602); *Himmelische Harmaney oder ausserlesene Catholische Gesänger* (Graz, 1644); *Heil- und Hülfs-Mittel zum thätigen Christenthum* (Brix, 1767); and *Cantus Catholici ex Editione Szelepcseniana* (Nagy-Szombatban, 1738).

[26] *Das Katholische Deutsche Kirchenlied in seinen Singweisen* (Freiburg, 1883–1911).

eighteenth-century Austrian and German hymn-books using the melodic fragment under consideration here, as in Ex. 22*a*.[27] This example, from an early Viennese source,[28] is a particularly notable instance of an entire melody dominated by the single melodic figure. Here, the first two melodic units are filled out, and the third has the open rising fourth followed by the descending stepwise pattern.

This melodic fragment can be found in association with other types of death song. One of these types relates specifically to Christ's crucifixion, an example of which, Ex. 22*b*, is a folksong from Lower Austria.[29] Another type of death song is that used at wakes, and examples of this have been collected by Klier, whose main sources were eighteenth- and nineteenth-century circulars printed at various locations in Burgenland.[30] In Ex. 22*c*, as in Symphony No. 100, the beginning variant of an open fourth is followed by a shape much closer to the prototype. In Klier's collection, one finds particularly fine examples of the prototype of the melodic fragment and other instances of it as the melodies are extended.[31] Ex. 22*d*, a *Totenlied* from the Sonnleithner-Sammlung which suggests the *Totenwacht* by its text, begins with a melodic shape not unlike that of the opening of Symphony No. 94. Aside from a large section of *Passionslieder*, hymn-books also often had a category called 'Songs of Death and the Life to Come'. This also is the most common type of death song in the manuscript sources. Ex. 22*e* is one of a very large number of songs of this type beginning with the rising fourth and descending stepwise line.[32] Early hymn-books also contain sections which deal with sin, and here one can make a connection with death through the biblical sense of sin's consequence. Under the section 'Songs of Atonement and Forgiveness of Sins', Bäumker includes a song with the prototype of the melodic figure in question.[33]

By no means all the songs in the sources containing this melodic figure refer to death, sin, or sorrow. Many are life-affirming, although even

---

[27] Two other good examples can be found in *Heil- und Hülfs-Mittel*, p. 600; and Bäumker, *Das Katholische Deutsche Kirchenlied*, iv. p. 706, no. 377, an example which first appeared in Cologne in 1748 and is in numerous German hymn-books until 1866.

[28] David Gregor Corner (ed.), *Gross Catholisch Gesangbuch* (Vienna, 1631).

[29] Other examples of this type are found in *Himmelische Harmoney*, p. 48; *Cantus Catholici*, p. 149; and Bäumker, *Das Katholische Deutsche Kirchenlied*, p. 476, no. 75.

[30] *Das Totenwacht-Singen in Burgenland* (Eisenstadt, 1956), p. 15.

[31] Ibid., nos. 1*c* and 14 (variant).

[32] The pertinent *Sterbenleider* from the Sonnleithner-Sammlung include the following: Neiderösterreich, nos. I/11b, XI/41, and XIII/5; *Totenlieder*, nos. 11(2), 16, 17, 37, 49, 50(2), 53, 54 (1, 3, 5, 6), 62, 64 (4, 5), 68(4), and 70; Oberösterreich, nos. XI/4 (1, 2) and D/8.XIX (3, 4). Good examples in Bäumker, *Das Katholische Deutsche Kirchelied* include: vol. 2, p. 301, no. 327; p. 306, no. 334; p. 309, nos. 338 and 339; and vol. 4, p. 697, no. 364.

[33] The example Bäumker gives in vol. 2, p. 262, no. 266 appeared in Rheinfels, 1666; Nordern, 1671; Münster, 1677; and Fulda, 1695. Another example of this type is found in *Heil- und Hülfs-Mittel*, p. 178, and it suggests the beginning of Symphony No. 84.

Ex. 22

a. Bäumker, ii. No. 354 II, p. 323

Der-je-nig Tag dess Zorns ein Tag, die Welt inn Fewr auff-löst mit klag, nach Da-vid und Sy-bil-la sag.

b. S–S/GdMf, Niederösterreich, XII/13

Nun ist das Lamb ge - schlach-tet, das Op - fer ist voll - bracht;

c. Klier, No. 23

Al - les schläft den To - des - schlum-mer hier in die - ser ö - den Flur;

d. S–S/GdMf, *Totenlieder*, 54.7

Äl - tem hör - et auf zu — wein - en ü - ber uns - ers — Kin - des — Tod.

e. S–S/GdMf, *Totenlieder*, 50.1

Lebt man schon hun-dert Jahr

here the sense of death can be directly apparent or implied. Again, the biblical point of view of life is defined in reference to death—the death of Christ and the death of the person's old way of life. Easter songs that refer to both death and resurrection are most obvious examples.[34] Similarly in songs which are statements of belief, one often finds that the eschatological basis of the religious consciousness is implied.[35] In songs that are exclusively concerned with Christian joy, the text may indirectly imply an association with death. In some cases the text will refer to the change which God has brought about in man, something which the devout would associate with Christ's death.[36]

The death-related association of this melodic figure has other sources

[34] See *Katholisches Gesangbuch auf Befehl Marien Theresiens*, no. XII.
[35] See *Cantus Catholici*, p. 253.
[36] A specific example of this is found in *Davidische Harmonia*, p. 198.

Ex. 23

with which Haydn may have been familiar. Two others include operatic and madrigal sources, and these are discussed by Ellen Rosand in the following way: 'During the fourth and fifth decades of the seventeenth century, a particular bassline pattern, the descending minor tetrachord, came to assume a quite specific function associated almost exclusively with a single expressive genre, the lament.'[37] Rosand refers to specific examples from Monteverdi, Frescobaldi, Sances, Pesenti, Ferrari, Manelli, and Cavalli which contain the descending tetrachord in laments. At the conclusion of the article, Rosand notes that later composers, including Purcell, Handel, and Bach, used the same figure as the basis of their lament arias, and she also provides an instrumental example, the 'Lament' from Bach's Capriccio in B flat major 'on the departure of his dearly Beloved Brother', of 1704 (p. 358). Here, then, in a work without a text, one finds that 'the pattern itself declares its precise iconographic significance, an emblem of lament' (p. 359).

While Haydn may not have encountered this figure with its association in earlier operatic sources or even in the works of Bach and Handel, he clearly was aware of it from liturgical sources. Aside from the types already cited, a striking example is the musical realization of the Passion story from the *Cantus Ecclesiasticus* which he used in Symphony No. 26 in D minor. Here the entire passage, regardless of the speaker (Evangelist, Christ, or the crowd (Vox populi)), is based on descending tetrachords (see *Chron.* ii. 292), figures which look very much like those used in later symphonies (Ex. 23). Also, his use of one of the 'Alphabet Lamentations' in the second movement continues the musical image. Here a descending figure is also the predominant melodic feature,

---

[37] 'The Descending Tetrachord: An Emblem of Lament', *Musical Quarterly*, 65 (1979), p. 346.

although in this case it is a third rather than a fourth. This variant of the prototype corresponds with the introductions of Nos. 84, 90, and 99.

Haydn's use of melodic source material offers an opportunity to look deeper into his creative process. The polarities which are defined by slow introductions and 'allegro' themes take on a new dimension when seen in the light of their potential sources, a dimension which affirms an archetypal human principle. In these images at the beginning of symphonies, Haydn is drawing from his national heritage and producing works of great dramatic power with a marked individual character. This meeting of national heritage and individual consciousness is by no means unique to Haydn, and is expressed as an aesthetic principle by as unlikely a musician as Maurice Ravel:

each creative artist has within him laws peculiar to his own being. These laws, peculiar to the artist himself, are, perhaps, the most momentous elements at play in the whole process of musical creation; they seem to be determined through an interplay of national and individual consciousness; and they can be imparted to the artist by no teacher, for they spring from his own heritage, and are first perceived only by himself.[38]

[38] 'Contemporary Music', *Rice Institute Pamphlet* (April 1928), p. 136. Quoted by Arbie Orenstein in 'Maurice Ravel's Creative Process', *Musical Quarterly*, 53 (1967), p. 469.

Symphonies and the Salomon Concerts

HAYDN's decision to spend a few years in England has been a source of satisfaction to most English observers, in the twentieth as well as the eighteenth century. Among some writers in the present century, in fact, this feeling has been extended to include a view of mutual advantage, a sense that rubbing shoulders with the English released in Haydn 'the still untapped spring of creative life within him'.[1] Some non-English Haydn scholars have taken exception to this ascendant view of his London works, and one in particular has reflected that 'in light of his total output their importance has been exaggerated'.[2] The English works are in a sense special, but not, of course, because of some newly discovered inspiration which makes them superior to previously written works. The differences clearly are not qualitative. Indeed, in the case of the symphonies, one could argue that the works written for the first season of Salomon Concerts are no more advanced than most of the symphonies written for performance in Paris. The difference concerns the manner in which one is able to examine these works since Haydn's presence in England afforded him the opportunity to observe his audience at first hand and build a certain type of relationship with that audience. He was determined, as Charlotte Papendiek correctly pointed out,[3] that his first efforts should endear him to the English public. However, he was equally resolved that his symphonies should challenge the listeners in moral or thoughtful ways, and over the sequence of the English Symphonies, one is able to see the shifts in balance which occur between popular appeal and intellectual challenge.

Observing the production of the English Symphonies in the light of reception is in large measure possible because of the wealth of documentation concerning this body of works, made accessible through the efforts of H. C. Robbins Landon in particular. It has been possible, for example, to give accurate dates of first performances of the London Symphonies with the exception of the two written for the 1791 season (*Chron.* iii. 496),[4] unlike the Paris Symphonies where chronologies of any

[1] Rosemary Hughes, *Haydn String Quartets* (London, 1961), p. 43.
[2] A. Peter Brown, 'Critical Years for Haydn's Instrumental Music: 1787–90', *Musical Quarterly*, 62 (1976), p. 375.
[3] See above, Chapter 8, p. 96.
[4] All subsequent references to this source in this chapter give volume and page numbers only.

type remain open to question. As a result, it is possible to observe changes which may have been made in response to the reception of previous works, or in any event to observe a compositional sequence determined by the effect he wished particular works to have on the audience.

No group of works by Haydn has been subjected to as much scrutiny as the English Symphonies, but much of this has been directed to purely analytical and stylistic considerations. As such, the changes which occur within the group tend to be seen as ongoing experiments or attempts to solve purely musical issues. The examination of these symphonies to be put forward in this chapter will attempt to place them in a perspective which accounts for compositional goals which are not purely musical, a perspective in which the audience is seen to have a bearing on production. The assessment of this role, however, cannot be as precise in relation to each work as one might wish. Unlike comparable literary situations, Gellert's, for example, where contemporary critics write at length about the details of a new work and the author often replies in writing to the criticism,[5] the reviews of Haydn's symphonies are almost always of a general nature, not singling out specifics of the work in question. In fact, the reviews almost invariably express unreserved praise.

Similarly, we lack documented replies by Haydn aside from his open letters of gratitude to the audience for its approbation. It is known that certain movements received greater applause than others or were given encores, but it is not likely that Haydn's fundamental compositional choices would be determined by a crude gauging of applause. What seems more probable is that Haydn, while in England, developed a strategy for the way he wished to reach his audience. The strategy was very simple: the initial works should ensure his popularity, and these should be followed by works which provide a greater challenge to the listener and address issues such as morality. The evidence that he adopted such a strategy lies not so much in external documentation as in the works themselves. It is in his changing approach from one work to the next concerning dramatic polarities, complex unfolding, conclusions which account for prior events, or processes which actually guide the listener that his strategy is apparent. The external evidence, as outlined in previous chapters, provides confirmation in a general sense that he was deeply concerned both about approbation and moral or intellectual goals.

The works will be discussed in the sequence in which they were presented to the London audience. The major division is determined by

---

[5] See John Van Cleve, *Harlequin Besieged: The Reception of Comedy in Germany during the Early Enlightenment* (Berne, 1980), pp. 90–103.

Haydn's two sojourns in England, and these can be further subdivided by the two separate seasons of each visit. The number of works to be included will be thirteen instead of twelve since the first symphony given at the Salomon Concerts was not one of the twelve written specifically for these concerts. The evidence points strongly to No. 92 as the first performed symphony, a previously composed work which the English would not yet have had the opportunity to hear (iii. 53–5). Aside from the fact that this was his most recent symphony before coming to London, its choice was an inspired one since its first movement is an unusually fine combination of the two effects of symphonic writing that Haydn was determined his works should have on the English audience. As an existing work it exemplified the best of his symphonic writing and provided a type of preview of the direction he would take in later seasons.

FIRST SEASON: 1791

No. 92

If Haydn was attempting to gain approbation and challenge the audience with the performance of No. 92 on 11 March 1791, the first of the Salomon Concerts, there was no question in the mind of the reviewer from the *Diary; or Woodfall's Register* that he succeeded: 'A new grand overture by HAYDN, was received with the highest applause, and universally deemed a composition as pleasing as scientific' (iii. 50). The same writer informed his readers in this review of 12 March that the audience had the second movement encored and attempted the same for the third. Also on 12 March Haydn was compared to Shakespeare in the *Morning Chronicle*. This writer held up the first movement as the highlight of No. 92:

His *new Grand Overture* was pronounced by every scientific ear to be a most wonderful composition; but the first movement in particular rises in grandeur of subject, and in the rich variety of *air* and passion, beyond any even of his own productions. The *Overture* has four movements—An Allegro—Andante—Minuet—and Rondo—They are all beautiful, but the first is pre-eminent in every charm. (iii. 49–50)

All subsequent writers, including Tovey, Rosen, and Landon, have recognized this symphony as one of Haydn's great achievements. In the first movement a sense of polarity is very clearly drawn, it is worked through in a comprehensible way, and there is an arrival at a definite conclusion. The counterpoint used in this process has more in common with that of the ensemble of comic opera than the stricter procedures of the first half of the eighteenth century.

The slow introduction of No. 92 is more closely related to those of English Symphonies than most earlier works in that it begins with material which has stable harmony and phrasing, and then moves to something which breaks down the stability. In this case the two clearly defined opening four-bar phrases are followed by fragmentation, and the tonic–dominant harmony of the opening gives way in the final eight bars to an emphasis of the augmented sixth chord. Like Nos. 90 and 91, there are thematic connections between the introduction and the material immediately ensuing, in this case a sustained tone followed by a descending passage.

The opening 'allegro spiritoso' thematic material contains both ambiguity and stability as it has an off-tonic beginning which moves to the tonic after four bars. The opening four bars are on the dominant, creating another link with the introduction which had prepared them with the augmented sixth chord. The polarity set up early in this work involves the two distinctly different facets of the opening thematic material. The unstable part is emphasized by its connection with the introduction. The contrasting parts of the first theme are linked together as well as delineated by similar sixteenth-note passages, ascending in one and descending in the next (Ex. 24). With the arrival of the new key, the unstable aspect of this theme is emphasized. It now begins on the dominant of D, but instead of following this with the original thematic material which gave stability, Haydn launches into a brief excursion in D minor, using material which belongs to the unstable part of the theme. Stability now comes with the dance-like closing theme which in fact is related to the earlier stable material. A strong feature of the closing theme is the use of a turn, a figure which is associated with the stable part of the early exposition (bar 35).

In the late symphonies one expects the three main sections of the first movement to be fairly equal in length. Here the exposition is eighty-two bars, the development a mere forty-three, and the recapitulation 107, placing the middle of the movement near the end of the development. This short development presents the important thematic and motivic material in a new arrangement, either individually or contrapuntally, such as the combination of the beginning of the first theme and the turn at bars 95–100 (Ex. 25). In this contrapuntal passage, the two contrasting elements are brought into direct interaction with each other. The counterpoint also generates some tonal ambiguity, finally settling on E minor at bar 110. The passage which follows is very similar to the disruptive D minor passage of the exposition, which now facilitates the arrival of the recapitulation by moving chromatically to the dominant of the dominant.

After this very short development section, the process of development is continued in the lengthy recapitulation. But before that happens, the

Ex. 24

Ex. 25

opening of the recapitulation repeats the beginning of the exposition almost without deviation for twenty bars, providing the formal function of return. The cue for something new to happen is the E flat in the bass at bar 145, and the new developmental treatment begins at bar 149, using the leap of a tenth which originated in the fourth bar of the theme. In the bass, one finds a chromatic descent answered by a diatonic ascent. In this new development there is a contrapuntal setting of the closing theme (bars 159–65) and a reinterpretation of the opening theme beginning at bar 175, now set against syncopation in the first violin. After the rest at bar 204, the coda begins with a restatement of the first four bars of the main theme and adds three more bars based on the large leap, a reference to the developmental treatment of this material in the recapitulation, but now in a context of complete tonal stability. Cadentially these bars lead to the tonic, so the listener is surprised by the arrival of the flattened submediant at bar 212 with the return of the passage which had been a disruptive factor in the exposition (in D minor). The passage is now longer than it had been in either the exposition or development, and is less stable as the chromatic progression is extended. The strong cadential preparation for the tonic at the end of this passage (bars 218–19) in fact fails to lead to the tonic chord. What follows is the original theme which in its earlier setting had started on C and had an off-tonic opening (see Ex. 24). At bar 220 the theme begins on G, the tonic, but it is now even further removed from the home key since its harmonic support is a diminished triad which must resolve to the dominant. With the final appearance of the closing theme at bar 225, the two polar forces of the movement are heard, as in No. 83, simply standing side by side. The conclusion does not provide a resolution but instead presents a coexistence; like No. 83, there is a message here concerning tolerance.

Nos. 96 and 95

Considering the enormous success of No. 92, it appears that there was no particular need to depart from writing that type of work. With the first two symphonies written specifically for London, Nos. 96 and 95, however, Haydn completely abandoned the direction he had taken in the first movement of No. 92 as well as other recent symphonies. The challenging aspect, so conspicuous in the symphonies of the late eighties, is now almost entirely absent. Conversely, his desire to achieve popular appeal seems to be intensified in these two works, as he turned to procedures which had ensured the popularity of certain earlier works. One can only speculate on Haydn's reasons for returning to these types of works. He may, indeed, have done precisely as Mrs Papendiek suggested he had in the first season, which is to observe the audience and write in such a way as to guarantee approval. It is also possible that he felt at this stage the significance of a work such as No. 92 was lost on the new audience, and that he would have to lead gradually to the type of complexity contained in this work.

The pattern here bears some resemblance to that of the Paris Symphonies, since as a pair Nos. 96 and 95 are not unlike Nos. 87 and 83, the presumed first works of that set. Nos. 96 and 87 in particular have features in common, despite the lack of a slow introduction in No. 87. The nature of the thematic writing and its expansion is similar, and neither work sets up polarities which engage in an inexorable drive towards a conclusion. Although these two focus on popular features, that is not to say there is no challenge to the listener. The challenge, however, is of a different nature, as it lies in the task of following the motivic working. Unlike Nos. 96 and 87, Nos. 95 and 83 have little more than the obvious in common, which is that No. 95 is the first symphony in a minor key since No. 83. The elaborate process which gives rise to intelligibility in No. 83 simply does not happen in No. 95. No. 95 has more in common with the pre-Paris symphonies Nos. 78 (also in C minor) and 80.

That ambiguity will not be a serious factor in No. 96 is first of all evident in the introduction. The opening is about as stable as music can be, defining a strong tonic chord. And as this relatively short introduction proceeds, it does not lead into instability. Instead, it simply states the opening passage in the tonic minor and settles quickly on the dominant which prepares the first 'allegro' theme. Also contrasting with recent works is the fact that there is no thematic connection between introduction and 'allegro' other than a rhythmic similarity between the end of the introduction and the beginning of the new theme. There is, however, a thematic connection between the introduction and Finale. In the exposition of the first movement, Haydn moves to the dominant with a fairly straightforward modulation. One of the few surprises in the transition is a C major cadence (the modulation is from D to A), and Haydn exploits this in the development by allowing C and G to be two of the strong tonal areas. In fact, after silence for almost three bars there is a false recapitulation on G. In keeping with the rest of the movement, the recapitation is predominantly stable. The only surprise here occurs near the end when the expectation of a strong tonic is diverted by a flattened submediant, which, however, is harmlessly turned into an augmented sixth that resolves conventionally to the dominant.

As for No. 95, the first two bars can be compared with No. 83 in that there is a melodic tritone emphasized by its appearance on the strong beats. And further, this is followed by a passage which outlines the tonic chord, thereby establishing an early polarity. Throughout the movement, however, including the development, these passages do not interact with each other and do not appear to have any influence on each other. The lack of a dramatic process here seems to suggest that the individual expansions of these passages are done more for affective purposes. In the end there is no conclusion drawn since there has been no issue requiring summation.

Concerning reception, less is known about Nos. 96 and 95 than any of the other English Symphonies. Since it has not been possible to specify their performance dates, it is also not possible to gauge audience or critical reaction. Landon has surmised that as piano trio arrangements they did not sell particularly well and that they therefore did not especially appeal to the English public (iii. 515–6). This may very well be the case since both types were not used again by Haydn. If Landon is correct, then it appears that Haydn's bid to appeal to his audience through the popular means of previous works was a miscalculation. In the following season this issue is remedied, although Haydn appears to have been convinced that his basic premise of first gaining approbation was correct, since his first symphony of 1792 sets out to do precisely that.

No. 93

The first concert of the second season took place on 17 February, and appears to have been greeted with even more enthusiasm than the first concert of 1791. Haydn's New Grand Overture on this concert was No. 93, and Haydn himself identified it as being in the key of D (iii. 133). With both the audience and the critics this work was an overwhelming success. The next day in the *Morning Herald* it was judged to be 'a composition of very extraordinary merit', and in the *Diary; or Woodfall's Register* it was said to exhibit 'all the fire of his bold imagination, and which in the opinion of every musical critic, was a composition at once grand, scientific, charming and original' (iii. 134–5). Even in *The Times*, which was not in the habit of reviewing musical performances, it was described in the following way: 'Such a combination of excellence was contained in every movement, as inspired all the performers as well as the audience with enthusiastic ardour. Novelty of idea, agreeable caprice, and whim combined with all *Haydn's* sublime and wonten grandeur, gave additional consequence to the *soul* and feelings of every individual present' (iii. 134). Haydn himself confirms this response of the audience, noting that the second movement was encored and that the Finale had a profound effect on the listeners. After the second performance of this work on 24 February, the writer for the *Oracle* went so far as to say that 'for the most powerful effects of the Science, no one of his compositions can compare with it' (iii. 137).

This work appealed to the audience in diverse ways, including through sublime effects as well as whim. Most critics and the audience at large had no difficulty with these features appearing in the same work. Unlike most of the other English Symphonies in which one can examine the dramatic process in first movements in isolation, No. 93 cannot be considered without taking the other movements into account. Compared with later symphonies, the first movement of this work is not especially complex or challenging to the listener. As in No. 96, however, the treatment of motivic material is of considerable interest, particularly in the relationship of the development to the exposition. The unusual feature of this work is that the motivic working of the first movement goes beyond that movement, setting up unmistakable links with later movements. Furthermore, while the first movement is relatively stable and undramatic, the third and fourth movements are unusually active and dramatic.

The Finale presents a particularly interesting problem, since this is the one which Haydn told Maria Anna von Genzinger was too weak in comparison with the first movement, as both he and the audience had recognized, and was therefore in need of alteration (iii. 140). Since the first movement is not powerful by any stretch of the imagination, and the Finale as we know it is one of the most intricate and potent of all Haydn's finales, it seems that he did indeed alter it. There is no other extant version of this Finale, and one can only speculate on how he may have altered it if he in fact did. The format of the opening of the Finale is that of a rondo or sonata-rondo with the double bars and repeats. But as the movement proceeds it decidedly settles into sonata form, suggesting that he may have made this conversion without discarding the opening. The new theme in the dominant at bar 118 is also significant in that its melodic and accompanimental similarities with the second theme of the first movement are unmistakable. It appears that the alteration of the Finale may have included both strengthening and the increasing of thematic associations with other parts of the work, changes which Haydn was prepared to make at least in part in response to reception. However, a shift in balance in favour of a stronger finale did not become the trend of subsequent symphonies.

In the slow introduction of No. 93, Haydn returned to the model of No. 92, although there is no overt connection between 'adagio' and 'allegro assai' thematic material. Just as the second part of the introduction in No. 92 is an extended augmented sixth chord, similarly in No. 93 he uses a Neapolitan sixth chord which resolves to the dominant in ample time to prepare the highly stable first theme. The type of theme used here is new for Haydn: not only is its harmony and phrasing completely stable but the melodic beauty is accentuated by its clearly defined arch shape. This clarity is matched by the second theme which now has a strongly defined dance character, as was noted in Ex. 20*b* of the previous chapter. The thematic stability of this exposition is scarcely challenged by any disruptive material, suggesting that the themes should simply be enjoyed for their beauty and charm. The only disruption (if one can call it that) which does occur in the exposition is of a metric nature, involving off-beat emphasis both before and after the second theme. Curiously this metric 'problem' is entirely avoided in the motivic working of the development. Finally in the recapitulation this matter does receive some new consideration, as the off-beat emphasis is extended to draw attention to the motivic material which will be a factor in linking the various movements (Ex. 26).

Since the second movement was encored, it appears that the English shared Haydn's sense of humour. It is near the end of this movement that the great bassoon joke occurs. In the third movement the link with the first movement is made in different ways, the strongest being the return of the rhythmic motive in which two eighth-notes fall on the last beat of the bar. Haydn adds a new twist in the Minuet, placing the eighth-note pair on the middle beat as well, thereby generating a type of

Ex. 26

metric displacement. At the beginning of the B section the metric issue is intensified as dynamic accents are placed on the weak beats. In the trio, harmony also becomes a factor since there is a progression to the relative minor and limited chromaticism. In this work there is a balance between popularity and challenge, but it is unlike most other Haydn symphonies in that the dual function is carried by separate movements. The first movement with its melodic charm and the second with its humour seem designed to win audience approval. The third and fourth movements, which are normally lighter movements for Haydn, in this case are the ones which place the greater demands on the listener.

No. 98

Because of the catalogue placement of No. 98, it can be assumed that it was written after No. 94, although Haydn elected to present it to the audience before No. 94. In his second London notebook, Haydn writes that the new symphony in B flat was given in the third concert (2 March 1792) and that the first and last movements were encored (iii. 139). While this was regarded as one of the grandest compositions ever heard, it was given less space in reviews than the Concertante with which it was performed on 9 March. The reason for this would appear to have less to do with quality than the fact that the Concertante offered more opportunity for the discussion of solo performance. Comparing the first movements of Nos. 98 and 94, No. 94 is the more complex and therefore appropriately follows No. 98. However, No. 98 is not without complexity, as there is a process leading to a conclusion which requires reflective listening in order to be followed.

If there had been any question in previous works about a connection between the slow introduction and first 'allegro' theme, there is none whatever in this work. Furthermore, the idea of combining thematic similarity with affective distinctiveness is taken to an extreme here as the 'adagio' introduction opens in B flat minor while the first 'allegro' theme is in B flat major. The subsequent harmonic direction of this introduction, which Tovey describes as being 'severely solemn and dark' (Tovey also uses the words 'sceptred pall'), is also of interest and has implications for other parts of the movement. After B flat minor there are shifts to G flat minor and D flat major before ending on the dominant. Having established this context for the hearing of the opening 'allegro' theme, one would expect that theme to be the basis for any dramatic interaction in this movement, and that indeed is the case. As the theme is presented at the beginning of the allegro section it has by no means ceased to be problematic as there is some metric ambiguity after the first few bars (Ex. 27). This sense of division or complexity in the theme is emphasized in the development as the separate components of the theme interact in a lively contrapuntal presentation (Ex. 28). Late in the recapitulation this issue is addressed again as the theme is presented once with metric ambiguity intensified (Ex. 29*a*), and later in a way which could not be more stable (Ex. 29*b*). Following the pattern of earlier complex works the forces of opposition are presented here side by side at the end. In fact, even in the concluding material, emphasis on the off-beat has not been eliminated.

The audience also demanded an encore of the Finale, and it too is in sonata form. However, the attraction of this movement was not its drama. Instead, it contains a solo violin part which allowed Salomon to display his tone, and even has a short solo keyboard passage near the end which Haydn himself performed.

No. 94

The second movement of No. 94 was the most discussed of all Haydn's symphonic movements for the obvious reason that reviewers could enjoy the effects of his sense of humour on drowsy listeners. The first movement of this work, however, presents a new level of complexity which challenges the listeners to a much greater extent than anything performed earlier. While it appears this work was written in 1791, Haydn appropriately delayed its performance until the audience had had the opportunity to be exposed to these types of procedures in less demanding contexts. In the *Diary; or Woodfall's Register* it was described

Ex. 27

Ex. 28

Ex. 29

a.

b.

on 24 March, the day after its first performance, as a work of 'very extraordinary merit', and was also said to be 'simple, profound and sublime' (iii. 149). When using the word simple, one assumes that the writer was not describing the first movement, unless in the context of the description in the *Morning Herald*: 'His novelty of last night was a grand Overture, the subject of which was remarkably simple, but extended to vast complication, exquisit[e]ly modulated, and striking in effect. Critical applause was fervid and abundant' (iii. 149). The description of the applause as 'critical' is not unlike Shaftesbury's dictum concerning the ancients, who 'refined the public ear and framed it right, that in return they might be rightly and lastingly applauded'. A review in the same publication of the same work performed on 13 April emphasizes this even further in describing it as a work with great 'taste'. At least one writer appeared to sense that there was something special about this work as Haydn was now going further in forming his audience and refining the public ear. In so doing, Haydn took a new step here in achieving moral objectives.

The opening figure of the slow introduction is the closest of any works to this date to the figure of a rising fourth and descending tetrachord identified in the previous chapter, and the forzato at bar 5 seems designed to heighten awareness of the interval of a fourth. Continuing with the general procedure established in No. 92, Haydn divides the introduction into two parts, the first being two four-bar phrases, and the second departing from periodicity, tonal stability, and thematicism. The division is brought about by the iterated G (beginning at bar 8) with its potential for ambiguity (Ex. 30), a potential which is subsequently achieved to some extent as the iteration becomes a chromatic upward movement. Thematic material does not entirely disappear in the second part, as an inverted version can now be found in the lower strings.

There are a number of connections between the introduction and the 'vivace assai', and the first of these is the similarity of thematic material. The 'vivace assai' opens with an off-tonic theme, an element of ambiguity which is magnified as a result of the thematic association with the introduction. Another connection can be found between the introduction and certain transitional points in the exposition, all being the iteration of a single note with a linking function based on the repeated G in the introduction. One of these occurs just before the main theme reappears in what should be the new key (Ex. 31a) and another is the final three bars of the exposition (Ex. 31b). These are the major formal divisions in the early part of the work, and in both cases, as with the similar point in the introduction, the movement is from relative stability to instability. The thematic return at bar 54 does not coincide with the arrival of the dominant (because of the off-tonic opening of the theme), even though the dominant has been thoroughly prepared. And, at the end of the exposition, the iterated B leaves a relatively stable dominant to go either to the beginning of the exposition or into the development, both of which are in different keys and are something less than stable.

Another parallel which can be drawn between this work and No. 92 is the way that the dominant arrives in each. Both works have an off-tonic main theme which returns at the point that the dominant is expected, and in both cases, this fails to lead to a firm dominant but instead moves to the dominant minor. The minor material in No. 92, as we have seen, has a disruptive impact with an important bearing on the movement, and the minor passage in No. 94 (bars 62 ff.) also recurs at important places.

The iterated note is again a factor in the development, and, beginning at bar 131, the procedure bears a strong resemblance to that of the introduction. Just as the iteration in the introduction had led into a chromatic passage, so also here, the repeated A finally leads chromatically to E sharp (Ex. 32). The diminished seventh chord at bar 140 leads to F sharp, the dominant of B, which was, of course, the important

Ex. 30

Ex. 31

a.

b.

Ex. 32

iterated note in the exposition. In the development, B makes a prominent arrival at bar 148, now iterated in the first violin for seven bars before leading back to the first theme and the beginning of the recapitulation.

Further similarities can be found with No. 92 in the recapitulation, as a large portion of the opening of the exposition (nineteen bars) is now given verbatim. The departure from this to new material is significant as a passage is used which ties together a number of important points in the movement. At bar 176, the iterated G in the winds, which stands against the rising passage in the strings (Ex. 33), is not unlike bar 9 of the introduction (see iii. 528). This passage also bears resemblance to various other points in the exposition and development, all of which are transitional and unstable. The remainder of the recapitulation is relatively stable, and as a result this brief passage, in being a focus of the unstable points of the movement, is given a heightened dramatic importance. Again there is a coexistence, now offered to the listener as early as the introduction.

No. 97

On 3 May 1792 a benefit concert for Haydn was held at the Hanover Square Rooms, and Landon speculates that Haydn would have saved his new symphony in C for this occasion (iii. 161). The second season of Salomon Concerts would last scarcely another two weeks, and Haydn intended to return to his patron as soon as possible, not at all certain whether or not he would return to England. No. 97, being the last symphony of the season (it was performed at the Salomon Concerts on 4 May) and possibly the final symphony of Haydn's tenure in London, had to be special. Haydn chose to write a work in C major, a festive key, which could serve as a celebration and provide a fitting tone for his departure from England. However, while he undoubtedly wished to be remembered fondly, he was not about to put forward an empty-headed work simply intended to secure endearment. In the first movement of this work he introduced some of the boldest procedures yet, particularly concerning the connection between the introduction and other parts of the movement. Perhaps most notable here is the directness of the application, giving his treatment a new level of accessibility. Thus, he is taking his listener by the hand, leading him simply and eloquently to a point of discovery.

Ex. 33

As it stands, the introduction to No. 97 is fairly unassuming: it is unusually short and does little more than give a cadential formula, thus providing an apparently ideal introduction for a festive work. As the 'vivace' section begins, one encounters nothing to suggest anything other than a celebration as the key of C major gets the strongest possible emphasis with the arpeggiation of the theme. In the transition, however, things become less straightforward. In fact it is not entirely clear where the second group begins. The dance-like material which begins at bar 54 has received dominant preparation, but we are not given any sort of cadential arrival in the new key for another six bars. With the arrival of G major, there is no stability as Haydn immediately launches into a chromatic passage which moves to the Neapolitan of G (see also Landon's analysis, iii. 543). The new theme at bar 76 brings firm stability.

The exposition ends, much to the listener's surprise, with a restatement of the material from the introduction followed by a highly stable concluding passage (Ex. 34). While the introduction had not been especially problematic, its placement in this context, with a cheerful dance-like passage, forces one to hear it in a different way. It now appears to exist in a potentially dramatic context which is all the more striking since it does not appear until the end of the exposition. The listener is placed on alert and, of course, attention is later rewarded.

In the short development section, Haydn initially returns to the festive quality, setting out with the opening 'vivace' material in E flat. The recapitulation also remains very stable aside from a digression to the flattened submediant. It is, however, worth noting that the dance-like passage, which in the exposition provides a tonally ambivalent beginning to the second group, is now absent. The listener's reward for noticing the material of the introduction in the codetta of the exposition now comes in the coda beginning at bar 240. Here Haydn reintroduces the material of the introduction and extends it through various tonal digressions to the extraordinary length of twenty-eight bars. The procedure was unprecedented, and at this point Haydn exerts an unusually direct influence on the listener's sense of expectation. The

Ex. 34

listener is not likely to miss what follows, and what does follow is a return of the dance-like theme which had been omitted earlier in the recapitulation, now in the dark key of D minor (Ex. 35). As it continues, it moves back towards the tonic, thereby allowing this passage (which was unsettled even in the exposition) to be a fusion of opposing affective states. This fusion at the end of the movement makes No. 97 much more than simply a celebration. The dramatic issue which is presented in the clearest possible way demands response in both musical and moral terms.

THIRD SEASON: 1794

No. 99

Haydn appears to have had little difficulty in persuading Prince Anton Eszterházy to allow him to make a second visit to England, and early in 1794, after an absence of a year and a half, he arrived in London ready for a new season of Salomon's concerts. The first concert took place on 10 February, and for this reintroduction to the London audience he presented a new symphony, No. 99 in E flat, which he had composed in advance. Haydn evidently felt that after a hiatus of a year and a half there was no need to re-establish his popular appeal with this audience, since with the first movement of No. 99 he offered something much more complex than his listeners had encountered previously. Even in the symphonies which followed (No. 102 being the exception), he tended not to place such extraordinary demands on the listener's capacity for reflective listening. Unlike No. 97, where the listener is very much guided through the process, No. 99 requires the audience to pick out some very subtle points to be able to follow the process. Haydn had had ample opportunity to observe his audience by this point, and he appears to have calculated correctly since the first movement, according the *Morning Chronicle*, was the one movement which was encored at the second performance on 17 February.

While away from England Haydn no doubt was able to reflect on the impact he was having on this audience. Concerning approbation there

Ex. 35

was no question of success. During his first sojourn he had established this to an extraordinary degree, so much so that the rival Professional Concerts using his pupil Pleyel had collapsed for lack of support. He had also gradually introduced more thought-provoking features during the 1792 season, but these had always been balanced by popular appeal. While away, he appears to have considered that since his rapport with the audience no longer needed to be nurtured, he could now strive without restraint to achieve his higher objective in symphonic writing which would allow these works to 'be of use to the world'. As a result of his friendship with a moralist such as Burney, with whom he could share ideas on Metastasio, his resolve in this regard may very well have been strengthened. Haydn, now returning to England with portraits of Metastasio for Burney, may have decided that this was the time to make his own most convincing moral statement to the English audience. The response in London to this symphony was overwhelming. In the *Morning Chronicle* after the first concert one could read that 'the incomparable HAYDN, produced an Overture of which it is impossible to speak in common terms. It is one of the grandest efforts of art that we ever witnessed. It abounds with ideas, as new in music as they are grand and impressive; it rouses and affects every emotion of the soul.—It was received with rapturous applause' (iii. 234). And, in the *Sun*, it was described as 'a composition of the most exquisite kind, rich, fanciful, bold, and impressive' (iii. 235).

The bold new steps taken by Haydn in this symphony are immediately apparent in the slow introduction. While the opening of this introduction, with periodic phrases and diatonic harmony, is conventional, that which follows is not. The new treatment beginning at bar 8 is emphasized by a striking dynamic contrast (*p* to *ff*). Starting at this point (Ex. 36), there are two types of chromatic movement, a short melodic one (B flat–A–A flat), and a more extended one in the bass which has implications for the tonal structure (B flat–C flat (B)–C). The C at bar 13 leads to G which curiously is the tonal arrival for the end of the introduction. Since this is not the dominant, Haydn inserts an unexpected dominant seventh chord at the end, giving the arrival of the tonic at the beginning of the 'vivace assai' an almost solecistic quality.

In Nos. 94 and 97 it became apparent that the connection between the introduction and 'allegro' was no longer a simple thematic one but was a sophisticated part of the drama, as the sense of ambiguity in the introduction was carried by means of subtle or overt links to various parts of the 'allegro'. In the early stages of the exposition of No. 99, one finds a very subtle achievement of that type of dramatic function. After the division of the introduction into highly stable and unstable parts, a similar division occurs between the theme and the transitional material of the exposition, and the ambiguity of the transition is directly related

Ex. 36

to that of the introduction. The first theme of the vivace assai is a simple theme with a dance character and periodic phrasing, with two primary eight-bar phrases which are virtually identical. In the sixteenth bar (bar 34), the thematic material comes to an end and the gesture of the dance is disrupted by a forzato which places the accent on the second beat of the bar. Unlike some works in which the transitional material is derived motivically from the first theme, the material beginning at bar 34 stands very much in contrast, the only association being an accompanimental one. The forzati, as disruptions, draw attention to themselves as they continue over the next few bars, and the most alert listener may notice that they are significant in another way. The tonal ambiguity of the introduction results from the chromatic movement B flat–C flat–C, leading to the non-dominant G, and it is precisely those notes, emphasized by forzati, which are prominently displayed in bars 34–7 at this early point of the transition (Ex. 37). While G in the introduction had proved to be a dead end, in the transition it is the beginning of a motion in fifths (G–C–F) leading to the dominant key, B flat.

Ex. 37

It has been noted that in those works which reintroduce the first theme in the dominant, one can normally expect some discontinuity of the theme as well as further procrastination about the firm arrival of the dominant key, and No. 99 is no exception to this expectation. The return to the original theme at bar 48 is short-lived, as changes occur after only two bars through a continued descending motion. The real disruption, however, comes after four bars, as new ascending eighth-note passages are flanked by syncopation and suspension. Before the return to stability, a passage begins at bar 64 which links the off-beat forzati of the transition with the turn of the first theme, fusing the polarities into a single unit (Ex. 38). When the closing theme arrives at bar 71, it brings the stability which had been lacking earlier, although before the exposition ends there are further examples of metric displacement.

The development follows a procedure very similar to that of No. 83 as it opens with a fragment of the first theme, moves directly to a modulatory expansion of the closing theme, and then embarks on an extended passage of complex and highly dramatic counterpoint. Also as in No. 83, the beginning of the significant counterpoint, in this case at bar 104, is marked by a strong dynamic contrast (p to f). The counterpoint continues for seventeen bars (104–20), and involves virtually every fragment of thematic, motivic, or transitional material from the exposition (Ex. 39). A further similarity with No. 83 is in the placement of previously stable material in an unstable context. Here it is the turn from the opening theme which appears in the context of forzato off-beats (Ex. 38) instead of the way it appears in the first theme. Following the counterpoint, the remaining seventeen bars of the development are calm, reinterpreting the motivic unit of the closing theme and enacting the retransition.

The recapitulation is much abbreviated: the theme is stated only once, transitional material is removed, and the presentation of the first theme (along with the new ambiguity near the beginning of the of the second group) is also absent. In fact, Haydn arrives at the closing theme after only twenty bars, in contrast to the exposition where it takes fifty-three bars. Of the prior disruptive material, the passage which had a chromatic similarity to the introduction is given in a slightly altered form (its arrival is now on D flat instead of G), but the passage in the second group which combined the forzato off-beats and the turn (Ex. 38) is now missing. Following the first statement of the closing theme, there is a lengthy extension of this material, taking into account the transformations which it has undergone in the development. In this extended treatment Haydn again builds up the listener's expectation, and the point of discovery comes at bar 191 with the return of the original theme. This theme, however, is no longer in its original form, but now has been adjusted to take into account the unfolding of the

Ex. 38

entire movement. In fact, this adjustment yields a new fusion of the polarities, as the fourth beat of the first bar does not go back to the tonic but instead continues a chromatic descent from E flat to C (Ex. 40).

Here, then, the chromaticism introduced in the slow introduction and the stability of the opening 'vivace assai' theme are united, confirming the dramatic principle that musical entities or themes, like the characters of a play, cannot be the same at the end as they were at the beginning. They encounter conflict and the forces of the conflict become a part of them. In this work, however, Haydn presents a dramatic unfolding which is by no means easy to follow. On the one hand the intricate process far exceeds anything previously offered, but on the other hand he could not realistically hope that many listeners would be able to hear these complexities. Possibly realizing that this type of enlightened process would reach only the select few, he was prepared in most subsequent symphonies to give the listener stronger directions leading to a point of understanding.

No. 101

With the complexity of his first symphony of the 1794 season, Haydn in effect served notice to his listeners that they must be ready for anything. No. 101, first performed on 3 March, proved to be an equally challenging work, but in a most unexpected way. Each new symphony invited greater superlatives from the reviewers, and No. 101 was no exception. In the *Morning Chronicle* on 5 March we find more than the usual one or two sentences:

But as usual the most delicious part of the entertainment was a new grand Overture by HAYDN; the inexhaustible, the wonderful, the sublime HAYDN! The first two movements were encored; and the character that pervaded the whole composition was heartfelt joy. Every new Overture he writes, we fear, till it is heard, he can only repeat himself; and we are every time mistaken. Nothing can be more original than the subject of the first movement; and having found a happy subject, no man knows like HAYDN how to produce incessant variety, without once departing from it. (iii. 241)

This writer proceeds to mention the second and third movements but completely neglects the finale, a rather serious blunder which suggests he was unable to follow Haydn's striking new process in this work.

The few simply chosen words in the *Oracle* on 10 March seem to come

Ex. 39

Ex. 40

closer to understanding the essence of the work: 'HAYDN, like VIRGIL's fame, *vires acquirit eundo*, has latterly written a symphony, which the connoisseurs admit to be his best work.' Reference to Virgil may strike one as not particularly in place, unless one reflects on Shaftesbury's view concerning the nature of the relationship between the classical writers and their audiences. The possible reference to the artist who shapes and forms his audience is reinforced by George Dance, for whom Haydn sat for a portrait on 20 March 1794. Dance was deeply impressed by Haydn and wrote that the 'beneficial influence [of Salomon's Concerts] upon the taste and judgement of the rising generation cannot be doubted.'[6]

The slow introduction to No. 101 was Haydn's longest yet, by a significant margin compared with most early symphonies. In fact, it is made to seem even longer than it is, in that it does not begin in the usual stable and periodic manner. Like No. 98, this introduction begins in the tonic minor (Ex. 41), and the opening is distinguished by a rising scale passage and a three-note motive in the first violin (balanced by contrary motion in the bass part). As the introduction proceeds it becomes progressively more chromatic, and ambiguity is compounded by the use of forzati on weak beats. Given the unusual character of this introduction, including its length, mode, and intensity, the listener, on the basis of previous experience, would be entirely justified in expecting that such an introduction would have a profound bearing on the subsequent unfolding of the first movement. Indeed there is a thematic link as the 'presto' begins with a rising scale passage, now of course in the major, followed by a descending third. However, following this direct connection, one does not find the strong links so apparent in some other works. Possible exceptions include the motivic figure which is so ubiquitous in the development (three eighth-notes involving a rising third and falling second), and the parallel between the chromatic passages at bars 8–10 and 110–13. In fact, the most notable thing about this movement is its cheerfulness and stability, and the absence of a complex or dramatic process. This is not to say that it is conventional. The recapitulation is given very considerable interest when the motivic counterpoint of the development reappears at bar 250 and lasts for sixteen bars. However, in dramatic terms it does not seem especially problematic, and the movement ends with a restatement of the first theme and no apparent accounting for what was a problematic introduction. It appears, in fact,

[6] *A Collection of Portraits Sketched from the Life*, ii (London, 1814), n.p.

Ex. 41

that Haydn decided to present a popular first movement not unlike those of 1791.

By this point Haydn had done some fairly extraordinary things with introductions, connecting them with transitions, codettas, or codas. In No. 101 he went a major step beyond these previous realizations, not disappointing those listeners who were left hanging by the relatively sparse use of the introduction in the first movement. In this case, the association is taken beyond the first movement, to the Minuet, and in a most extraordinary way to the Finale. Landon rightly observes that this is the most powerful of the English Finales, and it is one of the few times that Haydn shifts the balance of power to the end of the work. Only in No. 93, where Haydn described the need for a stronger Finale, does one see a parallel to this. Formally these two Finales are also similar as this one is a type of hybrid sonata-rondo.

The connection between the Finale and the introduction is immediately apparent in that the theme of the Finale is based on a rising scale passage, now starting on the mediant (Ex. 42). And further, the motivic extension of the theme at bar 9 uses a three-note figure which is a rising second and falling third (Ex. 43), identical to the first violin part in the first four bars of the introduction (see Ex. 41). The opening of the Minuet stands as a link between the introduction and Finale: the three-note motive is now inverted as a falling second and rising third, and the rhythm of bar 2 of the Finale is similar to the second bar of the Minuet (half-note followed by four sixteenths). In fact, since there is a strong possibility that the Minuet was composed first (see iii. 492), the linking function may very well have been a point of origin. In the episode which follows in the Finale, there is a modulation to the dominant, giving a strong sense of sonata form. The thematic material in the dominant is derived from the first theme, but as it now unfolds it begins to take into account the metric disruption which had been a factor in the introduction (Ex. 44). The next episode stands as a type of development section, and, since it is in the key of D minor, evokes a particularly strong connection with the introduction. In this extended minor section (bars 138–88) the ambiguous aspects of the introduction are given full

Ex. 42

Ex. 43

Ex. 44

realization, as the tonal progression is often chromatic and there is much metric displacement.

What follows at bar 189 is a recapitulation in the truest sense since the tonic is not immediately restabilized, and the theme itself begins to digress after fewer than three bars. In fact, it takes forty-four bars before the tonic is stabilized. Even at this point the theme remains in an altered form, and there is still more chromatic motion. The final statement of the theme in its original condition at bar 250 appears to be the fulfilling of the formal function of the rondo, and does not alter the fact that transformation has taken place. Haydn's discovery in this work concerning the interrelationship of movements and the strength of the finale in relation to the first movement (procedures which became so fundamental to Beethoven's language) did not become the basis for his own future endeavours. What happens here appears to be the natural outgrowth of the ways in which he had previously applied slow introductions. The particular treatment in this case confirms in a new and special way the critical dramatic importance of the introduction, now for the entire work rather than simply the first movement.

It was probably this work which inspired the London correspondent for the *Journal des Luxus und der Moden* to write the following: 'But what would you now say to his new symphonies composed expressly for these concerts, and directed by himself at the piano? It is truly wonderful what sublime and august thoughts this master weaves into his works.

Passages often occur which render it impossible to listen to them without becoming excited' (iii. 245–6).

No. 100

After presenting the audience with two extraordinarily challenging symphonies at the beginning of 1794, Haydn decided to end the season with a highly accessible and popular work. This appeal of No. 100 was recognized by the writer for the *Allgemeine Musikalische Zeitung*: 'It is somewhat less learned, and easier to take in, than some of the other newest works by him, but it is just as rich in new ideas' (iii. 566). The success of this work was staggering, and it was not only the second movement, giving this work the epithet 'Military' because of its use of 'Turkish' instruments, which the audience adored. Its Finale was also enormously popular, the theme becoming a favourite for the makers of musical clocks.

The only feature of this work which did not gain universal approval was Haydn's choice to reintroduce the percussion instruments of the second movement into the end of the finale. The review in the *Morning Chronicle* on 5 May found this to be objectionable since it was, in the writer's opinion, a frivolous use of 'discordant, grating, and offensive' sounds. His objection was not to discord itself but to its application. In the second movement, he was very ready to accept these instruments, since here he believed they serve a programmatic function: 'they inform us that the army is marching to battle, and, calling up all the ideas of the terror of such a scene, give it reality. Discordant sounds are then sublime; for what can be more horribly discordant to the heart than thousands of men meeting to murder each other' (iii. 250–1). Once again we have strong approval for the use of dissonance in a dramatic context by a contemporary of Haydn.

In all the clamour about the second movement, the first movement tended to be ignored, but one can only imagine that it did not hurt the enthusiasm for this work in the least. This movement has contrast and surprises, but at the same time it is entirely accessible, achieving its effects through highly audible devices. At the same time, the folk character of the themes makes them attractive, as had been the case in No. 93. The slow introduction returns to the well-established format of beginning with clarity and moving in the latter half towards something more ambiguous, which in this case borders on the ominous. It is the timpani roll at bars 14–15 which underlines the darker character of the motion through minor chords to the augmented sixth. The introduction and first 'allegro' theme are connected by the interval of a fourth, the figure which places this introduction in the category of those discussed in the previous chapter.

The dance-like 'allegro' theme is one of Haydn's most stable of this type, moving to the dominant at the end of eight bars and returning to the tonic after sixteen. This is followed by an eleven-bar passage which is riveted to the tonic. After the modulatory transition and a long and thorough preparation of the dominant, the first allegro theme returns in the dominant, and, as the listener expects, this does not provide a stable arrival of the new key. Disrupting a theme as stable as this will be particularly noticeable, and here the disruption begins after only five bars of restatement. The material which breaks down the even flow of the theme is, in fact, related to the modulatory transitional material. The instability is now continued as there is a tonal digression to D minor before the firm arrival of the dominant. Again it is not the opening theme which provides stability in the second group but a closing theme which is rhythmically related to the end of the first theme.

The development tends to concentrate on closing theme material, and its modulatory character now places it in an unstable context. Indeed, Landon goes so far as to say that there is an ominous sense here as Haydn reintroduces the timpani roll on two occasions in the development, suggesting its use in the introduction (iii. 561). Metric displacement also becomes a factor in the development, in an extended passage in which closing theme material, with a dance rhythm, is set against syncopation and off-beat forzati (Ex. 45).

Ex. 45

At the beginning of the very short recapitulation, the first eight bars of the first theme appear as they had at the beginning of the exposition. The tutti answering phrase, instead of leading to the tonic, is diverted as it had been in the new key section of the exposition, temporarily losing its phrase structure and tonal stability. Perhaps the most striking moment of the movement occurs at bar 239 with an abrasive, dynamically emphasized arrival of the flattened submediant, a not unusual device in his G major works. What follows is an unusually long coda of over fifty bars, the first event of which is a reworking of the closing theme material. At bar 248 the E flat chord becomes an augmented sixth chord, reminding the listener of the end of the introduction. The first ten bars of the coda, highlighted by tonality and dynamics, amalgamate the antagonists of this movement as the stable closing theme is presented in a context of distortion. With this less complex and more accessible presentation, however, there is no less an assertion of the principles of earlier symphonies. At the end of the 1794 season, Haydn returned to the type of work in which the listener is guided more directly by the composer.

FOURTH SEASON: 1795

No. 102

Haydn regarded his three years in England as the happiest time of his life, but the thought of staying on indefinitely probably did not cross his mind. The pace was hectic and there was a price to be paid for celebrity status. Now in his early sixties, after thirty years of extraordinarily hard work and productivity, a quieter life in Vienna had obvious attractions. His first stay in England had been about a year and a half, and no doubt in 1794 he saw his current visit following the same pattern and as his last. Considerations such as these probably had a bearing on his final symphonic productions for the English audience. Prior to the beginning of the 1795 season he could look back on his symphonic achievements to date with obvious satisfaction. He had achieved popularity beyond his wildest dreams: he was now without question the most famous living composer. Certainly he needed to do nothing further to consolidate his reputation or his rapport with his audience. Indeed, he now found himself in a most enviable position, since, no longer needing to gain approbation, he could write whatever kinds of symphonies he saw fit.

The decision on the types of works to present in his final season was made early, since No. 102, the first of the final three, was written in 1794. Judging from this work and those which follow, it is clear that Haydn elected in his final year in England to challenge his audience in the extreme. These symphonies are thought-provoking beyond all precedent, and it is notable that the most complex of the three, as was true of the 1794 season, is the first. With this work Haydn appealed to his most sophisticated listeners, the connoisseurs, but nevertheless in a manner which would not detach the listener from traditional processes of arriving at intelligibility. Again one can see Haydn's works in the context of literary achievements and the shared belief in the power of rhetoric.

As we learn from intellectuals such as van Swieten, Burney, and numerous others, interest in rhetoric was by no means dead at the end of the eighteenth century. The interest at this time was no longer in the techniques of classical rhetoric, but in a more general sense concerned the effect that works should have on readers or listeners. It is remarkable, however, how similar some of Haydn's symphonic procedures are to the classical techniques, particularly in slow introductions. An oratorical introduction was expected to have a tone of gravity and dignity. It should be divided into two parts, the first to make the listener attentive and the second to steal into the listener's mind by dissimulation.

The introduction of No. 102 appears to fit the pattern particularly well. This introduction, which has been compared to the largo 'Representation of Chaos' at the beginning of *The Creation*, is very slow and begins quietly. The first ten bars are essentially melodic, and this is followed by a type of contrapuntal passage which places an elaboration of the melodic material against a rising chromatic line which has the additional destabilizing feature of syncopation. The opening bars of this introduction provide, as was proposed in the previous chapter, the prototype for the melodic fragment from source material associated with death (Ex. 46). With this solemn opening statement, the listener's attention is riveted. In this introduction Haydn moves smoothly from the melodic first part to a more contrapuntal section, using an extension of the initial melodic fragment, now in the bass voices. In the second part the melodic extension is set against an off-beat iterated note which eventually begins to move chromatically from F to B flat. A type of counterpoint is therefore established, drawing thematic and non-thematic material together, constituting an appropriate dissimulation. The links between this introduction and the rest of the movement are varied and sophisticated, and in fact the links once again extend beyond the first movement.

As the exposition proceeds, there is very little that is not motivically connected to something else, and at the centre of the various fusions stands the first vivace theme (Ex. 47). The connection between this theme and the beginning of the introduction is unmistakable, and the extension at bars 38–9 makes the link even stronger. The contrapuntal

Ex. 46

Ex. 47

transitional material beginning at bar 56 presents a type of double link. On the one hand it can be seen to be derived from the 'vivace' theme, the second violin part from 'b', and the figure in the cellos and basses (and its inversion in the first violin) from 'a' (Ex. 48). On the other hand, a relationship with bars 11–6 of the introduction is also apparent as the reiterated C relates to the F in the introduction, and the rising seventh figure in the 'cellos and basses relates to those instruments at bar 10 (see Ex. 46). The line of repeated notes here has the added dimension of a lowered semitone at the beginning of each bar, an effect which is strengthened with forzato marks, emphasizing the dissonance of a semitone between the basso and second violin and a tritone between bass and first violin. The relationship of this passage with the introduction transfers the spirit of the introduction to the transition, and

Ex. 48

also allows a new conception of the first theme, giving it a sense of ambivalence. The recurrence of this passage in the new key area gives it added weight.

All commentators are in agreement that the development section of this movement is extraordinary. The importance of the transitional passage (Ex. 48), with its apparent associations with the introduction and first theme, is borne out by the development. The different aspects of Ex. 48 are individually used to bring about some unexpected key changes and generate some highly abstruse counterpoint (bars 120–32 and 160–83). This high degree of tension, generated by rising sevenths, off-beat forzati, and suspension, is given contrast by a false recapitulation on the key of C. The relaxation is short-lived, however, as a new section of tension begins at bar 191, this time based on the iterated material with the semitone from the second violin part of Ex. 48. Much of the development, then, is an alternation of passages of extreme stability and instability.

Beginning at bar 209, however, a new and intensive counterpoint starts which brings various facets of the movement together, placing the polarities directly against each other (Ex. 49). The outer string parts at bar 209, carried over from the previous section, give the iterated material (from Ex. 48, second violin). The rising seventh of an earlier contrapuntal section becomes a rising fourth in the violas, returning to the interval of the introduction. Ambiguity is built into this line by means of suspension. Other reflections of the introduction at this point include a chromatic bass line and further emphasis on off-beats in the upper winds. The counterpoint is completed by 'c' of the first 'vivace' theme, now in the first and second violins. The exchange between the two violin parts directly parallels bars 101–4 of the end of the exposition, a point of the exposition characterized by stability. Here, then, not unlike at certain points of tension in operatic ensembles, the different dramatic forces come together and are embroiled in a period of high intensity.

Ex. 49

After a truncated early section, the recapitulation ends very much as the exposition had, and the insertion of new material at bars 282–302 therefore takes on a special significance in addressing the dramatic events of the movement. The first theme returns at bar 289, and the way in which this theme participated in the tension and motion of the movement is graphically illustrated just before the fermata at bar 297 (Ex. 50). The second bar of the theme ('b' in Ex. 47) is isolated for closer scrutiny by the rhetorical devices of repetition and augmentation. Once again its associations are affirmed with the second violin part of Ex. 48, the section of the development in which this material was to generate very considerable tension, as well as with the introduction. And again, the point is made following the fermata, as the same material (now at a forte level) reminds one of its various contexts throughout the movement. The emphasis on the main theme at this point is a reflection on its ambivalence; this theme proves to be a fusion of the entire dramatic problem of the movement.

If Haydn was using the techniques of rhetoric in this and other works, the application was by no means rigorous. This apparent use may very well be similar to that of melodic sources and their associative possibilities. Rather than applying rhetoric consciously, he may, in the pursuit of moral goals, have inadvertently used a procedure which was well tried in the past and honoured throughout his own century.

Ex. 50

No. 103

These final symphonies of Haydn's career are works of extremes. In No.
102 the level of challenge to the listener reaches a peak. This challenge is
not only in the complexity and intensity of the first movement, but also
extends to the second movement, which generates its own dramatic
problems and sense of something ominous. In No. 103 Haydn achieved
another extreme position, and this was in his preparedness to direct the
listening of his audience. In this case he practically does take the listener
by the hand and pull him towards a very specific realization. The
audience is not given the option of sitting back and allowing pleasant
sounds to waft by in the first movement of this work. Towards the end of
the movement, Haydn jolts the listener into awareness of his moral
intention. This movement, more than any other work by Haydn, offers
the ultimate example of a fusion of opposites.

The uniqueness of this symphony is apparent in the first bar of the
work, an unaccompanied tympani roll. And as the 'adagio' introduction
proceeds, it bears little resemblance to any previous introduction, as the
listener hears only the lowest strings and bassoon in low tessituras at a
piano level. It may very well require concentration in order to hear, and
what emerges is something not unlike the beginning of the 'Dies Irae'
plainchant. That association may be no more than coincidental, but if it
is, it is a coincidence which supports an overall feeling. In previous
introductions, Haydn began with material which was generally stable,
saving ambiguity for the second part of the introduction. In this work
instability is the predominant characteristic from the beginning, as
neither the key nor the sense of metre is defined. While Haydn places his
introduction in a triple metre, there is nothing in the musical line to
suggest that a triple metre is more appropriate than a duple, and the
adagio tempo obscures that even further (Ex. 51). As this section
continues, its sense of importance intensifies as it grows in length,

Ex. 51

eventually reaching thirty-nine bars, which makes it by far the longest of Haydn's introductions. The solo E flat in the timpani at the beginning offers no certainty as to the key, and the line which follows quickly leads away from E flat.

As the initial ambiguities are removed by the dominant and tonic cadences at bars 7 and 12, new difficulties begin to emerge. Curiously, this introduction has a phrasing regularity which Haydn had not used before, and this generates new uncertainties for the listener. After three six-bar phrases, another dominant cadence is reached, and while this would offer an introduction of typical length, phrasing balance prevents stopping at this point. While the next phrase solves the phrasing issue, closure at this point is prevented by the tonic cadence which could not prepare the 'allegro' theme. Immediately following this cadence, Haydn adds a seventh to the tonic, giving it a secondary dominant function and leading off into new tonal regions. The introduction finally ends on a unison G which does not prepare the 'allegro con spirito' in the least, and the last few bars also contain off-beat forzati, again suggesting metric ambiguity. The fact that the introduction does not end on the dominant suggests a type of independence of function. While G does not provide harmonic preparation, there is a pivotal relationship with the first theme which begins on the mediant of E flat with a G–A flat–G figure. The usual role of preparation, then, is largely absent here and, considering the length of this introduction, a sense of dramatic importance is magnified.

While the harmonic movement of this exposition is for the most part very stable, there is one brief excursion during the modulation which in fact provides the first link of the 'allegro con spirito' with the introduction. Instead of moving to B flat at this point, the harmonic progression leads towards G with a strong cadential preparation. The chord of arrival, however, is not G major but is a diminished seventh which resolves to F. G, of course, was the last note of the introduction, and its thwarted arrival here recalls its non-functional harmonic placement in the introduction.

The arrival of the dominant is somewhat deceptive but exceedingly important. It happens so quickly after the diminished seventh chord which prevented the arrival of G that it does not appear to have been adequately prepared. The progression in fact is two bars of the diminished seventh, one bar of dominant preparation, and arrival of B flat. This fleeting and almost deceptive arrival of the new key is most appropriate, since the connection with the introduction which the G suggested leads directly into the most unusual connection between introduction and allegro in all of Haydn's works. In bars 73–4, the arrival of the dominant, a fleeting melodic passage occurs which contains the melodic contour of the opening phrase of the slow introduction. By this, the listener is reminded of the darker, possibly death-related character of the beginning of the work. The context here, however, is clearly not sombre, since the apparent dance-like rhythm is distinctly related to the cheerful dance theme (now firmly in the dominant) which begins at bar 79 (Ex. 52*c*). In this short passage of two bars, then, Haydn has fused together the opposing dark and cheerful forces of the movement. As it appears at this point of the exposition, it is most likely to escape the listener's notice since it is so fleeting, but yet it is crucial to an understanding of the movement. In fact, a second level of duality exists here in that this passage places a triple pattern (3/4) in the violins against the duple metre (6/8) maintained in the lower strings and bassoons (Ex. 52*b*).[7] The fusion in this passage, because of its placement, emphasizes a sense of opposition within an ongoing context.

Most of the thematic material from the introduction and exposition appears in the development, often in contrapuntal contexts. The tension in the development, however, is not related to material from the introduction but is now generated by material which was previously stable. Fragments of the dance themes are well suited to complex counterpoint, and a passage begins at bar 103 which places motives of the first and second themes against each other (Ex. 53). The previously stable second theme has now given way to metric ambiguity. After a rest extended by a fermata, the material from the introduction makes an appearance in the development, but now, in contrast to its ambiguous character in both the introduction and exposition, it is clearly in the 6/8 metre (Ex. 54). Not only are the previous metric problems completely aligned here, but the added 'commentary' in the upper strings makes the new context seem even more jovial. Later in the development, the two dance-like themes are brought together again, with all metric regularity restored. The second theme now occurs in the unlikely key of D flat, and some adjustments are needed to get back to the dominant.

One can hear the emphasis of significant dramatic material at the end of the first movement in a number of late symphonies, but in no work is the point made as forcefully as in No. 103. Again there is elision at the beginning of the recapitulation as the previous thirty-one bars between

---

[7] Numerous other writers, of course, have noted this passage. A diagram similar to Ex. 52*a* and *b* is given in Eugene K. Wolf, 'The Recapitulations in Haydn's London Symphonies', *Musical Quarterly*, 52 (1966), p. 78.

Ex. 52

Ex. 53

Ex. 54

the two themes are now reduced to twelve. The complex parts of the
exposition, such as the harmonic movement to G and the passage which
fused the opening of the introduction with the second theme, are now

absent as the transitional passage here is designed to bring in the second theme in the tonic as quickly as possible. Following the statement of the themes, the listener is placed on alert that something new will happen. The highly unusual step of allowing part of the slow introduction (including the drum-roll) to return near the end of the movement guarantees the listener's attention (Ex. 55). The return to allegro con spirito (or tempo primo) at bar 213 reintroduces the astonished listener to the passage first heard at bars 73–4. While the listener may have been no more than marginally aware of this passage in the exposition, Haydn makes it impossible to miss near the end of the movement, reaffirming its importance as a fusion of opposites.

If fusions such as this are grasped, the process which yields intelligibility is fulfilled. While Haydn allows portions of slow introductions to return in other recapitulations, the striking effect here is unparalleled. With the verbatim return of the first part of the introduction, the continuity is broken. The listener, placed off guard by that which is unorthodox, feels a keen sense of expectation. By presenting the important two-bar passage as he does, Haydn is, in a sense, offering a lesson in listening, building the key for understanding into the work itself. The opposition of archetypal opposites is left as it had been earlier, in a context of ambiguity, motion, and continuity. The coexistence of opposites put forward in this image, then, can be seen as something perpetual.

No. 104

On 4 May 1795, at the New Room, King's Theatre, Haydn presented his final symphony at a benefit concert for himself. In his notebook, he gave a detailed list of the works performed, including his 'new Symphony in D, the twelfth and the last of the English'. The evening was a great success in more ways than one. He could happily reflect that 'the whole company was thoroughly pleased and so was I'. Aside from the satisfaction of hearing the response of the audience, he had another obvious reason to be pleased: 'I made four thousand Gulden on this evening. Such a thing is only possible in England' (iii. 309). To put things into perspective, this sum was twice the amount of his total savings prior to coming to England. As usual, the critical reception of this work was everything he could have hoped for. Two days after the concert he could read the following opinion and prophecy in the *Morning Chronicle*:

He rewarded the good intentions of his friends by writing a new Overture for the occasion, which for fullness, richness, and majesty, in all its parts, is thought by some of the best judges to surpass all his other compositions. A Gentleman, eminent for his musical knowledge, taste, and sound criticism, declared this to

Ex. 55

be his opinion, That, for fifty years to come Musical Composers would be little better than imitators of Haydn; and would do little more than pour water on his leaves. We hope the prophecy may prove false; but probability seems to confirm the prediction. (iii. 308)

This opinion was echoed by Haydn's good friend Burney, who, writing four days after this benefit, described the new symphonies as being 'such as were never heard before, of any *mortal's* production; of what Apollo & the Muses compose or perform we can only judge by such productions as these' (iii. 307).

Considering the extraordinary variety in the English Symphonies to this point, it should come as no surprise that he would attempt something unique in his final symphony. Of the various musical means he had used to define polarities, one which he had not yet employed was contrasting intervallic relationships. For confirmation that intervallic relationships in fact had this potential, we can consider the views of Haydn's own English pupil John Callcott. Callcott's classification of intervals (octave, fifth, fourth, thirds, and sixths as consonant and seconds, sevenths, and the tritone as dissonant) was of course by no means unique.[8] However, Callcott was prepared to apply these classifications to melodic contexts as well as chords or counterpoint, pointing out that 'according to this classification, every passage of Melody which moves by *Degrees*, consists of dissonant Intervals' (p. 106). Stepwise motion becomes consonant if there is transient or passing motion between thirds or other consonant intervals. However, if seconds stand by themselves without a passing context, they remain dissonant intervals. As such they can stand in contrast to consonant intervals or consonant passing motion.

Analysis which depends solely on intervallic relationships is, as numerous endeavours of this type attest, much more likely than other approaches to slip into the realm of analytical sophistry. As resistant as one might be to this approach, Haydn leaves little room in the D minor introduction of No. 104 to see any other possibility. In the first two bars

[8] *A Musical Grammar*, 2nd edn. (London, 1809), p. 104.

he presents a fifth (and inverts it as a fourth), and in the next four bars he gives seconds, with a large dynamic contrast between the two (Ex. 56). This is followed by the same relationship in the relative major. No. 104 is the most analysed of all Haydn's symphonies, and many of the analyses, such as Landon's (iii. 609–18), focus on the intervallic issue. Landon and others have seen this as embracing all four movements (iii. 610), arguing that Haydn has unified the entire work through his concentration on specific intervals. Acceptance of that position does require a certain amount of faith since the intervals in question are common and are likely to be prominently displayed in any work. However, since there is little question that specific intervals are the focus of the introduction, the possibility of extending this to the rest of the work does indeed exist.

With the opening 'allegro' theme one finds the same intervals displayed, but since a third is now also included, it seems probable that the interest in intervals is in the differentiation of consonant and dissonant ones. Following that direction, the first two bars (along with the beginning of the third) focus on consonant intervals, while the second two bars isolate the second, which is dissonant. The stepwise motion of the next four bars places a dissonant interval in a consonant

Ex. 56

Ex. 57

context (Ex. 57). Further interest is added in the second half of this arched phrase (the first of its type as an opening 'allegro' theme since No. 93) by means of syncopation in the second violin. After the statement of the theme, the intervallic interest is maintained as bars 32–3 and 34–5 give strong-beat emphasis to the fourth while bars 36–7 and 38 do the same for the second.

The apparent focus on intervals is maintained throughout the remainder of the exposition and the development, as can be observed in Landon's discussion (iii. 610–2). This has an effect on the first theme which, in its second statement in the recapitulation, appears with a new countermelody (Ex. 58). Here the important structural note is A along with the seconds above and below it. This movement has a coda almost as long as the one in No. 100, and the original issue remains the focus of this section. This is particularly true of the final tutti in which the entire orchestra is divided into two, the upper melodic parts presenting a fourth and all other instruments the second (Ex. 59).

While one could dispute the intervallic relationships at various other points in the work, the conclusion of the Finale again brings them into particular prominence. The figure which is the second two-bar phrase of the Finale now contains forzato reinforcement of the second (Ex. 60a).

Ex. 58

Ex. 59

Ex. 60

a.

b.

And similarly, the forzato on the unison E in the third bar from the end emphasizes the second along with the fifth which naturally occurs in the final cadence (Ex. 60*b*). In his final symphony, Haydn again establishes strong polarities, allows them to interact throught the first movement and other points of the work, and has them coexisting at the end. The technique used here provided a new challenge for the listener, but at the same time the melodic charm of the first 'allegro' theme offered a type of sensory pleasure which looked back to the 1791 season (No. 93). Thus, Haydn can be seen in his final symphony to be joining the two fundamental characteristics of the symphony. This synthesis allowed him to be the most esteemed living composer, and so he remained until his death. The intellectual and moral challenge was very much present, but within a context of giving pleasure.

Conclusion

HAYDN's late symphonies, written near the end of the eighteenth century, can be seen in retrospect to have provided an extraordinary bridge between the past and the future. While these works may have been somewhat out of step with the most current or progressive literary endeavours, they nevertheless have a sense of timelessness about them. Concerning the past, they are a fulfilment of the principles put forward a century earlier by visionaries such as Shaftesbury, principles which were grounded in the discourses and practices of the poets, philosophers, and orators of antiquity. As for subsequent generations, these works never completely vanished from the repertoire, even during the nineteenth century. In the past half-century it has become impossible to imagine the symphonic repertoire without Haydn, and it is not a collector's curiosity for artefacts which keeps these works alive. On the contrary, they have as much to offer us as they did to the eighteenth century, a fact which reinforces the significance of the eighteenth century in relation to our own. At the same time, it is impossible to conceive of the symphonic repertoire as it has unfolded in the almost two centuries since Haydn's last symphonies without the aesthetic foundation which he put into place.

If Haydn did not know Shaftesbury's prescription that 'there must be an art of hearing found ere the performing arts can have their due effect, or anything exquisite in the kind be felt or comprehended', he certainly anticipated it on his own. The 'art of hearing' is not something achieved through external education, but in an effective work it is already built in. A composer of public compositions such as symphonies could not assume musical sophistication on the part of his audience. Aside from the small connoisseur element of the audience, the most the composer could hope was that his audience would be prepared to listen with concentration. Like Shaftesbury, Haydn believed the artist should walk his audience through a process of discovery, and he put this into practice in his symphonies. Haydn holds the listener's hand more firmly in some works than others, but in every case the audience is moved towards the composer's position, a position which in fact is the common moral ground that the artist shares with his public. As is true of literary works, it could be argued in the case of the symphony that the listener is built into the work itself, since the values he discovers are by and large his own. This, of course, is generalized by the composer on the basis of his assumptions concerning existing values, a projection which for Haydn was reinforced by his contacts with people such as Burney, Holcroft, Salomon, Latrobe, and Twining. These were men who possessed the highest intellectual, moral, and musical qualities, who were refined in the way that Shaftesbury and others saw as the ultimate goal.

A study which focuses on an author–audience relationship, of course, runs the risk of ignoring the value of the works to subsequent generations and audiences of the present in particular. If works were written for a specific audience at a particular time, how does one account for durability, or the way that succeeding generations respond? What is the capability of these works to engage the interests of audiences removed in time and social conditions from the society for which the works were intended? Following his departure from England in 1795, critical commentary on Haydn remained active for about three decades, reflecting the period of time his works remained in the mainstream of music in England. The first issue of the *Harmonicon* (1823), beginning with the 'Memoir of Haydn' after its 'Prefatory Address', reflected that Haydn was still much revered. The article illustrates the early nineteenth-century inclination towards extramusical or programmatic interpretation. For the next half-century, one finds few published commentaries on Haydn in Britain, and this parallels the relative infrequency of performance with the exception of *The Creation* during that time. It is, however, of interest that writers such as Edward Rimbault spoke of him in 1877 (in *The Leisure Hour*) 'as a name to be honoured, both in music and in morals'.

While Haydn was never completely lost from public view, it was nevertheless necessary for a revival of his works to take place in the twentieth century. If one considers the relationship of popularity and challenge which applied to the original reception, it is much less the popular aspect than the challenge which has guaranteed Haydn's durability and place in the current repertoire. Concerning the latter, the composer was not only writing for his contemporary audience but also for posterity. The values which the artist could share with his own audience can, of course, be shared with other generations as well. While Haydn, like other artists and writers of the Enlightenment, was attempting to inculcate a certain view of morality, that sense of values has a more universalized aspect which the twentieth century has by no means entirely abandoned. In fact, this century is able to look to the Enlightenment as the source of those values which we continue to hold as being important concerning social structure, education, political organization, and all the various freedoms and liberties which are now taken entirely for granted (although in all too few countries). It should come as no surprise that the composer who devised musical means for imparting these values and who directly or indirectly set the standard for all subsequent symphonists should continue to engage the imagination of the present age.

Bibliography

Abafi, Ludwig, *Geschichte der Freimaurerei in Österreich-Ungarn* (5 vols.; Budapest, 1890–4).

Abelmann, Charlotte, 'Der Codex Vietoris. Ein Beitrag zur Musikgeschichte des ungarisch-tschechoslowakischen Grenzgebietes', D. Phil. thesis (University of Vienna, 1946).

Abrams, M. H., 'Art-as-Such: The Sociology of Modern Aesthetics', *Bulletin of the American Academy of Arts and Sciences*, 38/6 (1985), 8–33.

Allanbrook, Wye Jamison, *Rhythmic Gesture in Mozart:* Le nozze di Figaro *and* Don Giovanni (Chicago, 1983).

Allison, Henry E., *Lessing and the Enlightenment* (Ann Arbor, 1966).

Alvarez, A., 'The Delinquent Aesthetic', *Hudson Review*, 19 (1966–7), 590–600.

Alxinger, Johann Baptist von, *Gedichte* (2 vols.; Vienna, 1812).

Arnason, Heidrun, 'Christian Fürchtegott Gellert's Literary–Critical Ideas', Ph.D. thesis (University of Waterloo, 1976).

Bach, C. P. E., *Essays on the True Art of Playing Keyboard Instruments*, trans. and ed. W. J. Mitchell (New York, 1949).

Bartha, Dénes, 'Volkstanz-Stilisierung in Joseph Haydns Finale-Themen', in Ludwig Finscher and Christoph-Hellmut Mahling (eds.), *Festschrift für Walter Wiora zum 30. Dezember 1966*, (Kassel, 1967), 375–84.

—— and Somfai, László, *Haydn als Operkapellmeister* (Budapest, 1960).

Bäumker, Wilhelm, *Das Katholische Deutsche Kirchenlied in seinen Singweisen* (4 vols.; Freiburg, 1883–1911).

Becker–Cantarino, Bärbel, *Aloys Blumauer and the Literature of Austrian Enlightenment* (Berne 1973).

Beenk, Eugene L., 'Laendler Elements in the Symphonic Minuets of Joseph Haydn', Ph. D. thesis (University of Iowa, 1969).

Bernard, Paul P., *Jesuits and Jacobins: Enlightenment and Enlightened Despotism in Austria* (Urbana, 1971).

Besseler, Heinrich, 'Einflüsse der Kontratanzmusik auf Joseph Haydn', in *Bericht über die Internationale Konferenz zum Andenken Joseph Haydns* (Budapest, 1961), 25–40.

Beuttner, Nicolaum (ed.), *Catholisch Gesang-Buch* (Graz, 1602).

Beythien, Jürgen, 'Der Einfluß des Kontretanzes auf die Orchestermusik der Deutschen Frühklassik', D. Phil. thesis (University of Jena, 1957).

Blackall, Eric, *The Emergence of German as a Literary Language* (Cambridge, 1959).

Blumauer, Aloys, *Beobachtungen über Oesterreichs Aufklärung und Litteratur* (Vienna, 1782).

—— 'Rede über den Karakter des Maurers', *Journal für Freymaurer*, 1/1 (1784), 187–92.

—— *Sämmtliche Werke* (4 vols.; Königsberg, 1827).

—— 'Vorerinnerung über die Veranlassung, den Zweck, und die eigentliche Bestimmung dieses Journals', *Journal für Freymaurer*, 1/1 (1784), 3–14.

Böhme, Franz M., *Geschichte des Tanzes in Deutschland* (2 vols.; Leipzig, 1886).

Brand, Carl Maria, *Die Messen von Joseph Haydn* (Würzburg, 1941).

Breitinger, J. J., *Critische Dichtkunst* (2 vols.; Zurich, 1740).

Brown, A. Peter, 'Critical Years for Haydn's Instrumental Music: 1787–90', *Musical Quarterly*, 62 (1976), 374–94.

—— 'Joseph Haydn and C. P. E. Bach: The Question of Influence', in Jens Peter Larsen, Howard Serwer, and James Webster (eds.), *Haydn Studies* (New York, 1981), 158–64.

Burgh, A., *Anecdotes of Music, Historical and Biographical; in a Series of Letters from a Gentleman to His Daughter* (3 vols.; London, 1814).

Burney, Charles, *A General History of Music from the Earliest Ages to the Present Period*, ed. Frank Mercer (2 vols.; New York, 1957).

—— *Memoirs of the Life and Writings of the Abate Metastasio* (3 vols.; London, 1796).

—— MS Letters, Osborn Collection, Beinecke Library, Yale University.

Burney, Fanny, *Diary & Letters of Madame d'Arblay (1778–1840) as Edited by her Niece Charlotte Barrett*, v (London, 1905).

Busby, Thomas, *A General History of Music, from the Earliest Times to the Present* (2 vols.; London, 1819).

Callcott, John Wall, *A Musical Grammar*, 2nd edn. (London, 1809).

Cantus Catholici ex Editione Szelepcseniana (Nagy-Szombatban, 1738).

Cantus Ecclesiasticus Sacrae Historiae Passionis Domini Nostri Jesu Christi. Secondum Quatuor Evangelistas nec non Lamentationum et Lectionum (Vienna, 1761).

Carpani, Guisseppe, *Le Haydine, ovvero lettere su la vita e le opere del celebre maestro Guiseppe Haydn* (Milan, 1812).

A Catalogue of the Library of Books, of Mr Thomas Holcroft (London, 1806).

Catalogus Bibliothecae Bornianae Publica Auctione Ventetur (Vienna, 1791).

Chafe, Eric, 'J. S. Bach's *St Matthew Passion*: Aspects of Planning, Structure, and Chronology', *Journal of the American Musicological Society*, 35 (1982), 49–114.

Chailley, Jacques, 'Joseph Haydn and the Freemasons', in H. C. Robbins Landon and Roger E. Chapman (eds.), *Studies in Eighteenth-Century Music: A Tribute to Karl Geiringer on his Seventieth Birthday* (London, 1970), 117–24.

Chew, Geoffrey, 'The Night-Watchman's Song Quoted by Haydn and its Implications', *Haydn-Studien*, 3 (1974), 106–24.

Corner, David Gregor (ed.), *Geistliche Nachtigal. Das ist Ausserlesene Catholische Gesänge* (Vienna, 1674).

—— (ed.), *Gross Catholisch Gesangbuch* (Vienna, 1631).

Cotte, Roger, *La Musique maçonnique et ses musiciens* (Braine-le-Comte, 1975).

Crotch, William, *Substance of Several Courses of Lectures on Music* (London, 1831).

Cushman, David Steven, 'Joseph Haydn's Melodic Material: An Exploratory Introduction to the Primary and Secondary Sources together with an Analytical Catalogue and Tables of Proposed Melodic Correspondence and/or Variance', Ph.D. thesis (Boston University, 1972).

Dahlhaus, Carl, 'Romantische Musikästhetik und Wiener Klassik', *Archiv für Musikwissenschaft*, 29 (1972), 167–81.

Dance, George, *A Collection of Portraits Sketched from the Life since the Year 1793* (2 vols.; London, 1814).

Davidische Harmonia. Das ist Christlich Catholische Gesänge (Vienna, 1659).

Dent, Edward J., 'Italian Opera in the Eighteenth Century, and its Influence on the Music of the Classical Period', *Sammelbände der Internationalen Musikgesellschaft*, 13 (1912–13), 500–9.

Deutsch, Otto Erich, 'Haydn bleibt Lehrling: Nach den Freimaurer-Akten des Österreichischen Staatsarchivs', *Musica*, 5 (1959), 289–90.

Deutsch, Walter, ' "Volkstümliche" Wirkungen in der Musik Joseph Haydns', *Musikerzeihung*, 14 (1960), 88–92.

—— and Hofer, Gerlinde, *Die Volksmusiksammlung der Gesellschaft der Musikfreunde in Wein (Sonnleithner-Sammlung)* (Vienna, 1969).

Dies, Albert Christoph, *Biographische Nachrichten von Joseph Haydn*, in Vernon Gotwals (trans. and ed.), *Haydn: Two Contemporary Portraits* (Madison, 1968).

Dittersdorf, Karl Ditters von, *Lebensbeschreibung. Seinem Sohne in die Feder diktirt* (Leipzig, 1801).

Domokos, Pál Péter, 'Magyar Táncdallamok a XVIII. Századból' (Hungarian Dance Melodies from the Eighteenth Century), *Zenetudomány: Tanulmányok*, 9 (1961), 269–94.

Duff, Sir M. E. Grant, *The Club, 1764–1905* (London, 1905).

Eggert, Elda Marie M., 'The Influence of Certain English Moral Philosophers upon the Writings of C. F. Gellert', MA thesis (University of California at Berkeley, 1928).

Einstein, Alfred, *Mozart: His Character, His Work*, trans. Arthur Mendel and Nathan Broder (New York, 1945).

—— '*Orlando furioso* and *La Gerusalemme liberata* as Set to Music during the 16th and 17th Centuries', *Notes*, 8 (1950–1), 623–8.

Elschek, Oskar (ed.), *Methoden der Klassifikation von Volksliedweisen* (Bratislava, 1969).

Fischer, Wilhelm, 'Zur Entwicklungsgeschichte des Wiener klassischen Stils', *Studien zur Musikwissenschaft*, 3 (1915), 24–84.

Foster, Jonathan, 'The Tempora Mutantur Symphony of Joseph Haydn', *Haydn Yearbook*, 9 (1975), 328–9.

Gassmann, Florian, *L'Amore artigiano* (handcopy from 1911 in Library of Congress, Washington, DC).

Geiringer, Karl, *Haydn: A Creative Life in Music* (Berkeley and Los Angeles, 1968).

Gellert, C. F., *Sämmtliche Schriften* (10 vols.; Leipzig, 1769–74).

Gesellschaft der Musikfreunde, Vienna, MS (1819), Sonnleithner–Sammlung, Vienna.

Giese, Alexander, 'Einige Bemerkungen über Joseph Haydn als Freimaurer und die Freimaurerei seiner Zeit', in Gerda Mraz, Gottfried Mraz, and Gerald Schlag (eds.), *Joseph Haydn in seiner Zeit* (Eisenstadt, 1982), 168–71.

Gott-Lob singendes Jahr. Das ist geistliche Gesänger (Vienna, 1737).

Grant, Kerry S., *Dr Burney as Critic and Historian of Music* (Ann Arbor, 1983).

Green, Robert A., ' "Il Distratto" of Regnard and Haydn: A Re-examination', *Haydn Yearbook*, 11 (1980), 183–95.

Griesinger, Georg August, *Biographische Notizen über Joseph Haydn*, in Vernon Gotwals (trans. and ed.), *Haydn: Two Contemporary Portraits* (Madison, 1968).

Hadow, W. Henry, *A Croation Composer: Notes toward the Study of Haydn* (London, 1897).

Haidinger, Karl, 'Ueber die Fortschritte der Aufklärung', *Journal für Freymaurer*, 2/4 (1785), 54–60.

Harich, János, 'Das Repertoire des Opernkapellmeisters Joseph Haydn in Esterháza (1780–1790)', *Haydn Yearbook*, 1 (1962), 9–110.

Hawkins, John, *A General History of the Science and Practice of Music*, ed. Charles Cudworth (2 vols.; New York, 1963).

Haydn, Joseph, *Werke* (Munich and Duisberg, 1958–).

'Haydn's Diary while in England', *Harmonicon*, 5 (1827), 5–7.

Heartz, Daniel, 'Haydn und Gluck im Burgtheater um 1760: Der neue krumme Teufel, Le Diable à quatre und die Sinfonie "Le Soire"', in Christoph-Hellmut Mahling and Sigrid Wiesmann (eds.), *Bericht über den Internationalen Musikwissenschaftlichen Kongreß Bayreuth 1981* (Kassel, 1984), 120–35.

Heier, Edmund, *L. H. Nicolay (1737–1820) and his Contemporaries: Diderot, Rousseau, Voltaire* (The Hague, 1965).

Heil- und Hülfs-Mittel zum thätigen Christenthum (Brix, 1767).

Himmlische Harmaney oder ausserlesene Catholische Gesänger (Graz, 1644).

Hoboken, Anthony van, 'Nunziato Porta und der Text von Joseph Haydns Oper "Orlando Paladino"', in Friedrich Wilhelm Riedel and Hubert Unverricht (eds.), *Symbolae Historiae Musicae. Hellmut Federhofer zum 60. Geburtstag*, (Mainz, 1971), 170–9.

Holcroft, Thomas, *The Life of Thomas Holcroft. Written by Himself; and continued to the Time of his Death from his Diary, Notes & Other Papers by William Hazlitt; and now newly Edited with Introduction and Notes by Elbridge Colby* (2 vols.; London, 1925).

—— *Memoirs of Thomas Holcroft Written by Himself and Continued by William Hazlitt* (Oxford, 1926).

—— *The Theatrical Recorder* (2 vols.; London, 1805).

Holzmeister, Joseph von, 'Ueber die Harmonie. Bey der Aufnahme des Br. H ** n', *Journal für Freymaurer*, 2/2 (1785), 175–81.

Horányi, Mátyás, *The Magnificence of Eszterháza*, trans. András Deák (London, 1962).

Hörwarthner, Maria, 'Joseph Haydns Bibliothek—Versuch einer literarhistorischen Rekonstruktion', in Herbert Zeman (ed.), *Joseph Haydn und die Literatur seiner Zeit* (Eisenstadt, 1976), 157–207.

Hosler, Bellamy, *Changing Aesthetic Views of Instrumental Music in 18th-Century Germany* (Ann Arbor, 1981).

Hughes, Rosemary, *Haydn* (London, 1962).

—— *Haydn String Quartets* (London, 1961).

Hunter, Mary, 'Haydn's Aria Forms: A Study of the Arias in the Italian Operas written at Esterháza, 1766–1783', Ph.D. thesis (Cornell University, 1982).

Hurwitz, Joachim, 'Haydn and the Freemasons', *Haydn Yearbook*, 16 (1985), 5–98.

Ilgner, Richard M., *The Romantic Chivalrous Epic as a Phenomenon of the German Rococo* (Berne, 1979).

Jackson, William, *Observations on the Present State of Music in London*, 2nd edn. (London, 1791).

Jacob, Heinrich Eduard, *Joseph Haydn: His Art, Times, and Glory*, trans. Richard and Clara Winston (London, 1950).

Jauss, Hans Robert, *Toward an Aesthetic of Reception*, trans. Timothy Bahti (Minneapolis, 1982).

Journal für Freimaurer. Als Manuskript gedruckt für Brüder und Meister des Ordens (Vienna, 1784–7).

Kann, Robert A., *A Study in Austrian Intellectual History: From Late Baroque to Romanticism* (New York, 1960).

Katholisches Gesangbuch auf allerhöchsten Befehl Ihrer k. k. Majestät Marien Theresiens (Vienna, 1750).

Kerman, Joseph, *Opera as Drama* (New York, 1956).

—— 'Tovey's Beethoven', in Alan Tyson (ed.), *Beethoven Studies*, ii (London, 1977), 172–9.

Kirkendale, Warren, 'Ciceronians versus Aristotelians on the Ricercar as Exordium, from Bembo to Bach', *Journal of the American Musicological Society*, 32 (1979), 1–44.

Klier, Karl M., 'Haydns Thema aus dem Andante der "Symphonie mit dem Paukenschlag"', *Völkische Musikerziehung*, 6 (1940), 55–8.

—— *Das Totenwacht-Singen in Burgenland* (Eisenstadt, 1956).

Kling, H., 'Haydn und Mozart und die Freimaurerei', *Neue musikalische Rundschau* [Munich], 1/5 (1908), 6–9.

Knigge, Adolf, *Über den Umgang mit Menschen*, trans. P. Will as *Practical Philosophy of Social Life* (2 vols.; London, 1799).

Koch, Heinrich Christoph, *Introductory Essays on Composition: The Mechanical Rules of Melody, Sections 3 and 4*, trans. Nancy Kovaleff Baker (New Haven, 1983).

—— *Versuch einer Anleitung zur Composition* (3 vols.; Leipzig, 1782–93).

Kratter, Franz, *Drei Briefe über die neueste Maurerrevolution in Wien* (Prague, 1785).

Kuhač, Franjo Saverije, *Josip Haydn i hrvatske narodne popievke* (Zagreb, 1880).

Lach, Robert, *Zur Geschichte des Gesellschaftstanzes im 18. Jahrhundert* (Vienna, 1920).

Landon, H. C. Robbins (ed.), *The Collected Correspondence and London Notebooks of Joseph Haydn* (London, 1959).

—— *Haydn: Chronicle and Works* (5 vols.; London, 1976–80).

—— 'Haydn's Marionette Operas and the Repertoire of the Marionette Theatre at the Eszterháza Castle', *Haydn Yearbook*, i (1962), 111–97.

—— (ed.), *Joseph Haydn: Critical Edition of the Complete Symphonies* (12 vols.; Vienna, 1961–7).

—— *Mozart and the Masons: New Light on the Lodge 'Crowned Hope'* (London, 1982).

—— *The Symphonies of Joseph Haydn* (London, 1955).

—— and Bartha, Dénes (eds.), *Joseph Haydn: Gesammelte Briefe und Aufzeichnungen* (Kassel, 1965).

Lang, Paul Henry, *The Experience of Opera* (New York, 1973).

Larsen, Jens Peter, 'Haydn, (Franz) Joseph', in *The New Grove Dictionary of Music and Musicians* (London, 1980), viii. 328–407.

—— 'The Symphonies', in H. C. Robbins Landon and Donald Mitchell (eds.), *The Mozart Companion* (New York, 1969), 156–99.

Latrobe, Christian Ignatius, *Letters to My Children: Written at Sea during a Voyage to the Cape of Good Hope in 1815, Containing a Memorial of some Occurrences in My Past Life*, ed. J. A. Latrobe (London, 1851).

Lavater, Johann Caspar, *Aphorisms on Man*, trans. William Blake (London, 1788).

—— *Physiognomische Fragmente. Zur Beförderung der Menschenkenntnis und Menschenliebe* (Leipzig and Winterthur, 1775–8).

Lazarevich, Gordana, 'The Neapolitan Intermezzo and its Influence on the Symphonic Idiom', *Musical Quarterly*, 57 (1971), 294–313.

—— 'The Role of the Neapolitan Intermezzo in the Evolution of Eighteenth-Century Musical Style: Literary, Symphonic and Dramatic Aspects, 1685–1735', Ph.D. thesis (Columbia University, 1970).

Lenneberg, Hans, 'Johann Mattheson on Affect and Rhetoric in Music', *Journal of Music Theory*, 2 (1958), 47–84, 193–236.

Lonsdale, Roger, *Dr Charles Burney: A Literary Biography* (Oxford, 1965).

McClymonds, Marita, 'Haydn and his Contemporaries: "Armida abbandonata"', in *Joseph Haydn: Proceedings of the International Joseph Haydn Congress, Wien, Hofburg, 5.–12. September 1982*, ed. Eva Badura-Skoda (Munich, 1986), 325–32.

Mahler, Gustav, 'The Influence of the Folk-song on German Musical Arts', *Etude*, 29 (1911), 301–2.

Major, Erwin, 'Ungarische Tanzmelodien in Haydns Bearbeitung', *Zeitschrift für Muskwissenschaft*, 11 (1928–9), 601–4.

Markwardt, Bruno, *Geschichte Deutschen Poetik* (2 vols.; Berlin, 1956).

Martens, Wolfgang, *Die Botschaft der Tugend. Die Aufklärung im Spiegel der deutschen moralischen Wochenschriften* (Stuttgart, 1968).

Mayer, Joseph, 'Ueber die Verbindung der Künste und Wissenschaften mit der Maurerey', *Journal für Freymaurer*, 1/2 (1784), 65–104.

'Memoir of Haydn', *Harmonicon*, 1 (1823), 2–5, 17–21.

'Memoir of Johann Peter Salomon', *Harmonicon*, 8 (1830), 45–7.

Merian, Wilhelm, *Der Tanz in den deutschen Tabulaturbüchern* (Leipzig, 1927).

Milligan, Thomas B., *The Concerto and London's Musical Culture in the Late Eighteenth Century* (Ann Arbor, 1983).

Mozart, Wolfang Amadeus, *Neue Ausgabe sämtlicher Werke* (Kassel, 1955–).

National Széchényi Library, Budapest, MS Linus (1786).

Nettl, Paul, *Das Wiener Lied im Zeitalter des Barock* (Vienna and Leipzig, 1934).

Neubauer, John, *The Emancipation of Music from Language: Departure from Mimesis in Eighteenth-Century Aesthetics* (New Haven, 1986).

Nicolovius, D. Alfred, *Johann Georg Schlossers Leben und literarisches Wirken* (Bonn, 1844).

Nowak, Leopold, *Joseph Haydn. Leben, Bedeutung und Werk* (Vienna, 1959).

Olleson, D. Edward, 'Gottfried, Baron van Swieten, and his Influence on Haydn and Mozart', D. Phil. thesis (University of Oxford, 1967).

Papendiek, Charlotte, *Court and Private Life in the Time of Queen Charlotte: Being the Journal of Mrs Papendiek, Assistant Keeper of the Wardrobe and Reader to Her Majesty*, ed. Mrs Vernon Delves Broughton (2 vols.; London, 1887).

Parakilas, James, 'Mozart's *Tito* and the Music of Rhetorical Strategy', Ph.D. thesis (Cornell University, 1979).

Paul, Steven, 'Wit, Comedy and Humour in the Instrumental Music of Franz Joseph Haydn', Ph.D. thesis (University of Cambridge, 1981).

Pergolesi, Giovanni B., *La serva padrona*, ed. Karl Geiringer (Vienna, n.d.).

Pichler, Caroline, *Denkwürdigkeiten aus meinem Leben*, i (Vienna, 1844).

Pohl, Carl Ferdinand, *Joseph Haydn* (3 vols.; Leipzig, 1878, 1882, 1927).

Pope, Alexander, *An Essay on Man*, ed. Maynard Mack, in John Butt (ed.), *The Twickenham Edition of the Poems of Alexander Pope*, iii. i (London, 1950).

Price, Lawrence Marsden, *The Reception of English Literature in Germany* (Berkeley, 1932).

Radcliffe, Philip, *Beethoven's String Quartets* (New York, 1968).

Ratner, Leonard D., *Classic Music: Expression, Form, and Style* (New York, 1980).

—— 'Eighteenth-Century Theories of Musical Period Structure', *Musical Quarterly*, 42 (1956), 439–54.

Ravel, Maurice, 'Contemporary Music', *Rice Institute Pamphlet* (April 1928).

Rees, Abraham (ed.), *The Cyclopedia; or the Universal Dictionary of Arts, Science, and Literature* (39 vols.; London, 1819).

Rice, John A., 'Sarti's Giulio Sabino, Haydn's Armida, and the arrival of opera seria at Eszterháza', *Haydn Yearbook*, 15 (1984), 181–98.

Robinson, Herbert Spencer, *English Shakespearian Criticism in the Eighteenth Century* (New York, 1968).

Rosand, Ellen, 'The Descending Tetrachord: An Emblem of Lament', *Musical Quarterly*, 65 (1979), 346–59.

Rosen, Charles, *The Classical Style: Haydn, Mozart, Beethoven* (New York, 1972).

—— *Sonata Forms* (New York, 1980).

Rosenstrauch-Königsberg, Edith, *Freimaurerei im Josephinischen Wien: Aloys Blumauers Weg vom Jesuiten zum Jakobiner* (Vienna, 1975).

Sandberger, Adolf, 'Zur Geschichte des Haydnschen Streichquartetts', *Altbayerische Monatshefte* (1900), 1–24.

Schittlersberg, Augustin von, 'Ueber die Beobachtung der maurerischen Gleichheit', *Journal für Freymaurer*, 2/1 (1785), 77–82.

Schlosser, Johann Georg, *Ueber Schaftsbury von der Tugend, an Born* (Basel, 1785).

Schmid, Ernst Fritz, *Joseph Haydn. Ein Buch von Vorfahren und Heimat des Meisters* (Kassel, 1934).

Schneider, Ute, *Der Moralische Charakter. Ein Mittel aufklärerischer Menschendarstellung in den frühen deutschen Wochenschriften* (Stuttgart, 1976).

Schroeder, David P., 'Audience Reception and Haydn's London Symphonies', *International Review of the Aesthetics and Sociology of Music*, 16 (1985), 57–72.

—— 'Haydn and Gellert: Parallels in Eighteenth-Century Music and Literature', *Current Musicology*, 35 (1983), 7–18.

—— 'Melodic Source Material and Haydn's Creative Process', *Musical Quarterly*, 68 (1982), 496–515.

Segers, Rien T., 'Readers, Text and Author: Some Implications of Rezeptionsästhetik', *Yearbook of Comparative and General Literature*, 24 (1975), 15–23.

Selby, Scott Finn, 'Soliloquy, Colloquy, and Dialectic: The Rhetorical Strategies of Shaftesbury's *Characteristics*', Ph.D. thesis (University of California at Berkeley, 1982).

Shaftesbury, Anthony Ashley Cooper, Third Earl of, *Characteristics of Men, Manners, Opinions, Times*, 4th edn. (3 vols.; London, 1727).

Smith, Adam, *The Theory of Moral Sentiments*, ed. D. D. Raphael and A. L. MacFie (Oxford, 1976).

Somfai, László, 'The London Revision of Haydn's Instrumental Style', *Proceedings of the Royal Musical Association*, 100 (1973–4), 159–74.

Strommer, Roswitha, 'Wiener literarische Salons zur Zeit Joseph Haydns', in Herbert Zeman (ed.), *Joseph Haydn und die Literatur seiner Zeit* (Eisenstadt, 1976), 97–121.

Suleiman, Susan R., and Crossman, Inge (eds.), *The Reader in the Text: Essays on Audience and Interpretation* (Princeton, 1980).

Szabolcsi, Bence, 'Haydn und die Ungarische Musik', in *Bericht über die Internationale Konferenz zum Andenken Joseph Haydns* (Budapest, 1961), 159–75.

Taylor, John, *Records of My Life: 1757–1832* (2 vols.; London, 1832).

Tillotson, Geoffrey, *The Moral Poetry of Pope* (Newcastle upon Tyne, 1946).

Timbs, John, *Clubs and Club Life in London* (London, 1872).

Timpe, Eugene F., 'Lorenz Leopold Haschka: One Further Contrast', *Germanic Notes*, 10 (1979), 56–8.

Tovey, Donald Francis, *Essays in Musical Analysis*, i. *Symphonies* (London, 1935).

Troy, Charles E., *The Comic Intermezzo: A Study in the History of Eighteenth-Century Italian Opera* (Ann Arbor, 1979).

Tuveson, Ernest, 'Shaftesbury and the Age of Sensibility', in Howard Anderson and John S. Shea (eds.), *Studies in Criticism and Aethetics, 1600–1800: Essays in Honor of Samuel Holt Monk* (Minneapolis, 1967), 73–93.

Twining, Thomas, *Aristotle's Treatise on Poetry, Translated, with Notes, and Two Dissertations on Poetical and Musical Imitation* (London, 1789).

—— *Recreations and Studies of a Country Clergyman of the Eighteenth Century, Being Selections from the Correspondence of the Rev. Thomas Twining, M. A.* (London, 1882).

Van Cleve, John Walter, *Harlequin Besieged: The Reception of Comedy in Germany during the Early Enlightenment* (Berne, 1980).

Wangermann, Ernst, *Aufklärung und staatsbürgerliche Erziehung: Gottfried van Swieten als Reformator der österreichischen Unterrichtswesens 1781–1791* (Munich, 1978).

—— 'Reform Catholicism and Political Radicalism in the Austrian Enlightenment', in Roy Porter and Mikuláš Teich (eds.), *The Enlightenment in National Context* (Cambridge, 1981).

Weber, William, 'The Contemporaneity of Eighteenth-Century Musical Taste', *Musical Quarterly*, 70 (1984), 175–94.

Weiss, Piero, and Taruskin, Richard (eds.), *Music in the Western World: A History in Documents* (New York, 1984).

Wellek, René, *History of Modern Criticism, 1750–1950*, i. *The Later Eighteenth Century* (New Haven, 1955).

Wheelock, Gretchen Ann, 'Wit, Humor, and the Instrumental Music of Joseph Haydn', Ph.D. thesis (Yale University, 1979).

Wilson, W. Daniel, 'Readers in Texts', *Publications of the Modern Language Association*, 96 (1981), 848–63.

Wimsatt, William K., *The Verbal Icon* (London, 1970).

Wiora, Walter, 'Ethnomusicology and the History of Music', *Studia Musicologica Academiae Scientiarum Hungaricae*, 7 (1965), 187–93.

—— *European Folk Song: Common Forms in Characteristic Modifications*, iv. K. G. Fellerer (ed.), *Anthology of Music*, trans. R. Kolben (Cologne, 1966).

—— 'On the Methods of Comparative Melodic Research', *Journal of the International Folk Music Council*, 9 (1957), 55–8.

Wirth, Helmut, *Joseph Haydn als Dramatiker: Sein Bühnenschaffen als Beitrag zur Gesichchte der deutschen Oper* (Wolfenbüttel and Berlin, 1940).

Witgeest, Simon, *Natürliches Zauber-Buch* (Nuremberg, 1762).

Wolf, Eugene, 'The Recapitulations in Haydn's London Symphonies', *Musical Quarterly*, 52 (1966), 71–87.

Yuill, W. E., 'A Genteel Jacobin: Adolf Freiherr von Knigge', in Hinrich Siefken and Alan Robinson (eds.), *'Erfahrung und Überlieferung': Festschrift for C. P. Magill* (Cardiff, 1974).

Zeman, Herbert (ed.), *Joseph Haydn und die Literatur seiner Zeit* (Eisenstadt, 1976).

Ziska, Franz, and Schottky, J. M. (eds.), *Oesterreichische Volkslieder mit ihren Singweisen* (Budapest, 1819).

Zoder, Raimund, *Altösterreichische Volkstänze* (Vienna, 1937).

—— 'Haydn-Menuett und ein Steyrischer', *Volkslied, Volkstanz, Volksmusik, 48 (1947), 28–9*.

Index